CW01303402

Ninja Dual Zone Air Fryer Cookbook UK

Super Speedy Tasty & Healthy Air Fryer Recipes for Beginners, Incl.Tips and Tricks to Master Your Smart Dual Zone Air Fryer

Phyllis R. Rich

CONTENTS

Breakfast Recipes

Buttermilk Biscuits With Roasted Stone Fruit Compote

Servings:4

Cooking Time: 20 Minutes

Ingredients:

- FOR THE BISCUITS
- 1⅓ cups all-purpose flour
- 2 teaspoons sugar
- 2 teaspoons baking powder
- ½ teaspoon baking soda
- ½ teaspoon kosher salt
- 4 tablespoons (½ stick) very cold unsalted butter
- ½ cup plus 1 tablespoon low-fat buttermilk
- FOR THE FRUIT COMPOTE
- 2 peaches, peeled and diced
- 2 plums, peeled and diced
- ¼ cup water
- 2 teaspoons honey
- ⅛ teaspoon ground ginger (optional)

Directions:

1. To prep the biscuits: In a small bowl, combine the flour, sugar, baking powder, baking soda, and salt. Using the large holes on a box grater, grate in the butter. Stir in the buttermilk to form a thick dough.
2. Place the dough on a lightly floured surface and gently pat it into a ½-inch-thick disc. Fold the dough in half, then rotate the whole thing 90 degrees, pat into a ½-inch thick disc and fold again. Repeat until you have folded the dough four times.
3. Pat the dough out a final time into a ½-inch-thick disc and use a 3-inch biscuit cutter to cut 4 biscuits from the dough (discard the scraps).
4. To prep the fruit compote: In a large bowl, stir together the peaches, plums, water, honey, and ginger (if using).
5. To cook the biscuits and compote: Install a crisper plate in the Zone 1 basket, place the biscuits in the basket, and insert the basket in the unit. Place the fruit in the Zone 2 basket and insert the basket in the unit.
6. Select Zone 1, select AIR FRY, set the temperature to 400°F, and set the time to 10 minutes.
7. Select Zone 2, select ROAST, set the temperature to 350°F, and set the time to 20 minutes. Select SMART FINISH.
8. Press START/PAUSE to begin cooking.
9. When the Zone 2 timer reads 10 minutes, press START/PAUSE. Remove the basket and stir the compote. Reinsert the basket and press START/PAUSE to resume cooking.
10. When cooking is complete, the biscuits will be golden brown and crisp on top and the fruit will be soft. Transfer the biscuits to a plate to cool. Lightly mash the fruit to form a thick, jammy sauce.
11. Split the biscuits in half horizontally and serve topped with fruit compote.

Nutrition:

- (Per serving) Calories: 332; Total fat: 12g; Saturated fat: 7.5g; Carbohydrates: 50g; Fiber: 2.5g; Protein: 6g; Sodium: 350mg

Morning Patties

Servings: 4

Cooking Time: 13 Minutes.

Ingredients:

- 1 lb. minced pork
- 1 lb. minced turkey
- 2 teaspoons dry rubbed sage
- 2 teaspoons fennel seeds
- 2 teaspoons garlic powder
- 1 teaspoon paprika
- 1 teaspoon of sea salt
- 1 teaspoon dried thyme

Directions:

1. In a mixing bowl, add turkey and pork, then mix them together.
2. Mix sage, fennel, paprika, salt, thyme, and garlic powder in a small bowl.
3. Drizzle this mixture over the meat mixture and mix well.
4. Take 2 tablespoons of this mixture at a time and roll it into thick patties.
5. Place half of the patties in Zone 1, and the other half in Zone 2, then spray them all with cooking oil.
6. Return the crisper plate to the Ninja Foodi Dual Zone Air Fryer.
7. Choose the Air Fry mode for Zone 1 and set the temperature to 390 degrees F and the time to 13 minutes.
8. Select the "MATCH" button to copy the settings for Zone 2.
9. Initiate cooking by pressing the START/STOP button.
10. Flip the patties in the drawers once cooked halfway through.
11. Serve warm and fresh.

Nutrition:

- (Per serving) Calories 305 | Fat 25g |Sodium 532mg | Carbs 2.3g | Fiber 0.4g | Sugar 2g | Protein 18.3g

Breakfast Casserole

Servings:4

Cooking Time:10

Ingredients:

- 1 pound of beef sausage, grounded
- 1/4 cup diced white onion
- 1 diced green bell pepper
- 8 whole eggs, beaten
- ½ cup Colby jack cheese, shredded
- ¼ teaspoon of garlic salt
- Oil spray, for greasing

Directions:

1. Take a bowl and add ground sausage to it.
2. Add in the diced onions, bell peppers, eggs and whisk it well.
3. Then season it with garlic salt.
4. Spray both the baskets of the air fryer with oil spray.
5. Divide this mixture among the baskets; remember to remove the crisper plates.
6. Top the mixture with cheese.
7. Now, turn ON the Ninja Foodie 2-Basket Air Fryer zone 1 and select AIR FRY mode and set the time to 10 minutes at 390 degrees F.
8. Select the MATCH button for zone 2 baskets, and hit start.

9. Once the cooking cycle completes, take out, and serve.
10. Serve and enjoy.

Nutrition:

- (Per serving) Calories 699| Fat 59.1g | Sodium 1217 mg | Carbs 6.8g | Fiber 0.6g| Sugar 2.5g | Protein33.1 g

Sausage With Eggs

Servings:2

Cooking Time:13

Ingredients:

- 4 sausage links, raw and uncooked
- 4 eggs, uncooked
- 1 tablespoon of green onion
- 2 tablespoons of chopped tomatoes
- Salt and black pepper, to taste
- 2 tablespoons of milk, dairy
- Oil spray, for greasing

Directions:

1. Take a bowl and whisk eggs in it.
2. Then pour milk, and add onions and tomatoes.
3. Whisk it all well.
4. Now season it with salt and black pepper.
5. Take one cake pan, that fit inside the air fryer and grease it with oil spray.
6. Pour the omelet in the greased cake pans.
7. Put the cake pan inside zone 1 air fryer basket of Ninja Foodie 2-Basket Air Fryer.
8. Now place the sausage link into the zone 2 basket.
9. Select bake for zone 1 basket and set the timer to 8-10 minutes at 300 degrees F.
10. For the zone 2 basket, select the AIR FRY button and set the timer to 12 minutes at 390 degrees.
11. Once the cooking cycle completes, serve by transferring it to plates.
12. Chop the sausage or cut it in round and then mix it with omelet.
13. Enjoy hot as a delicious breakfast.

Nutrition:

- (Per serving) Calories 240 | Fat 18.4g| Sodium 396mg | Carbs 2.8g | Fiber0.2g | Sugar 2g | Protein 15.6g

Air Fried Bacon And Eggs

Servings: 1

Cooking Time: 10 Minutes

Ingredients:

- 2 eggs
- 2 slices bacon

Directions:

1. Grease a ramekin using cooking spray.
2. Install the crisper plate in the zone 1 drawer and place the bacon inside it. Insert the drawer into the unit.
3. Crack the eggs and add them to the greased ramekin.
4. Install the crisper plate in the zone 2 drawer and place the ramekin inside it. Insert the drawer into the unit.
5. Select zone 1 to AIR FRY for 9–11 minutes at 400 degrees F/ 200 degrees C. Select zone 2 to AIR FRY for 8–9 minutes at 350 degrees F/ 175 degrees C. Press SYNC.
6. Press START/STOP to begin cooking.
7. Enjoy!

Nutrition:

- (Per serving) Calories 331 | Fat 24.5g | Sodium 1001mg | Carbs 1.2g | Fiber 0g | Sugar 0.7g | Protein 25.3g

Brussels Sprouts Potato Hash

Servings: 4

Cooking Time: 10 Minutes

Ingredients:

- 455g Brussels sprouts
- 1 small to medium red onion
- 227g baby red potatoes
- 2 tablespoons avocado oil
- ½ teaspoon salt
- ½ teaspoon black pepper

Directions:

1. Peel and boil potatoes in salted water for 15 minutes until soft.
2. Drain and allow them to cool down then dice.
3. Shred Brussels sprouts and toss them with potatoes and the rest of the ingredients.
4. Divide this veggies hash mixture in both of the air fryer baskets.
5. Return the air fryer basket 1 to Zone 1, and basket 2 to Zone 2 of the Ninja Foodi 2-Basket Air Fryer.
6. Choose the "Air Fry" mode for Zone 1 with 375 degrees F temperature and 10 minutes of cooking time.
7. Select the "MATCH COOK" option to copy the settings for Zone 2.
8. Initiate cooking by pressing the START/PAUSE BUTTON.
9. Shake the veggies once cooked halfway through.
10. Serve warm.

Nutrition:

- (Per serving) Calories 305 | Fat 25g |Sodium 532mg | Carbs 2.3g | Fiber 0.4g | Sugar 2g | Protein 18.3g

Honey Banana Oatmeal

Servings: 4

Cooking Time: 8 Minutes

Ingredients:

- 2 eggs
- 2 tbsp honey

- 1 tsp vanilla
- 45g quick oats
- 73ml milk
- 30g Greek yoghurt
- 219g banana, mashed

Directions:

1. In a bowl, mix eggs, milk, yoghurt, honey, vanilla, oats, and mashed banana until well combined.
2. Pour batter into the four greased ramekins.
3. Insert a crisper plate in the Ninja Foodi air fryer baskets.
4. Place ramekins in both baskets.
5. Select zone 1 then select "air fry" mode and set the temperature to 390 degrees F for 8 minutes. Press "match" to match zone 2 settings to zone 1. Press "start/stop" to begin.

Nutrition:

- (Per serving) Calories 228 | Fat 4.6g |Sodium 42mg | Carbs 40.4g | Fiber 4.2g | Sugar 16.1g | Protein 7.7g

Sweet Potatoes Hash

Servings:2

Cooking Time:25

Ingredients:

- 450 grams sweet potatoes
- 1/2 white onion, diced
- 3 tablespoons of olive oil
- 1 teaspoon smoked paprika
- 1/4 teaspoon cumin
- 1/3 teaspoon of ground turmeric
- 1/4 teaspoon of garlic salt
- 1 cup guacamole

Directions:

1. Peel and cut the potatoes into cubes.
2. Now, transfer the potatoes to a bowl and add oil, white onions, cumin, paprika, turmeric, and garlic salt.
3. Put this mixture between both the baskets of the Ninja Foodie 2-Basket Air Fryer.
4. Set it to AIR FRY mode for 10 minutes at 390 degrees F.
5. Then take out the baskets and shake them well.
6. Then again set time to 15 minutes at 390 degrees F.
7. Once done, serve it with guacamole.

Nutrition:

- (Per serving) Calories691 | Fat 49.7g| Sodium 596mg | Carbs 64g | Fiber15g | Sugar 19g | Protein 8.1g

Sausage Breakfast Casserole
Servings: 4
Cooking Time: 10 Minutes
Ingredients:

- 455g hash browns
- 455g ground breakfast sausage
- 1 green capsicum diced
- 1 red capsicum diced
- 1 yellow capsicum diced
- ¼ cup sweet onion diced
- 4 eggs

Directions:

1. Layer each air fryer basket with parchment paper.
2. Place the hash browns in both the baskets.
3. Spread sausage, onion and peppers over the hash brown.
4. Return the air fryer basket 1 to Zone 1, and basket 2 to Zone 2 of the Ninja Foodi 2-Basket Air Fryer.
5. Choose the "Air Fry" mode for Zone 1 at 355 degrees F temperature and 10 minutes of cooking time.
6. Select the "MATCH COOK" option to copy the settings for Zone 2.
7. Initiate cooking by pressing the START/PAUSE BUTTON.
8. Beat eggs in a bowl and pour over the air fried veggies.
9. Continue air frying for 10 minutes.
10. Garnish with salt and black pepper.
11. Serve warm.

Nutrition:

- (Per serving) Calories 267 | Fat 12g |Sodium 165mg | Carbs 39g | Fiber 1.4g | Sugar 22g | Protein 3.3g

Breakfast Bacon
Servings: 4
Cooking Time: 14 Minutes.
Ingredients:

- ½ lb. bacon slices

Directions:

1. Spread half of the bacon slices in each of the crisper plate evenly in a single layer.
2. Return the crisper plate to the Ninja Foodi Dual Zone Air Fryer.
3. Choose the Air Fry mode for Zone 1 and set the temperature to 390 degrees F and the time to 14 minutes.
4. Select the "MATCH" button to copy the settings for Zone 2.
5. Initiate cooking by pressing the START/STOP button.
6. Flip the crispy bacon once cooked halfway through, then resume cooking.
7. Serve.

Nutrition:

- (Per serving) Calories 273 | Fat 22g |Sodium 517mg | Carbs 3.3g | Fiber 0.2g | Sugar 1.4g | Protein 16.1g

Baked Mushroom And Mozzarella Frittata With Breakfast Potatoes
Servings:4
Cooking Time: 35 Minutes
Ingredients:

- FOR THE FRITTATA
- 8 large eggs
- ⅓ cup whole milk
- 1 teaspoon kosher salt
- ½ teaspoon freshly ground black pepper
- 1 cup sliced cremini mushrooms (about 2 ounces)
- 1 teaspoon olive oil
- 2 ounces part-skim mozzarella cheese, cut into ½-inch cubes
- FOR THE POTATOES
- 2 russet potatoes, cut into ½-inch cubes
- 1 tablespoon olive oil
- ½ teaspoon garlic powder
- ¼ teaspoon kosher salt
- ¼ teaspoon freshly ground black pepper

Directions:

1. To prep the frittata: In a large bowl, whisk together the eggs, milk, salt, and pepper. Stir in the mushrooms.
2. To prep the potatoes: In a large bowl, combine the potatoes, olive oil, garlic powder, salt, and black pepper.
3. To cook the frittata and potatoes: Brush the bottom of the Zone 1 basket with 1 teaspoon of olive oil. Add the egg mixture to the basket, top with the mozzarella cubes, and insert the basket in the unit. Install a crisper plate in the Zone 2 basket. Place the potatoes in the basket and insert the basket in the unit.
4. Select Zone 1, select BAKE, set the temperature to 350°F, and set the time to 30 minutes.
5. Select Zone 2, select AIR FRY, set the temperature to 400°F, and set the time to 35 minutes. Select SMART FINISH.
6. Press START/PAUSE to begin cooking.
7. When the Zone 2 timer reads 15 minutes, press START/PAUSE. Remove the basket and shake the potatoes for 10 seconds. Reinsert the basket and press START/PAUSE to resume cooking.
8. When cooking is complete, the frittata will pull away from the edges of the basket and the potatoes will be golden brown. Transfer the frittata to a cutting board and cut into 4 portions. Serve with the potatoes.

Nutrition:

- (Per serving) Calories: 307; Total fat: 17g; Saturated fat: 5.5g; Carbohydrates: 18g; Fiber: 1g; Protein: 19g; Sodium: 600mg

Spinach Egg Muffins
Servings: 4
Cooking Time: 13 Minutes.
Ingredients:

- 4 tablespoons milk
- 4 tablespoons frozen spinach, thawed
- 4 large eggs
- 8 teaspoons grated cheese

- Salt, to taste
- Black pepper, to taste
- Cooking Spray

Directions:

1. Grease four small-sized ramekin with cooking spray.
2. Add egg, cheese, spinach, and milk to a bowl and beat well.
3. Divide the mixture into the four small ramekins and top them with salt and black pepper.
4. Place the two ramekins in each of the two crisper plate.
5. Return the crisper plate to the Ninja Foodi Dual Zone Air Fryer.
6. Choose the Air Fry mode for Zone 1 and set the temperature to 390 degrees F and the time to 13 minutes.
7. Select the "MATCH" button to copy the settings for Zone 2.
8. Initiate cooking by pressing the START/STOP button.
9. Serve warm.

Nutrition:

- (Per serving) Calories 237 | Fat 19g |Sodium 518mg | Carbs 7g | Fiber 1.5g | Sugar 3.4g | Protein 12g

Sweet Potato Hash

Servings: 4

Cooking Time: 15 Minutes

Ingredients:

- 3 sweet potatoes, peel & cut into ½-inch pieces
- ½ tsp cinnamon
- 2 tbsp olive oil
- 1 bell pepper, cut into ½-inch pieces
- ½ tsp dried thyme
- ½ tsp nutmeg
- 1 medium onion, cut into ½-inch pieces
- Pepper
- Salt

Directions:

1. In a bowl, toss sweet potatoes with the remaining ingredients.
2. Insert a crisper plate in Ninja Foodi air fryer baskets.
3. Add potato mixture in both baskets.
4. Select zone 1 then select "air fry" mode and set the temperature to 355 degrees F for 15 minutes. Press "match" to match zone 2 settings to zone 1. Press "start/stop" to begin.

Nutrition:

- (Per serving) Calories 167 | Fat 7.3g |Sodium 94mg | Carbs 24.9g | Fiber 4.2g | Sugar 6.8g | Protein 2.2g

Spinach And Red Pepper Egg Cups With Coffee-glazed Canadian Bacon
Servings:6
Cooking Time: 13 Minutes
Ingredients:

- FOR THE EGG CUPS
- 4 large eggs
- ¼ cup heavy (whipping) cream
- ¼ teaspoon kosher salt
- ¼ teaspoon freshly ground black pepper
- ½ cup roasted red peppers (about 1 whole pepper), drained and chopped
- ½ cup baby spinach, chopped
- FOR THE CANADIAN BACON
- ¼ cup brewed coffee
- 2 tablespoons maple syrup
- 1 tablespoon light brown sugar
- 6 slices Canadian bacon

Directions:

1. To prep the egg cups: In a medium bowl, whisk together the eggs and cream until well combined with a uniform, light color. Stir in the salt, black pepper, roasted red peppers, and spinach until combined.
2. Divide the egg mixture among 6 silicone muffin cups.
3. To prep the Canadian bacon: In a small bowl, whisk together the coffee, maple syrup, and brown sugar.
4. Using a basting brush, brush the glaze onto both sides of each slice of bacon.
5. To cook the egg cups and Canadian bacon: Install a crisper plate in each of the two baskets. Place the egg cups in the Zone 1 basket and insert the basket in the unit. Place the glazed bacon in the Zone 2 basket, making sure the slices don't overlap, and insert the basket in the unit. It is okay if the bacon overlaps a little bit.
6. Select Zone 1, select BAKE, set the temperature to 325°F, and set the time to 13 minutes.
7. Select Zone 2, select AIR FRY, set the temperature to 400°F, and set the time to 5 minutes. Select SMART FINISH.
8. Press START/PAUSE to begin cooking.
9. When the Zone 2 timer reads 2 minutes, press START/PAUSE. Remove the basket and use silicone-tipped tongs to flip the bacon. Reinsert the basket and press START/PAUSE to resume cooking.
10. When cooking is complete, serve the egg cups with the Canadian bacon.

Nutrition:

- (Per serving) Calories: 180; Total fat: 9.5g; Saturated fat: 4.5g; Carbohydrates: 9g; Fiber: 0g; Protein: 14g; Sodium: 688mg

Pepper Egg Cups
Servings: 4
Cooking Time: 18 Minutes.
Ingredients:

- 2 halved bell pepper, seeds removed
- 4 eggs
- 1 teaspoon olive oil
- 1 pinch salt and black pepper
- 1 pinch sriracha flakes

Directions:

1. Slice the bell peppers in half, lengthwise, and remove their seeds and the inner portion to get a cup-like shape.
2. Rub olive oil on the edges of the bell peppers.
3. Place them in the two crisper plates with their cut side up and crack 1 egg in each half of bell pepper.
4. Drizzle salt, black pepper, and sriracha flakes on top of the eggs.
5. Return the crisper plates to the Ninja Foodi Dual Zone Air Fryer.
6. Choose the Air Fry mode for Zone 1 and set the temperature to 390 degrees F and the time to 18 minutes.
7. Select the "MATCH" button to copy the settings for Zone 2.
8. Initiate cooking by pressing the START/STOP button.
9. Serve warm and fresh.

Nutrition:

- (Per serving) Calories 183 | Fat 15g |Sodium 402mg | Carbs 2.5g | Fiber 0.4g | Sugar 1.1g | Protein 10g

Donuts

Servings: 6
Cooking Time: 15 Minutes

Ingredients:

- 1 cup granulated sugar
- 2 tablespoons ground cinnamon
- 1 can refrigerated flaky buttermilk biscuits
- ¼ cup unsalted butter, melted

Directions:

1. Combine the sugar and cinnamon in a small shallow bowl and set aside.
2. Remove the biscuits from the can and put them on a chopping board, separated. Cut holes in the center of each biscuit with a 1-inch round biscuit cutter (or a similarly sized bottle cap).
3. Place a crisper plate in each drawer. In each drawer, place 4 biscuits in a single layer. Insert the drawers into the unit.
4. Select zone 1, then AIR FRY, then set the temperature to 360 degrees F/ 180 degrees C with a 10-minute timer. To match zone 2 settings to zone 1, choose MATCH. To begin cooking, select START/STOP.
5. Remove the donuts from the drawers after the timer has finished.

Nutrition:

- (Per serving) Calories 223 | Fat 8g | Sodium 150mg | Carbs 40g | Fiber 1.4g | Sugar 34.2g | Protein 0.8g

Breakfast Sausage Omelet

Servings:2
Cooking Time:8

Ingredients:

- ¼ pound breakfast sausage, cooked and crumbled
- 4 eggs, beaten
- ½ cup pepper Jack cheese blend
- 2 tablespoons green bell pepper, sliced

- 1 green onion, chopped
- 1 pinch cayenne pepper
- Cooking spray

Directions:

1. Take a bowl and whisk eggs in it along with crumbled sausage, pepper Jack cheese, green onions, red bell pepper, and cayenne pepper.
2. Mix it all well.
3. Take two cake pans that fit inside the air fryer and grease it with oil spray.
4. Divide the omelet mixture between cake pans.
5. Put the cake pans inside both of the Ninja Foodie 2-Basket Air Fryer baskets.
6. Turn on the BAKE function of the zone 1 basket and let it cook for 15-20 minutes at 310 degrees F.
7. Select MATCH button for zone 2 basket.
8. Once the cooking cycle completes, take out, and serve hot, as a delicious breakfast.

Nutrition:

- (Per serving) Calories 691| Fat52.4g | Sodium1122 mg | Carbs 13.3g | Fiber 1.8g| Sugar 7g | Protein 42g

Blueberry Coffee Cake And Maple Sausage Patties

Servings:6

Cooking Time: 25 Minutes

Ingredients:

- FOR THE COFFEE CAKE
- 6 tablespoons unsalted butter, at room temperature, divided
- ⅓ cup granulated sugar
- 1 large egg
- 1 teaspoon vanilla extract
- 1/4 cup whole milk
- 11/2 cups all-purpose flour, divided
- 1 teaspoon baking powder
- 1/4 teaspoon salt
- 1 cup blueberries
- 1/4 cup packed light brown sugar
- 1/2 teaspoon ground cinnamon
- FOR THE SAUSAGE PATTIES
- 1/2 pound ground pork
- 2 tablespoons maple syrup
- 1/2 teaspoon dried sage
- 1/2 teaspoon dried thyme
- 11/2 teaspoons kosher salt
- 1/2 teaspoon crushed fennel seeds
- 1/2 teaspoon red pepper flakes (optional)
- 1/4 teaspoon freshly ground black pepper

Directions:

1. To prep the coffee cake: In a large bowl, cream together 4 tablespoons of butter with the granulated sugar. Beat in the egg, vanilla, and milk.
2. Stir in 1 cup of flour, along with the baking soda and salt, to form a thick batter. Fold in the blueberries.
3. In a second bowl, mix the remaining 2 tablespoons of butter, remaining ½ cup of flour, the brown sugar, and cinnamon to form a dry crumbly mixture.
4. To prep the sausage patties: In a large bowl, mix the pork, maple syrup, sage, thyme, salt, fennel seeds, red pepper flakes (if using), and black pepper until just combined.
5. Divide the mixture into 6 equal patties about ½ inch thick.
6. To cook the coffee cake and sausage patties: Spread the cake batter into the Zone 1 basket, top with the crumble mixture, and insert the basket in the unit. Install a crisper plate in the Zone 2 basket, add the sausage patties in a single layer, and insert the basket in the unit.
7. Select Zone 1, select BAKE, set the temperature to 350°F, and set the time to 25 minutes.
8. Select Zone 2, select AIR FRY, set the temperature to 375°F, and set the time to 12 minutes. Select SMART FINISH.
9. Press START/PAUSE to begin cooking.
10. When the Zone 2 timer reads 6 minutes, press START/PAUSE. Remove the basket and use silicone-tipped tongs to flip the sausage patties. Reinsert the basket and press START/PAUSE to resume cooking.
11. When cooking is complete, let the coffee cake cool for at least 5 minutes, then cut into 6 slices. Serve warm or at room temperature with the sausage patties.

Nutrition:

- (Per serving) Calories: 395; Total fat: 15g; Saturated fat: 8g; Carbohydrates: 53g; Fiber: 1.5g; Protein: 14g; Sodium: 187mg

Yellow Potatoes With Eggs

Servings:2

Cooking Time:35

Ingredients:

- 1 pound of Dutch yellow potatoes, quartered
- 1 red bell pepper, chopped
- Salt and black pepper, to taste
- 1 green bell pepper, chopped
- 2 teaspoons of olive oil
- 2 teaspoons of garlic powder
- 1 teaspoon of onion powder
- 1 egg
- ¼ teaspoon of butter

Directions:

1. Toss together diced potatoes, green pepper, red pepper, salt, black pepper, and olive oil along with garlic powder and onion powder.
2. Put in the zone 1 basket of the air fryer.
3. Take ramekin and grease it with oil spray.
4. Whisk egg in a bowl and add salt and pepper along with ½ teaspoon of butter.
5. Pour egg into a ramekin and place it in a zone 2 basket.
6. Now start cooking and set a timer for zone 1 basket to 30-35 minutes at 400 degrees at AIR FRY mode.
7. Now for zone 2, set it on AIR FRY mode at 350 degrees F for 8-10 minutes.
8. Press the Smart finish button and press start, it will finish both at the same time.
9. Once done, serve and enjoy.

Nutrition:

- (Per serving) Calories252 | Fat7.5g | Sodium 37mg | Carbs 40g | Fiber3.9g | Sugar 7g | Protein 6.7g

Bacon And Eggs For Breakfast

Servings:1

Cooking Time:12

Ingredients:

- 4 strips of thick-sliced bacon
- 2 small eggs
- Salt and black pepper, to taste
- Oil spray for greasing ramekins

Directions:

1. Take 2 ramekins and grease them with oil spray.
2. Crack eggs in a bowl and season it salt and black pepper.
3. Divide the egg mixture between two ramekins.
4. Put the bacon slices into Ninja Foodie 2-Basket Air Fryer zone 1 basket, and ramekins in zone 2 baskets.
5. Now for zone 1 set it to AIR FRY mode at 400 degrees F for 12 minutes.
6. And for zone 2 set it 350 degrees for 8 minutes using AIR FRY mode.
7. Press the Smart finish button and press start, it will finish both at the same time.
8. Once done, serve and enjoy.

Nutrition:

- (Per serving) Calories131 | Fat 10g| Sodium 187mg | Carbs0.6 g | Fiber 0g | Sugar 0.6g | Protein 10.7

Banana And Raisins Muffins

Servings:2

Cooking Time:16

Ingredients:

- Salt, pinch
- 2 eggs, whisked
- 1/3 cup butter, melted
- 4 tablespoons of almond milk
- ¼ teaspoon of vanilla extract
- ½ teaspoon of baking powder
- 1-1/2 cup all-purpose flour
- 1 cup mashed bananas
- 2 tablespoons of raisins

Directions:

1. Take about 4 large (one-cup sized) ramekins and layer them with muffin papers.

2. Crack eggs in a large bowl, and whisk it all well and start adding vanilla extract, almond milk, baking powder, and melted butter
3. Whisk the ingredients very well.
4. Take a separate bowl and add the all-purpose flour, and salt.
5. Now, combine the add dry ingredients with the wet ingredients.
6. Now, pour mashed bananas and raisins into this batter
7. Mix it well to make a batter for the muffins.
8. Now pour the batter into four ramekins and divided the ramekins in the air fryer zones.
9. Set the timer for zone 1 to 16 minutes at 350 degrees F.
10. Select the MATCH button for the zone 2 basket.
11. Check if not done, and let it AIR FRY for one more minute.
12. Once it is done, serve.

Nutrition:

- (Per serving) Calories 727| Fat 43.1g| Sodium366 mg | Carbs 74.4g | Fiber 4.7g | Sugar 16.1g | Protein 14.1g

Healthy Oatmeal Muffins

Servings: 6

Cooking Time: 17 Minutes

Ingredients:

- 1 egg
- ¼ tsp ground ginger
- 1 tsp ground cinnamon
- ½ tsp baking soda
- ½ tsp baking powder
- 55g brown sugar
- ½ tsp vanilla
- 2 tbsp butter, melted
- 125g applesauce
- 61ml milk
- 68gm whole wheat flour
- 100gm quick oats
- Pinch of salt

Directions:

1. In a mixing bowl, mix together all dry the ingredients.
2. In a separate bowl, add the remaining ingredients and mix well.
3. Add the dry ingredients mixture into the wet mixture and mix until well combined.
4. Pour the batter into the silicone muffin moulds.
5. Insert a crisper plate in the Ninja Foodi air fryer baskets.
6. Place muffin moulds in both baskets.
7. Select zone 1 then select "bake" mode and set the temperature to 390 degrees F for 17 minutes. Press "start/stop" to begin.

Nutrition:

- (Per serving) Calories 173 | Fat 5.8g |Sodium 177mg | Carbs 26.6g | Fiber 2.1g | Sugar 8.7g | Protein 4.2g

Egg And Avocado In The Ninja Foodi
Servings:2
Cooking Time:12
Ingredients:

- 2 Avocados, pitted and cut in half
- Garlic salt, to taste
- Cooking for greasing
- 4 eggs
- ¼ teaspoon of Paprika powder, for sprinkling
- 1/3 cup parmesan cheese, crumbled
- 6 bacon strips, raw

Directions:

1. First cut the avocado in half and pit it.
2. Now scoop out the flesh from the avocado and keep intact some of it
3. Crack one egg in each hole of avocado and sprinkle paprika and garlic salt
4. Top it with cheese at the end.
5. Now put it into tin foils and then put it in the air fryer zone basket 1
6. Put bacon strips in zone 2 basket.
7. Now for zone 1, set it to AIR FRY mode at 350 degrees F for 10 minutes
8. And for zone 2, set it 400 degrees for 12 minutes AIR FRY mode.
9. Press the Smart finish button and press start, it will finish both at the same time.
10. Once done, serve and enjoy.

Nutrition:

- (Per serving) Calories609 | Fat53.2g | Sodium 335mg | Carbs 18.1g | Fiber13.5g | Sugar 1.7g | Protein 21.3g

Bagels
Servings: 8
Cooking Time: 15 Minutes
Ingredients:

- 2 cups self-rising flour
- 2 cups non-fat plain Greek yogurt
- 2 beaten eggs for egg wash (optional)
- ½ cup sesame seeds (optional)

Directions:

1. In a medium mixing bowl, combine the self-rising flour and Greek yogurt using a wooden spoon.
2. Knead the dough for about 5 minutes on a lightly floured board.
3. Divide the dough into four equal pieces and roll each into a thin rope, securing the ends to form a bagel shape.
4. Install a crisper plate in both drawers. Place 4 bagels in a single layer in each drawer. Insert the drawers into the unit.
5. Select zone 1, select AIR FRY, set temperature to 360 degrees F/ 180 degrees C, and set time to 15 minutes. Select MATCH to match zone 2 settings to zone 1. Select START/STOP to begin.
6. Once the timer has finished, remove the bagels from the units.

7. Serve and enjoy!

Nutrition:

- (Per serving) Calories 202 | Fat 4.5g | Sodium 55mg | Carbs 31.3g | Fiber 2.7g | Sugar 4.7g | Protein 8.7g

Strawberry Baked Oats Chocolate Peanut Butter Baked Oats

Servings:12

Cooking Time: 15 Minutes

Ingredients:

- FOR THE STRAWBERRY OATS
- 1 cup whole milk
- 1 cup heavy (whipping) cream
- ½ cup maple syrup
- 2 teaspoons vanilla extract
- 2 large eggs
- 2 cups old-fashioned oats
- 2 teaspoons baking powder
- ½ teaspoon ground cinnamon
- ¼ teaspoon kosher salt
- 1½ cups diced strawberries
- FOR THE CHOCOLATE PEANUT BUTTER OATS
- 2 very ripe bananas
- ½ cup maple syrup
- ¼ cup unsweetened cocoa powder
- 2 teaspoons vanilla extract
- 2 teaspoons baking powder
- 2 large eggs
- ½ teaspoon kosher salt
- 2 cups old-fashioned oats
- 2 tablespoons peanut butter

Directions:

1. To prep the strawberry oats: In a large bowl, combine the milk, cream, maple syrup, vanilla, and eggs. Stir in the oats, baking powder, cinnamon, and salt until fully combined. Fold in the strawberries.
2. To prep the chocolate peanut butter oats: In a large bowl, mash the banana with a fork. Stir in the maple syrup, cocoa powder, vanilla, baking powder, and salt until smooth. Beat in the eggs. Stir in the oats until everything is combined.
3. To bake the oats: Place the strawberry oatmeal in the Zone 1 basket and insert the basket in the unit. Place the chocolate peanut butter oatmeal in the Zone 2 basket. Add ½ teaspoon dollops of peanut butter on top and insert the basket in the unit.
4. Select Zone 1, select BAKE, set the temperature to 320°F, and set the time to 15 minutes. Select MATCH COOK to match Zone 2 settings to Zone 1.
5. Press START/PAUSE to begin cooking.
6. When cooking is complete, serve each oatmeal in a shallow bowl.

Nutrition:

- (Per serving) Calories: 367; Total fat: 19g; Saturated fat: 11g; Carbohydrates: 42g; Fiber: 3.5g; Protein: 8g; Sodium: 102mg

Egg With Baby Spinach
Servings:4
Cooking Time:12
Ingredients:

- Nonstick spray, for greasing ramekins
- 2 tablespoons olive oil
- 6 ounces baby spinach
- 2 garlic cloves, minced
- 1/3 teaspoon kosher salt
- 6-8 large eggs
- ½ cup half and half
- Salt and black pepper, to taste
- 8 Sourdough bread slices, toasted

Directions:

1. Grease 4 ramekins with oil spray and set aside for further use.
2. Take a skillet and heat oil in it.
3. Then cook spinach for 2 minutes and add garlic and salt black pepper.
4. Let it simmer for2more minutes.
5. Once the spinach is wilted, transfer it to a plate.
6. Whisk an egg into a small bowl.
7. Add in the spinach.
8. Whisk it well and then pour half and half.
9. Divide this mixture between 4 ramekins and remember not to overfill it to the top, leave a little space on top.
10. Put the ramekins in zone 1 and zone 2 baskets of the Ninja Foodie 2-Basket Air Fryer.
11. Press start and set zone 1 to AIR fry it at 350 degrees F for 8-12 minutes.
12. Press the MATCH button for zone 2.
13. Once it's cooked and eggs are done, serve with sourdough bread slices.

Nutrition:

- (Per serving) Calories 404| Fat 19.6g| Sodium 761mg | Carbs 40.1g | Fiber 2.5g| Sugar 2.5g | Protein 19.2g

Breakfast Cheese Sandwich
Servings: 2
Cooking Time: 8 Minutes
Ingredients:

- 4 bread slices
- 2 provolone cheese slice
- ¼ tsp dried basil
- 2 tbsp mayonnaise
- 2 Monterey jack cheese slice
- 2 cheddar cheese slice

- ¼ tsp dried oregano

Directions:

1. In a small bowl, mix mayonnaise, basil, and oregano.
2. Spread mayonnaise on one side of the two bread slices.
3. Top two bread slices with cheddar cheese, provolone cheese, Monterey jack cheese slice, and cover with remaining bread slices.
4. Insert a crisper plate in the Ninja Foodi air fryer baskets.
5. Place sandwiches in both baskets.
6. Select zone 1, then select "air fry" mode and set the temperature to 390 degrees F for 8 minutes. Press "match" to match zone 2 settings to zone 1. Press "start/stop" to begin. Turn halfway through.

Nutrition:

- (Per serving) Calories 421 | Fat 30.7g |Sodium 796mg | Carbs 13.9g | Fiber 0.5g | Sugar 2.2g | Protein 22.5g

Breakfast Frittata

Servings: 4

Cooking Time: 12 Minutes

Ingredients:

- 4 eggs
- 4 tablespoons milk
- 35g cheddar cheese grated
- 50g feta crumbled
- 1 tomato, deseeded and chopped
- 15g spinach chopped
- 1 tablespoon fresh herbs, chopped
- 2 spring onion chopped
- Salt and black pepper, to taste
- ½ teaspoon olive oil

Directions:

1. Beat eggs with milk in a bowl and stir in the rest of the ingredients.
2. Grease two small-sized springform pans and line them with parchment paper.
3. Divide the egg mixture into the pans and place one in each air fryer basket.
4. Return the air fryer basket 1 to Zone 1, and basket 2 to Zone 2 of the Ninja Foodi 2-Basket Air Fryer.
5. Choose the "Air Fry" mode for Zone 1 at 350 degrees F and 12 minutes of cooking time.
6. Select the "MATCH COOK" option to copy the settings for Zone 2.
7. Initiate cooking by pressing the START/PAUSE BUTTON.
8. Serve warm.

Nutrition:

- (Per serving) Calories 273 | Fat 22g |Sodium 517mg | Carbs 3.3g | Fiber 0.2g | Sugar 1.4g | Protein 16.1g

Sausage Hash And Baked Eggs
Servings:4
Cooking Time: 30 Minutes
Ingredients:

- FOR THE HASH
- 2 yellow potatoes (about 1 pound), cut into ½-inch pieces
- 4 garlic cloves, minced
- 1 teaspoon kosher salt
- ¼ teaspoon freshly ground black pepper
- 2 tablespoons olive oil
- ½ pound pork breakfast sausage meat
- 1 small yellow onion, diced
- 1 red bell pepper, diced
- 1 teaspoon Italian seasoning
- FOR THE EGGS
- Nonstick cooking spray
- 4 large eggs
- 4 tablespoons water

Directions:

1. To prep the hash: In a large bowl, combine the potatoes, garlic, salt, black pepper, and olive oil and toss to coat. Crumble in the sausage and mix until combined.
2. To prep the eggs: Mist 4 silicone muffin cups with cooking spray. Crack 1 egg into each muffin cup. Top each egg with 1 tablespoon of water.
3. To cook the hash and eggs: Install a crisper plate in the Zone 1 basket. Place the sausage and potato mixture in the Zone 1 basket and insert the basket in the unit. Place the egg cups in the Zone 2 basket and insert the basket in the unit.
4. Select Zone 1, select AIR FRY, set the temperature to 400°F, and set the time to 30 minutes.
5. Select Zone 2, select BAKE, set the temperature to 325°F, and set the time to 12 minutes. Select SMART FINISH.
6. Press START/PAUSE to begin cooking.
7. When the Zone 1 timer reads 20 minutes, press START/PAUSE. Remove the basket and add the onion, bell pepper, and Italian seasoning to the hash. Mix until combined, breaking up any large pieces of sausage. Reinsert the basket and press START/PAUSE to resume cooking.
8. When cooking is complete, serve the hash topped with an egg.

Nutrition:

- (Per serving) Calories: 400; Total fat: 23g; Saturated fat: 5.5g; Carbohydrates: 31g; Fiber: 2g; Protein: 19g; Sodium: 750mg

Banana Muffins
Servings: 10
Cooking Time: 15 Minutes
Ingredients:

- 2 very ripe bananas
- ⅓ cup olive oil
- 1 egg
- ½ cup brown sugar

- 1 teaspoon vanilla extract
- 1 teaspoon cinnamon
- ¾ cup self-rising flour

Directions:

1. In a large mixing bowl, mash the bananas, then add the egg, brown sugar, olive oil, and vanilla. To blend, stir everything together thoroughly.
2. Fold in the flour and cinnamon until everything is just blended.
3. Fill muffin molds evenly with the mixture (silicone or paper).
4. Install a crisper plate in both drawers. Place the muffin molds in a single layer in each drawer. Insert the drawers into the unit.
5. Select zone 1, select AIR FRY, set temperature to 360 degrees F/ 180 degrees C, and set time to 15 minutes. Select MATCH to match zone 2 settings to zone 1. Select START/STOP to begin.
6. Once the timer has finished, remove the muffins from the drawers.
7. Serve and enjoy!

Nutrition:

- (Per serving) Calories 148 | Fat 7.3g | Sodium 9mg | Carbs 19.8g | Fiber 1g | Sugar 10g | Protein 1.8g

Crispy Hash Browns

Servings: 4

Cooking Time: 13 Minutes.

Ingredients:

- 3 russet potatoes
- ¼ cup chopped green peppers
- ¼ cup chopped red peppers
- ¼ cup chopped onions
- 2 garlic cloves chopped
- 1 teaspoon paprika
- Salt and black pepper, to taste
- 2 teaspoons olive oil

Directions:

1. Peel and grate all the potatoes with the help of a cheese grater.
2. Add potato shreds to a bowl filled with cold water and leave it soaked for 25 minutes.
3. Drain the water and place the potato shreds on a plate lined with a paper towel.
4. Transfer the shreds to a dry bowl and add olive oil, paprika, garlic, and black pepper.
5. Make four flat patties out of the potato mixture and place two into each of the crisper plate.
6. Return the crisper plate to the Ninja Foodi Dual Zone Air Fryer.
7. Choose the Air Fry mode for Zone 1 and set the temperature to 390 degrees F and set the time to 13 minutes.
8. Select the "MATCH" button to copy the settings for Zone 2.
9. Initiate cooking by pressing the START/STOP button.
10. Flip the potato hash browns once cooked halfway through, then resume cooking.
11. Once done, serve warm.

Nutrition:

- (Per serving) Calories 190 | Fat 18g |Sodium 150mg | Carbs 0.6g | Fiber 0.4g | Sugar 0.4g | Protein 7.2g

Lemon-cream Cheese Danishes Cherry Danishes
Servings:4
Cooking Time: 15 Minutes
Ingredients:

- FOR THE CREAM CHEESE DANISHES
- 1 ounce (2 tablespoons) cream cheese, at room temperature
- 1 teaspoon granulated sugar
- ¼ teaspoon freshly squeezed lemon juice
- ⅛ teaspoon vanilla extract
- ½ sheet frozen puff pastry, thawed
- 2 tablespoons lemon curd
- 1 large egg yolk
- 1 tablespoon water
- FOR THE CHERRY DANISHES
- ½ sheet frozen puff pastry, thawed
- 2 tablespoons cherry preserves
- 1 teaspoon coarse sanding sugar

Directions:

1. To prep the cream cheese Danishes: In a small bowl, mix the cream cheese, granulated sugar, lemon juice, and vanilla.
2. Cut the puff pastry sheet into 2 squares. Cut a ½-inch-wide strip from each side of the pastry. Brush the edges of the pastry square with water, then layer the strips along the edges, pressing gently to adhere and form a border around the outside of the pastry.
3. Divide the cream cheese mixture between the two pastries, then top each with 1 tablespoon of lemon curd.
4. In a second small bowl, whisk together the egg yolk and water (this will be used for the cherry Danishes, too). Brush the exposed edges of the pastry with half the egg wash.
5. To prep the cherry Danishes: Cut the puff pastry sheet into 2 squares. Cut a ½-inch-wide strip from each side of the pastry. Brush the edges of the pastry square with water, then layer the strips along the edges, pressing gently to adhere and form a border around the outside of the pastry.
6. Spoon 1 tablespoon of cherry preserves into the center of each pastry.
7. Brush the exposed edges of the pastry with the remaining egg wash, then sprinkle with the sanding sugar.
8. To cook both Danishes: Install a crisper plate in each of the two baskets. Place the cream cheese Danishes in the Zone 1 basket and insert the basket in the unit. Place the cherry Danishes in the Zone 2 basket and insert the basket in the unit.
9. Select Zone 1, select AIR FRY, set the temperature to 330°F, and set the time to 15 minutes. Select MATCH COOK to match Zone 2 settings to Zone 1.
10. Press START/PAUSE to begin cooking.
11. When cooking is complete, transfer the Danishes to a wire rack to cool. Serve warm.

Nutrition:

- (Per serving) Calories: 415; Total fat: 24g; Saturated fat: 12g; Carbohydrates: 51g; Fiber: 1.5g; Protein: 7g; Sodium: 274mg

Roasted Oranges
Servings: 4
Cooking Time: 6 Minutes
Ingredients:

- 2 oranges, halved
- 2 teaspoons honey
- 1 teaspoon cinnamon

Directions:

1. Place the oranges in each air fryer basket.
2. Drizzle honey and cinnamon over the orange halves.
3. Return the air fryer basket 1 to Zone 1, and basket 2 to Zone 2 of the Ninja Foodi 2-Basket Air Fryer.
4. Choose the "Air Fry" mode for Zone 1 at 395 degrees F temperature and 6 minutes of cooking time.
5. Select the "MATCH COOK" option to copy the settings for Zone 2.
6. Initiate cooking by pressing the START/PAUSE BUTTON.
7. Serve.

Nutrition:

- (Per serving) Calories 183 | Fat 15g |Sodium 402mg | Carbs 2.5g | Fiber 0.4g | Sugar 1.1g | Protein 10g

Hash Browns
Servings: 4
Cooking Time: 5 Minutes
Ingredients:

- 4 frozen hash browns patties
- Cooking oil spray of choice

Directions:

1. Install a crisper plate in both drawers. Place half the hash browns in zone 1 and half in zone 2, then insert the drawers into the unit. Spray the hash browns with some cooking oil.
2. Select zone 1, select AIR FRY, set temperature to 390 degrees F/ 200 degrees C, and set time to 5 minutes.
3. Select MATCH to match zone 2 settings to zone 1. Press the START/STOP button to begin cooking.
4. When cooking is complete, remove the hash browns and serve.

Nutrition:

- (Per serving) Calories 130 | Fat 7g | Sodium 300mg | Carbs 15g | Fiber 2g | Sugar 0g | Protein 1g

Morning Egg Rolls
Servings: 6
Cooking Time: 13 Minutes.
Ingredients:

- 2 eggs
- 2 tablespoons milk
- Salt, to taste

- Black pepper, to taste
- ½ cup shredded cheddar cheese
- 2 sausage patties
- 6 egg roll wrappers
- 1 tablespoon olive oil
- 1 cup water

Directions:

1. Grease a small skillet with some olive oil and place it over medium heat.
2. Add sausage patties and cook them until brown.
3. Chop the cooked patties into small pieces. Beat eggs with salt, black pepper, and milk in a mixing bowl.
4. Grease the same skillet with 1 teaspoon of olive oil and pour the egg mixture into it.
5. Stir cook to make scrambled eggs.
6. Add sausage, mix well and remove the skillet from the heat.
7. Spread an egg roll wrapper on the working surface in a diamond shape position.
8. Add a tablespoon of cheese at the bottom third of the roll wrapper.
9. Top the cheese with egg mixture and wet the edges of the wrapper with water.
10. Fold the two corners of the wrapper and roll it, then seal the edges.
11. Repeat the same steps and divide the rolls in the two crisper plates.
12. Return the crisper plates to the Ninja Foodi Dual Zone Air Fryer.
13. Choose the Air Fry mode for Zone 1 and set the temperature to 375 degrees F and the time to 13 minutes.
14. Select the "MATCH" button to copy the settings for Zone 2.
15. Initiate cooking by pressing the START/STOP button.
16. Flip the rolls after 8 minutes and continue cooking for another 5 minutes.
17. Serve warm and fresh.

Nutrition:

- (Per serving) Calories 282 | Fat 15g |Sodium 526mg | Carbs 20g | Fiber 0.6g | Sugar 3.3g | Protein 16g

Cornbread

Servings: 6

Cooking Time: 15 Minutes

Ingredients:

- 1 cup cornmeal
- 1 cup all-purpose flour
- 1 tablespoon sugar
- 2 teaspoons baking powder
- ½ teaspoon baking soda
- ½ teaspoon salt
- 1 stick butter melted
- 1½ cups buttermilk
- 2 eggs
- 113g diced chiles

Directions:

1. Mix cornmeal with flour, sugar, baking powder, baking soda, salt, butter, milk, eggs and chiles in a bowl until smooth.

2. Spread this mixture in two greased 4-inch baking pans.
3. Place one pan in each air fryer basket.
4. Return the air fryer basket 1 to Zone 1, and basket 2 to Zone 2 of the Ninja Foodi 2-Basket Air Fryer.
5. Choose the "Air Fry" mode for Zone 1 at 330 degrees F and 15 minutes of cooking time.
6. Select the "MATCH COOK" option to copy the settings for Zone 2.
7. Initiate cooking by pressing the START/PAUSE BUTTON.
8. Slice and serve.

Nutrition:

- (Per serving) Calories 199 | Fat 11.1g |Sodium 297mg | Carbs 14.9g | Fiber 1g | Sugar 2.5g | Protein 9.9g

Snacks And Appetizers Recipes

Crispy Popcorn Shrimp

Servings: 4
Cooking Time: 6 Minutes

Ingredients:

- 170g shrimp, peeled and diced
- ½ cup breadcrumbs
- Salt and black pepper to taste
- 2 eggs, beaten

Directions:

1. Mix breadcrumbs with black pepper and salt in a bowl.
2. Dip the shrimp pieces in the eggs and coat each with breadcrumbs.
3. Divide the shrimp popcorn into the 2 Air Fryer baskets.
4. Return the air fryer basket 1 to Zone 1, and basket 2 to Zone 2 of the Ninja Foodi 2-Basket Air Fryer.
5. Choose the "Air Fry" mode for Zone 1 at 400 degrees F and 6 minutes of cooking time.
6. Select the "MATCH COOK" option to copy the settings for Zone 2.
7. Initiate cooking by pressing the START/PAUSE BUTTON.
8. Serve warm.

Nutrition:

- (Per serving) Calories 180 | Fat 3.2g |Sodium 133mg | Carbs 32g | Fiber 1.1g | Sugar 1.8g | Protein 9g

Jalapeño Popper Dip With Tortilla Chips

Servings:6
Cooking Time: 15 Minutes

Ingredients:

- FOR THE DIP
- 8 ounces cream cheese, at room temperature
- ½ cup sour cream
- 1 cup shredded Cheddar cheese
- ¼ cup shredded Parmesan cheese

- 1/4 cup roughly chopped pickled jalapeños
- 1/2 teaspoon kosher salt
- 1/2 cup panko bread crumbs
- 2 tablespoons olive oil
- 1/2 teaspoon dried parsley
- FOR THE TORTILLA CHIPS
- 10 corn tortillas
- 2 tablespoons fresh lime juice
- 1 tablespoon olive oil
- 1/2 teaspoon kosher salt

Directions:

1. To prep the dip: In a medium bowl, mix the cream cheese, sour cream, Cheddar, Parmesan, jalapeños, and salt until smooth.
2. In a small bowl, combine the panko, olive oil, and parsley.
3. Pour the dip into a 14-ounce ramekin and top with the panko mixture.
4. To prep the chips: Brush both sides of each tortilla with lime juice, then with oil. Sprinkle with the salt. Using a sharp knife or a pizza cutter, cut each tortilla into 4 wedges.
5. To cook the dip and chips: Install a crisper plate in each of the two baskets. Place the ramekin of dip in the Zone 1 basket and insert the basket in the unit. Layer the tortillas in the Zone 2 basket and insert the basket in the unit.
6. Select Zone 1, select BAKE, set the temperature to 350°F, and set the time to 15 minutes.
7. Select Zone 2, select AIR FRY, set the temperature to 375°F, and set the time to 5 minutes. Select SMART FINISH.
8. Press START/PAUSE to begin cooking.
9. When the Zone 2 timer reads 3 minutes, press START/PAUSE. Remove the basket from the unit and give the basket a good shake to redistribute the chips. Reinsert the basket and press START/PAUSE to resume cooking.
10. When cooking is complete, the dip will be bubbling and golden brown and the chips will be crispy. Serve warm.

Nutrition:

- (Per serving) Calories: 406; Total fat: 31g; Saturated fat: 14g; Carbohydrates: 22g; Fiber: 1g; Protein: 11g; Sodium: 539mg

Mozzarella Sticks

Servings: 8

Cooking Time: 1 Hour 15 Minutes

Ingredients:

- 8 mozzarella sticks
- 1/4 cup all-purpose flour
- 1 egg, whisked
- 1 cup panko breadcrumbs
- 1/2 teaspoon each onion powder, garlic powder, smoked paprika, salt

Directions:

1. Freeze the mozzarella sticks for 30 minutes after placing them on a parchment-lined plate.
2. In the meantime, set up your "breading station": Fill a Ziploc bag halfway with flour. In a small dish, whisk the egg. In a separate shallow bowl, combine the panko and spices.

3. To bread your mozzarella sticks: Toss the sticks into the bag of flour, seal it, and shake to coat the cheese evenly. Take out the sticks and dip them in the egg, then in the panko, one at a time. Put the coated sticks back on the plate and put them in the freezer for another 30 minutes.
4. Place a crisper plate in each drawer, then add the mozzarella sticks in a single layer to each. Insert the drawers into the unit.
5. Select zone 1, then AIR FRY, then set the temperature to 400 degrees F/ 200 degrees C with a 15-minute timer. To match zone 2 settings to zone 1, choose MATCH. To begin, select START/STOP

Nutrition:

- (Per serving) Calories 131 | Fat 5.3g | Sodium 243mg | Carbs 11.3g | Fiber 1.1g | Sugar 0.3g | Protein 9.9g

Chicken Stuffed Mushrooms

Servings: 6

Cooking Time: 15 Minutes.

Ingredients:

- 6 large fresh mushrooms, stems removed
- Stuffing:
- ½ cup chicken meat, cubed
- 1 (4 ounces) package cream cheese, softened
- ¼ lb. imitation crabmeat, flaked
- 1 cup butter
- 1 garlic clove, peeled and minced
- Black pepper and salt to taste
- Garlic powder to taste
- Crushed red pepper to taste

Directions:

1. Melt and heat butter in a skillet over medium heat.
2. Add chicken and sauté for 5 minutes.
3. Add in all the remaining ingredients for the stuffing.
4. Cook for 5 minutes, then turn off the heat.
5. Allow the mixture to cool. Stuff each mushroom with a tablespoon of this mixture.
6. Divide the stuffed mushrooms in the two crisper plates.
7. Return the crisper plate to the Ninja Foodi Dual Zone Air Fryer.
8. Choose the Air Fry mode for Zone 1 and set the temperature to 375 degrees F and the time to 15 minutes.
9. Select the "MATCH" button to copy the settings for Zone 2.
10. Initiate cooking by pressing the START/STOP button.
11. Serve warm.

Nutrition:

- (Per serving) Calories 180 | Fat 3.2g |Sodium 133mg | Carbs 32g | Fiber 1.1g | Sugar 1.8g | Protein 9g

Fried Halloumi Cheese

Servings: 6

Cooking Time: 12 Minutes.

Ingredients:

- 1 block of halloumi cheese, sliced
- 2 teaspoons olive oil

Directions:

1. Divide the halloumi cheese slices in the crisper plate.
2. Drizzle olive oil over the cheese slices.
3. Return the crisper plate to the Ninja Foodi Dual Zone Air Fryer.
4. Choose the Air Fry mode for Zone 1 and set the temperature to 360 degrees F and the time to 12 minutes.
5. Flip the cheese slices once cooked halfway through.
6. Serve.

Nutrition:

- (Per serving) Calories 186 | Fat 3g |Sodium 223mg | Carbs 31g | Fiber 8.7g | Sugar 5.5g | Protein 9.7g

Tasty Sweet Potato Wedges

Servings: 4

Cooking Time: 20 Minutes

Ingredients:

- 2 sweet potatoes, peel & cut into wedges
- 1 tbsp BBQ spice rub
- ½ tsp sweet paprika
- 1 tbsp olive oil
- Pepper
- Salt

Directions:

1. In a bowl, toss sweet potato wedges with sweet paprika, oil, BBQ spice rub, pepper, and salt.
2. Insert a crisper plate in the Ninja Foodi air fryer baskets.
3. Add sweet potato wedges in both baskets.
4. Select zone 1 then select "air fry" mode and set the temperature to 390 degrees F for 20 minutes. Press "match" to match zone 2 settings to zone 1. Press "start/stop" to begin. Turn halfway through.

Nutrition:

- (Per serving) Calories 87 | Fat 3.6g |Sodium 75mg | Carbs 13.2g | Fiber 2.1g | Sugar 2.8g | Protein 1.1g

Bacon Wrapped Tater Tots

Servings: 8

Cooking Time: 14 Minutes

Ingredients:

- 8 bacon slices
- 3 tablespoons honey

- ½ tablespoon chipotle chile powder
- 16 frozen tater tots

Directions:

1. Cut the bacon slices in half and wrap each tater tot with a bacon slice.
2. Brush the bacon with honey and drizzle chipotle chile powder over them.
3. Insert a toothpick to seal the bacon.
4. Place the wrapped tots in the air fryer baskets.
5. Return the air fryer basket 1 to Zone 1, and basket 2 to Zone 2 of the Ninja Foodi 2-Basket Air Fryer.
6. Choose the "Air Fry" mode for Zone 1 at 350 degrees F and 14 minutes of cooking time.
7. Select the "MATCH COOK" option to copy the settings for Zone 2.
8. Initiate cooking by pressing the START/PAUSE BUTTON.
9. Serve warm.

Nutrition:

- (Per serving) Calories 100 | Fat 2g |Sodium 480mg | Carbs 4g | Fiber 2g | Sugar 0g | Protein 18g

Chicken Tenders
Servings:3
Cooking Time:12
Ingredients:

- 1 pound of chicken tender
- Salt and black pepper, to taste
- 1 cup Panko bread crumbs
- 2 cups Italian bread crumbs
- 1 cup parmesan cheese
- 2 eggs
- Oil spray, for greasing

Directions:

1. Sprinkle the tenders with salt and black pepper.
2. In a medium bowl mix Panko bread crumbs with Italian breadcrumbs.
3. Add salt, pepper, and parmesan cheese.
4. Crack two eggs in a bowl.
5. First, put the chicken tender in eggs.
6. Now dredge the tender in a bowl and coat the tender well with crumbs.
7. Line both of the baskets of the air fryer with parchment paper.
8. At the end spray the tenders with oil spray.
9. Divided the tenders between the baskets of Ninja Foodie 2-Basket Air Fryer.
10. Set zone 1 basket to AIR FRY mode at 350 degrees F for 12 minutes.
11. Select the MATCH button for the zone 2 basket.
12. Once it's done, serve.

Nutrition:

- (Per serving) Calories558 | Fat23.8g | Sodium872 mg | Carbs 20.9g | Fiber1.7 g| Sugar2.2 g | Protein 63.5g

Onion Rings
Servings: 4
Cooking Time: 7 Minutes
Ingredients:

- 170g onion, sliced into rings
- ½ cup breadcrumbs
- 2 eggs, beaten
- ½ cup flour
- Salt and black pepper to taste

Directions:

1. Mix flour, black pepper and salt in a bowl.
2. Dredge the onion rings through the flour mixture.
3. Dip them in the eggs and coat with the breadcrumbs.
4. Place the coated onion rings in the air fryer baskets.
5. Return the air fryer basket 1 to Zone 1, and basket 2 to Zone 2 of the Ninja Foodi 2-Basket Air Fryer.
6. Choose the "Air Fry" mode for Zone 1 at 350 degrees F and 7 minutes of cooking time.
7. Select the "MATCH COOK" option to copy the settings for Zone 2.
8. Initiate cooking by pressing the START/PAUSE BUTTON.
9. Shake the rings once cooked halfway through.
10. Serve warm.

Nutrition:

- (Per serving) Calories 185 | Fat 11g |Sodium 355mg | Carbs 21g | Fiber 5.8g | Sugar 3g | Protein 4.7g

Blueberries Muffins
Servings:2
Cooking Time:15
Ingredients:

- Salt, pinch
- 2 eggs
- 1/3 cup sugar
- 1/3 cup vegetable oil
- 4 tablespoons of water
- 1 teaspoon of lemon zest
- ¼ teaspoon of vanilla extract
- ½ teaspoon of baking powder
- 1 cup all-purpose flour
- 1 cup blueberries

Directions:

1. Take 4 one-cup sized ramekins that are oven safe and layer them with muffin papers.
2. Take a bowl and whisk the egg, sugar, oil, water, vanilla extract, and lemon zest.
3. Whisk it all very well.
4. Now, in a separate bowl, mix the flour, baking powder, and salt.

5. Now, add dry ingredients slowly to wet ingredients.
6. Now, pour this batter into ramekins and top it with blueberries.
7. Now, divide it between both zones of the Ninja Foodie 2-Basket Air Fryer.
8. Set the time for zone 1 to 15 minutes at 350 degrees F.
9. Select the MATCH button for the zone 2 basket.
10. Check if not done, and let it AIR FRY for one more minute.
11. Once it is done, serve.

Nutrition:

- (Per serving) Calories 781| Fat41.6g | Sodium 143mg | Carbs 92.7g | Fiber 3.5g| Sugar41.2 g | Protein 0g

Peppered Asparagus

Servings: 6

Cooking Time: 16 Minutes.

Ingredients:

- 1 bunch of asparagus, trimmed
- Avocado or Olive Oil
- Himalayan salt, to taste
- Black pepper, to taste

Directions:

1. Divide the asparagus in the two crisper plate.
2. Toss the asparagus with salt, black pepper, and oil.
3. Return the crisper plate to the Ninja Foodi Dual Zone Air Fryer.
4. Choose the Air Fry mode for Zone 1 and set the temperature to 390 degrees F and the time to 16 minutes.
5. Select the "MATCH" button to copy the settings for Zone 2.
6. Initiate cooking by pressing the START/STOP button.
7. Serve warm.

Nutrition:

- (Per serving) Calories 163 | Fat 11.5g |Sodium 918mg | Carbs 8.3g | Fiber 4.2g | Sugar 0.2g | Protein 7.4g

Dijon Cheese Sandwich

Servings:2

Cooking Time:10

Ingredients:

- 4 large slices sourdough, whole grain
- 4 tablespoons of Dijon mustard
- 1-1/2 cup grated sharp cheddar cheese
- 2 teaspoons green onion, chopped the green part
- 2 tablespoons of butter melted

Directions:

1. Brush the melted butter on one side of all the bread slices.

2. Then spread Dijon mustard on other sides of slices.
3. Then top the 2 bread slices with cheddar cheese and top it with green onions.
4. Cover with the remaining two slices to make two sandwiches.
5. Divide it between two baskets of the air fryer.
6. Turn on the air fry mode for zone 1 basket at 350 degrees f, for 10 minutes.
7. Use the match button for the second zone.
8. Once it's done, serve.

Nutrition:

- (Per serving) calories 617| fat 38 g| sodium 1213mg | carbs40.8 g | fiber 5g| sugar 5.6g | protein 29.5g

Chili-lime Crispy Chickpeas Pizza-seasoned Crispy Chickpeas

Servings:6

Cooking Time: 20 Minutes

Ingredients:

- FOR THE CHILI-LIME CHICKPEAS
- 1½ cups canned chickpeas, rinsed and drained
- ¼ cup fresh lime juice
- 1 tablespoon olive oil
- 1½ teaspoons chili powder
- ½ teaspoon kosher salt
- FOR THE PIZZA-SEASONED CHICKPEAS
- 1½ cups canned chickpeas, rinsed and drained
- 1 tablespoon olive oil
- 1 tablespoon grated Parmesan cheese
- ½ teaspoon dried basil
- ½ teaspoon dried oregano
- ½ teaspoon kosher salt
- ¼ teaspoon onion powder
- ¼ teaspoon garlic powder
- ¼ teaspoon fennel seeds
- ¼ teaspoon dried thyme
- ¼ teaspoon red pepper flakes (optional)

Directions:

1. To prep the chili-lime chickpeas: In a small bowl, mix the chickpeas, lime juice, olive oil, chili powder, and salt until the chickpeas are well coated.
2. To prep the pizza-seasoned chickpeas: In a small bowl, mix the chickpeas, olive oil, Parmesan, basil, oregano, salt, onion powder, garlic powder, fennel, thyme, and red pepper flakes (if using) until the chickpeas are well coated.
3. To cook the chickpeas: Install a crisper plate in each of the two baskets. Place the chili-lime chickpeas in the Zone 1 basket and insert the basket in the unit. Place the pizza-seasoned chickpeas in the Zone 2 basket and insert the basket in the unit.
4. Select Zone 1, select AIR FRY, set the temperature to 375°F, and set the time to 20 minutes. Select MATCH COOK to match Zone 2 settings to Zone 1.
5. Press START/PAUSE to begin cooking.
6. When both timers read 10 minutes, press START/PAUSE. Remove both baskets and give each basket a shake to redistribute the chickpeas. Reinsert both baskets and press START/PAUSE to resume cooking.

7. When both timers read 5 minutes, press START/PAUSE. Remove both baskets and give each basket a good shake again. Reinsert both baskets and press START/PAUSE to resume cooking.
8. When cooking is complete, the chickpeas will be crisp and golden brown. Serve warm or at room temperature.

Nutrition:

- (Per serving) Calories: 145; Total fat: 6.5g; Saturated fat: 0.5g; Carbohydrates: 17g; Fiber: 4.5g; Protein: 5g; Sodium: 348mg

Cauliflower Cheese Patties

Servings: 4

Cooking Time: 10 Minutes

Ingredients:

- 2 eggs
- 200g cauliflower rice, microwave for 5 minutes
- 56g mozzarella cheese, shredded
- 22g parmesan cheese, grated
- 11g Mexican cheese, shredded
- ½ tsp onion powder
- 1 tsp dried basil
- 1 tsp garlic powder
- 33g breadcrumbs
- Pepper
- Salt

Directions:

1. Add cauliflower rice and remaining ingredients into the mixing bowl and mix until well combined.
2. Insert a crisper plate in the Ninja Foodi air fryer baskets.
3. Make patties from the cauliflower mixture and place them in both baskets.
4. Select zone 1, then select "air fry" mode and set the temperature to 390 degrees F for 10 minutes. Press "match" to match zone 2 settings to zone 1. Press "start/stop" to begin. Turn halfway through.

Nutrition:

- (Per serving) Calories 318 | Fat 18g |Sodium 951mg | Carbs 11.1g | Fiber 1.8g | Sugar 2.2g | Protein 25.6g

Healthy Spinach Balls

Servings: 4

Cooking Time: 10 Minutes

Ingredients:

- 1 egg
- 29g breadcrumbs
- ½ medium onion, chopped
- 225g spinach, blanched & chopped
- 1 carrot, peel & grated
- 1 tbsp cornflour

- 1 tbsp nutritional yeast
- 1 tsp garlic, minced
- ½ tsp garlic powder
- Pepper
- Salt

Directions:

1. Add spinach and remaining ingredients into the mixing bowl and mix until well combined.
2. Insert a crisper plate in the Ninja Foodi air fryer baskets.
3. Make small balls from the spinach mixture and place them in both baskets.
4. Select zone 1, then select "air fry" mode and set the temperature to 390 degrees F for 10 minutes. Press "match" to match zone 2 settings to zone 1. Press "start/stop" to begin.

Nutrition:

- (Per serving) Calories 74 | Fat 1.7g |Sodium 122mg | Carbs 11.1g | Fiber 1.9g | Sugar 2g | Protein 4.2g

Garlic Bread

Servings: 4

Cooking Time: 10 Minutes

Ingredients:

- ½ loaf of bread
- 3 tablespoons butter, softened
- 3 garlic cloves, minced
- ½ teaspoon Italian seasoning
- Small pinch of red pepper flakes
- Optional
- ¼ cup shredded mozzarella cheese
- Freshly grated parmesan cheese
- Chopped fresh parsley for serving/topping

Directions:

1. Slice the bread in half horizontally or as appropriate to fit inside the air fryer.
2. Combine the softened butter, garlic, Italian seasoning, and red pepper flakes in a mixing bowl.
3. Brush the garlic butter mixture evenly over the bread.
4. Place a crisper plate in each drawer. Place the bread pieces into each drawer. Insert the drawers into the unit.
5. Select zone 1, then AIR FRY, then set the temperature to 360 degrees F/ 180 degrees C with a 6-minute timer. To match zone 2 settings to zone 1, choose MATCH. To begin, select START/STOP.
6. Remove the garlic bread from your air fryer, slice, and serve!

Nutrition:

- (Per serving) Calories 150 | Fat 8.2g | Sodium 208mg | Carbs 14.3g | Fiber 2.3g | Sugar 1.2g | Protein 4.9g

Potato Tater Tots
Servings: 4
Cooking Time: 27 Minutes.
Ingredients:

- 2 potatoes, peeled
- ½ teaspoon Cajun seasoning
- Olive oil cooking spray
- Sea salt to taste

Directions:

1. Boil water in a cooking pot and cook potatoes in it for 15 minutes.
2. Drain and leave the potatoes to cool in a bowl.
3. Grate these potatoes and toss them with Cajun seasoning.
4. Make small tater tots out of this mixture.
5. Divide them into the two crisper plates and spray them with cooking oil.
6. Return the crisper plates to the Ninja Foodi Dual Zone Air Fryer.
7. Choose the Air Fry mode for Zone 1 and set the temperature to 375 degrees F and the time to 27 minutes.
8. Select the "MATCH" button to copy the settings for Zone 2.
9. Initiate cooking by pressing the START/STOP button.
10. Flip them once cooked halfway through, and resume cooking.
11. Serve warm

Nutrition:

- (Per serving) Calories 185 | Fat 11g |Sodium 355mg | Carbs 21g | Fiber 5.8g | Sugar 3g | Protein 4.7g

Crispy Chickpeas
Servings: 4
Cooking Time: 15 Minutes
Ingredients:

- 1 (15-ounce) can unsalted chickpeas, rinsed and drained
- 1½ tablespoons toasted sesame oil
- ¼ teaspoon smoked paprika
- ¼ teaspoon crushed red pepper
- ⅛ teaspoon salt
- Cooking spray
- 2 lime wedges

Directions:

1. The chickpeas should be spread out over multiple layers of paper towels. Roll the chickpeas under the paper towels to dry both sides, then top with more paper towels and pat until completely dry.
2. In a medium mixing bowl, combine the chickpeas and oil. Add the paprika, crushed red pepper, and salt to taste.
3. Place a crisper plate in each drawer. Put the chickpeas in a single layer in each drawer. Insert the drawers into the unit.
4. Select zone 1, then ROAST, then set the temperature to 400 degrees F/ 200 degrees C with a 15-minute timer. To match zone 2 settings to zone 1, choose MATCH. To begin, select START/STOP.

Nutrition:

- (Per serving) Calories 169 | Fat 5g | Sodium 357mg | Carbs 27.3g | Fiber 5.7g | Sugar 0.6g | Protein 5.9g

Crab Cakes
Servings: 4
Cooking Time: 10 Minutes
Ingredients:

- 227g lump crab meat
- 1 red capsicum, chopped
- 3 green onions, chopped
- 3 tablespoons mayonnaise
- 3 tablespoons breadcrumbs
- 2 teaspoons old bay seasoning
- 1 teaspoon lemon juice

Directions:

1. Mix crab meat with capsicum, onions and the rest of the ingredients in a food processor.
2. Make 4 inch crab cakes out of this mixture.
3. Divide the crab cakes into the Ninja Foodi 2 Baskets Air Fryer baskets.
4. Return the air fryer basket 1 to Zone 1, and basket 2 to Zone 2 of the Ninja Foodi 2-Basket Air Fryer.
5. Choose the "Air Fry" mode for Zone 1 at 370 degrees F and 10 minutes of cooking time.
6. Select the "MATCH COOK" option to copy the settings for Zone 2.
7. Initiate cooking by pressing the START/PAUSE BUTTON.
8. Flip the crab cakes once cooked halfway through.
9. Serve warm.

Nutrition:

- (Per serving) Calories 163 | Fat 11.5g |Sodium 918mg | Carbs 8.3g | Fiber 4.2g | Sugar 0.2g | Protein 7.4g

Sweet Bites
Servings:4
Cooking Time:12
Ingredients:

- 10 sheets of Phyllo dough, (filo dough)
- 2 tablespoons of melted butter
- 1 cup walnuts, chopped
- 2 teaspoons of honey
- Pinch of cinnamon
- 1 teaspoon of orange zest

Directions:

1. First, layer together 10 Phyllo dough sheets on a flat surface.
2. Then cut it into 4 *4-inch squares.
3. Now, coat the squares with butter, drizzle some honey, orange zest, walnuts, and cinnamon.

4. Bring all 4 corners together and press the corners to make a little like purse design.
5. Divide it amongst air fryer basket and select zone 1 basket using AIR fry mode and set it for 7 minutes at 375 degrees F.
6. Select the MATCH button for the zone 2 basket.
7. Once done, take out and serve.

Nutrition:

- (Per serving) Calories 397| Fat 27.1 g| Sodium 271mg | Carbs31.2 g | Fiber 3.2g| Sugar3.3g | Protein 11g

Miso-glazed Shishito Peppers Charred Lemon Shishito Peppers

Servings:4

Cooking Time: 10 Minutes

Ingredients:

- FOR THE MISO-GLAZED PEPPERS
- 2 tablespoons vegetable oil
- 2 tablespoons water
- 1 tablespoon white miso
- 1 teaspoon grated fresh ginger
- ½ pound shishito peppers
- FOR THE CHARRED LEMON PEPPERS
- ½ pound shishito peppers
- 1 lemon, cut into ⅛-inch-thick rounds
- 2 garlic cloves, minced
- 2 tablespoons vegetable oil
- ½ teaspoon kosher salt

Directions:

1. To prep the miso-glazed peppers: In a large bowl, mix the vegetable oil, water, miso, and ginger until well combined. Add the shishitos and toss to coat.
2. To prep the charred lemon peppers: In a large bowl, combine the shishitos, lemon slices, garlic, vegetable oil, and salt. Toss to coat.
3. To cook the peppers: Install a crisper plate in each of the two baskets. Place the miso-glazed peppers in the Zone 1 basket and insert the basket in the unit. Place the peppers with lemons in the Zone 2 basket and insert the basket in the unit.
4. Select Zone 1, select AIR FRY, set the temperature to 390°F, and set the time to 10 minutes. Select MATCH COOK to match Zone 2 settings to Zone 1.
5. Press START/PAUSE to begin cooking.
6. When both timers read 4 minutes, press START/PAUSE. Remove both baskets and shake well. Reinsert the baskets and press START/PAUSE to resume cooking.
7. When cooking is complete, serve immediately.

Nutrition:

- (Per serving) Calories: 165; Total fat: 14g; Saturated fat: 2g; Carbohydrates: 9g; Fiber: 2g; Protein: 2g; Sodium: 334mg

Stuffed Mushrooms
Servings: 5
Cooking Time: 8 Minutes
Ingredients:

- 8 ounces fresh mushrooms (I used Monterey)
- 4 ounces cream cheese
- ¼ cup shredded parmesan cheese
- ⅛cup shredded sharp cheddar cheese
- ⅛ cup shredded white cheddar cheese
- 1 teaspoon Worcestershire sauce
- 2 garlic cloves, minced
- Salt and pepper, to taste

Directions:

1. To prepare the mushrooms for stuffing, remove their stems. Make a circle cut around the area where the stem used to be. Continue to cut until all of the superfluous mushroom is removed.
2. To soften the cream cheese, microwave it for 15 seconds.
3. Combine the cream cheese, shredded cheeses, salt, pepper, garlic, and Worcestershire sauce in a medium mixing bowl. To blend, stir everything together.
4. Stuff the mushrooms with the cheese mixture.
5. Place a crisper plate in each drawer. Put the stuffed mushrooms in a single layer in each drawer. Insert the drawers into the unit.
6. Select zone 1, then AIR FRY, then set the temperature to 360 degrees F/ 180 degrees C with an 8-minute timer. To match zone 2 settings to zone 1, choose MATCH. To begin, select START/STOP.
7. Serve and enjoy!

Nutrition:

- (Per serving) Calories 230 | Fat 9.5g | Sodium 105mg | Carbs 35.5g | Fiber 5.1g | Sugar 0.1g | Protein 7.1g

Roasted Tomato Bruschetta With Toasty Garlic Bread
Servings:4
Cooking Time: 12 Minutes
Ingredients:

- FOR THE ROASTED TOMATOES
- 10 ounces cherry tomatoes, cut in half
- 1 tablespoon balsamic vinegar
- 1 tablespoon olive oil
- ¼ teaspoon kosher salt
- ¼ teaspoon freshly ground black pepper
- FOR THE GARLIC BREAD
- 4 slices crusty Italian bread
- 1 tablespoon olive oil
- 3 garlic cloves, minced
- ¼ teaspoon Italian seasoning
- FOR THE BRUSCHETTA
- ¼ cup loosely packed fresh basil, thinly sliced
- ½ cup part-skim ricotta cheese

Directions:

1. To prep the tomatoes: In a small bowl, combine the tomatoes, vinegar, oil, salt, and black pepper.
2. To prep the garlic bread: Brush one side of each bread slice with the oil. Sprinkle with the garlic and Italian seasoning.
3. To cook the tomatoes and garlic bread: Install a broil rack in the Zone 1 basket (without the crisper plate installed). Place the tomatoes on the rack in the basket and insert the basket in the unit.
4. Place 2 slices of bread in the Zone 2 basket and insert the basket in the unit.
5. Select Zone 1, select AIR BROIL, set the temperature to 450°F, and set the time to 12 minutes.
6. Select Zone 2, select AIR FRY, set the temperature to 360°F, and set the time to 10 minutes. Select SMART FINISH.
7. Press START/PAUSE to begin cooking.
8. When the Zone 2 timer reads 5 minutes, press START/PAUSE. Remove the basket and transfer the garlic bread to a cutting board. Place the remaining 2 slices of garlic bread in the basket. Reinsert the basket in the unit and press START/PAUSE to resume cooking.
9. To assemble the bruschetta: When cooking is complete, add the basil to the tomatoes and stir to combine. Spread 2 tablespoons of ricotta onto each slice of garlic bread and top with the tomatoes. Serve warm or at room temperature.

Nutrition:

- (Per serving) Calories: 212; Total fat: 11g; Saturated fat: 2.5g; Carbohydrates: 22g; Fiber: 1.5g; Protein: 6g; Sodium: 286mg

Parmesan Crush Chicken

Servings:4

Cooking Time:18

Ingredients:

- 4 chicken breasts
- 1 cup parmesan cheese
- 1 cup bread crumb
- 2 eggs, whisked
- Salt, to taste
- Oil spray, for greasing

Directions:

1. Whisk egg in a large bowl and set aside.
2. Season the chicken breast with salt and then put it in egg wash.
3. Next, dredge it in breadcrumb then parmesan cheese.
4. Line both the basket of the air fryer with parchment paper.
5. Divided the breast pieces between the backsets, and oil spray the breast pieces.
6. Set zone 1 basket to air fry mode at 350 degrees F for 18 minutes.
7. Select the MATCH button for the zone 2 basket.
8. Once it's done, serve.

Nutrition:

- (Per serving) Calories574 | Fat25g | Sodium848 mg | Carbs 21.4g | Fiber 1.2g| Sugar 1.8g | Protein 64.4g

Cinnamon Sugar Chickpeas
Servings: 4
Cooking Time: 15 Minutes
Ingredients:

- 2 cups chickpeas, drained
- Spray oil
- 1 tablespoon coconut sugar
- ½ teaspoon cinnamon
- Serving
- 57g cheddar cheese, cubed
- ¼ cup raw almonds
- 85g jerky, sliced

Directions:

1. Toss chickpeas with coconut sugar, cinnamon and oil in a bowl.
2. Divide the chickpeas into the Ninja Foodi 2 Baskets Air Fryer baskets.
3. Drizzle cheddar cheese, almonds and jerky on top.
4. Return the air fryer basket 1 to Zone 1, and basket 2 to Zone 2 of the Ninja Foodi 2-Basket Air Fryer.
5. Choose the "Air Fry" mode for Zone 1 at 380 degrees F and 15 minutes of cooking time.
6. Select the "MATCH COOK" option to copy the settings for Zone 2.
7. Initiate cooking by pressing the START/PAUSE BUTTON.
8. Toss the chickpeas once cooked halfway through.
9. Serve warm.

Nutrition:

- (Per serving) Calories 103 | Fat 8.4g |Sodium 117mg | Carbs 3.5g | Fiber 0.9g | Sugar 1.5g | Protein 5.1g

Beef Jerky Pineapple Jerky
Servings:8
Cooking Time: 6 To 12 Hours
Ingredients:

- FOR THE BEEF JERKY
- ½ cup reduced-sodium soy sauce
- ¼ cup pineapple juice
- 1 tablespoon dark brown sugar
- 1 tablespoon Worcestershire sauce
- ½ teaspoon smoked paprika
- ¼ teaspoon freshly ground black pepper
- ¼ teaspoon red pepper flakes
- 1 pound beef bottom round, trimmed of excess fat, cut into ¼-inch-thick slices
- FOR THE PINEAPPLE JERKY
- 1 pound pineapple, cut into ⅛-inch-thick rounds, pat dry
- 1 teaspoon chili powder (optional)

Directions:

1. To prep the beef jerky: In a large zip-top bag, combine the soy sauce, pineapple juice, brown sugar, Worcestershire sauce, smoked paprika, black pepper, and red pepper flakes.
2. Add the beef slices, seal the bag, and toss to coat the meat in the marinade. Refrigerate overnight or for at least 8 hours.
3. Remove the beef slices and discard the marinade. Using a paper towel, pat the slices dry to remove excess marinade.
4. To prep the pineapple jerky: Sprinkle the pineapple with chili powder (if using).
5. To dehydrate the jerky: Arrange half of the beef slices in a single layer in the Zone 1 basket, making sure they do not overlap. Place a crisper plate on top of the beef slices and arrange the remaining slices in a single layer on top of the crisper plate. Insert the basket in the unit.
6. Repeat this process with the pineapple in the Zone 2 basket and insert the basket in the unit.
7. Select Zone 1, select DEHYDRATE, set the temperature to 150°F, and set the time to 8 hours.
8. Select Zone 2, select DEHYDRATE, set the temperature to 135°F, and set the time to 12 hours.
9. Press START/PAUSE to begin cooking.
10. When the Zone 1 timer reads 2 hours, press START/PAUSE. Remove the basket and check the beef jerky for doneness. If necessary, reinsert the basket and press START/PAUSE to resume cooking.

Nutrition:

- (Per serving) Calories: 171; Total fat: 6.5g; Saturated fat: 2g; Carbohydrates: 2g; Fiber: 0g; Protein: 25g; Sodium: 369mg

Crab Cake Poppers

Servings: 6

Cooking Time: 10 Minutes

Ingredients:

- 1 egg, lightly beaten
- 453g lump crab meat, drained
- 1 tsp garlic, minced
- 1 tsp lemon juice
- 1 tsp old bay seasoning
- 30g almond flour
- 1 tsp Dijon mustard
- 28g mayonnaise
- Pepper
- Salt

Directions:

1. In a bowl, mix crab meat and remaining ingredients until well combined.
2. Make small balls from the crab meat mixture and place them on a plate.
3. Place the plate in the refrigerator for 50 minutes.
4. Insert a crisper plate in the Ninja Foodi air fryer baskets.
5. Place the prepared crab meatballs in both baskets.
6. Select zone 1 then select "air fry" mode and set the temperature to 360 degrees F for 10 minutes. Press "match" to match zone 2 settings to zone 1. Press "start/stop" to begin.

Nutrition:

- (Per serving) Calories 86 | Fat 8.5g |Sodium 615mg | Carbs 2.7g | Fiber 0.1g | Sugar 0.4g | Protein 12g

Potato Chips
Servings: 4
Cooking Time: 16 Minutes
Ingredients:

- 2 large potatoes, peeled and sliced
- 1½ teaspoons salt
- 1½ teaspoons black pepper
- Oil for misting

Directions:

1. Soak potatoes in cold water for 30 minutes then drain.
2. Pat dry the potato slices and toss them with cracked pepper, salt and oil mist.
3. Spread the potatoes in the air fryer basket.
4. Return the air fryer basket 1 to Zone 1, and basket 2 to Zone 2 of the Ninja Foodi 2-Basket Air Fryer.
5. Choose the "Air Fry" mode for Zone 1 at 300 degrees F and 16 minutes of cooking time.
6. Select the "MATCH COOK" option to copy the settings for Zone 2.
7. Initiate cooking by pressing the START/PAUSE BUTTON.
8. Toss the fries once cooked halfway through.
9. Serve warm.

Nutrition:

- (Per serving) Calories 122 | Fat 1.8g |Sodium 794mg | Carbs 17g | Fiber 8.9g | Sugar 1.6g | Protein 14.9g

Mozzarella Balls
Servings: 6
Cooking Time: 13 Minutes
Ingredients:

- 2 cups mozzarella, shredded
- 3 tablespoons cornstarch
- 3 tablespoons water
- 2 eggs, beaten
- 1 cup Italian seasoned breadcrumbs
- 1 tablespoon Italian seasoning
- 1½ teaspoons garlic powder
- 1 teaspoon salt
- 1½ teaspoons Parmesan

Directions:

1. Mix mozzarella with parmesan, water and cornstarch in a bowl.
2. Make 1-inch balls out of this mixture.
3. Mix breadcrumbs with seasoning, salt, and garlic powder in a bowl.
4. Dip the balls into the beaten eggs and coat with the breadcrumbs.

5. Place the coated balls in the air fryer baskets.
6. Return the air fryer basket 1 to Zone 1, and basket 2 to Zone 2 of the Ninja Foodi 2-Basket Air Fryer.
7. Choose the “Air Fry” mode for Zone 1 and set the temperature to 360 degrees F and 13 minutes of cooking time.
8. Select the “MATCH COOK” option to copy the settings for Zone 2.
9. Initiate cooking by pressing the START/PAUSE BUTTON.
10. Toss the balls once cooked halfway through.
11. Serve.

Nutrition:

- (Per serving) Calories 307 | Fat 8.6g |Sodium 510mg | Carbs 22.2g | Fiber 1.4g | Sugar 13g | Protein 33.6g

Parmesan French Fries

Servings: 6
Cooking Time: 20 Minutes.

Ingredients:

- 3 medium russet potatoes
- 2 tablespoons parmesan cheese
- 2 tablespoons fresh parsley, chopped
- 1 tablespoon olive oil
- Salt, to taste

Directions:

1. Wash the potatoes and pass them through the fries’ cutter to get ¼-inch-thick fries.
2. Place the fries in a colander and drizzle salt on top.
3. Leave these fries for 10 minutes, then rinse.
4. Toss the potatoes with parmesan cheese, oil, salt, and parsley in a bowl.
5. Divide the potatoes into the two crisper plates.
6. Return the crisper plates to the Ninja Foodi Dual Zone Air Fryer.
7. Choose the Air Fry mode for Zone 1 and set the temperature to 360 degrees F and the time to 20 minutes.
8. Select the “MATCH” button to copy the settings for Zone 2.
9. Initiate cooking by pressing the START/STOP button.
10. Toss the chips once cooked halfway through, then resume cooking.
11. Serve warm.

Nutrition:

- (Per serving) Calories 307 | Fat 8.6g |Sodium 510mg | Carbs 22.2g | Fiber 1.4g | Sugar 13g | Protein 33.6g

Grill Cheese Sandwich

Servings:2
Cooking Time:10

Ingredients:

- 4 slices of white bread slices
- 2 tablespoons of butter, melted
- 2 slices of sharp cheddar

- 2 slices of Swiss cheese
- 2 slices of mozzarella cheese

Directions:

1. Brush melted butter on one side of all the bread slices and then top the 2 bread slices with slices of cheddar, Swiss, and mozzarella, one slice per bread.
2. Top it with the other slice to make a sandwich.
3. Divide it between two baskets of the air fryer.
4. Turn on AIR FRY mode for zone 1 basket at 350 degrees F for 10 minutes.
5. Use the MATCH button for the second zone.
6. Once done, serve.

Nutrition:

- (Per serving) Calories 577 | Fat38g | Sodium 1466mg | Carbs 30.5g | Fiber 1.1g| Sugar 6.5g | Protein 27.6g

Fried Pickles

Servings: 4

Cooking Time: 15 Minutes

Ingredients:

- 2 cups sliced dill pickles
- 1 cup flour
- 1 tablespoon garlic powder
- 1 tablespoon Cajun spice
- ½ tablespoon cayenne pepper
- Olive Oil or cooking spray

Directions:

1. Mix together the flour and spices in a bowl.
2. Coat the sliced pickles with the flour mixture.
3. Place a crisper plate in each drawer. Put the pickles in a single layer in each drawer. Insert the drawers into the unit.
4. Select zone 1, then AIR FRY, then set the temperature to 400 degrees F/ 200 degrees C with a 15-minute timer. To match zone 2 settings to zone 1, choose MATCH. To begin, select START/STOP.

Nutrition:

- (Per serving) Calories 161 | Fat 4.1g | Sodium 975mg | Carbs 27.5g | Fiber 2.2g | Sugar 1.5g | Protein 4g

Avocado Fries With Sriracha Dip

Servings: 4

Cooking Time: 6 Minutes

Ingredients:

- Avocado Fries
- 4 avocados, peeled and cut into sticks

- ¾ cup panko breadcrumbs
- ¼ cup flour
- 2 eggs, beaten
- ½ teaspoon garlic powder
- ½ teaspoon salt
- SRIRACHA-RANCH SAUCE
- ¼ cup ranch dressing
- 1 teaspoon sriracha sauce

Directions:

1. Mix flour with garlic powder and salt in a bowl.
2. Dredge the avocado sticks through the flour mixture.
3. Dip them in the eggs and coat them with breadcrumbs.
4. Place the coated fries in the air fryer baskets.
5. Return the air fryer basket 1 to Zone 1, and basket 2 to Zone 2 of the Ninja Foodi 2-Basket Air Fryer.
6. Choose the "Air Fry" mode for Zone 1 at 400 degrees F and 6 minutes of cooking time.
7. Select the "MATCH COOK" option to copy the settings for Zone 2.
8. Initiate cooking by pressing the START/PAUSE BUTTON.
9. Flip the fries once cooked halfway through.
10. Mix all the dipping sauce ingredients in a bowl.
11. Serve the fries with dipping sauce.

Nutrition:

- (Per serving) Calories 229 | Fat 1.9 |Sodium 567mg | Carbs 1.9g | Fiber 0.4g | Sugar 0.6g | Protein 11.8g

Ravioli

Servings: 2

Cooking Time: 6 Minutes

Ingredients:

- 12 frozen portions of ravioli
- ½ cup buttermilk
- ½ cup Italian breadcrumbs

Directions:

1. Place two bowls side by side. Put the buttermilk in one and breadcrumbs in the other.
2. Dip each piece of ravioli into the buttermilk then breadcrumbs, making sure to coat them as best as possible.
3. Place a crisper plate in both drawers. In each drawer, put four breaded ravioli pieces in a single layer. Insert the drawers into the unit.
4. Select zone 1, then AIR FRY, then set the temperature to 360 degrees F/ 180 degrees C with a 6-minute timer. To match zone 2 settings to zone 1, choose MATCH. To begin, select START/STOP.
5. Remove the ravioli from the drawers after the timer has finished.

Nutrition:

- (Per serving) Calories 481 | Fat 20g | Sodium 1162mg | Carbs 56g | Fiber 4g | Sugar 9g | Protein 19g

Mac And Cheese Balls
Servings: 4
Cooking Time: 20 Minutes
Ingredients:

- 1 cup panko breadcrumbs
- 4 cups prepared macaroni and cheese, refrigerated
- 3 tablespoons flour
- 1 teaspoon salt, divided
- 1 teaspoon ground black pepper, divided
- 1 teaspoon smoked paprika, divided
- ½ teaspoon garlic powder, divided
- 2 eggs
- 1 tablespoon milk
- ¼ cup ranch dressing, garlic aioli, or chipotle mayo, for dipping (optional)

Directions:

1. Preheat a conventional oven to 400 degrees F/ 200 degrees C.
2. Shake the breadcrumbs onto a baking sheet so that they're evenly distributed. Bake in the oven for 3 minutes, then shake and bake for an additional 1 to 2 minutes, or until toasted.
3. Form the chilled macaroni and cheese into golf ball-sized balls and set them aside.
4. Combine the flour, ½ teaspoon salt, ½ teaspoon black pepper, ½ teaspoon smoked paprika, and ¼ teaspoon garlic powder in a large mixing bowl.
5. In a small bowl, whisk together the eggs and milk.
6. Combine the breadcrumbs, remaining salt, pepper, paprika, and garlic powder in a mixing bowl.
7. To coat the macaroni and cheese balls, roll them in the flour mixture, then the egg mixture, and then the breadcrumb mixture.
8. Place a crisper plate in each drawer. Put the cheese balls in a single layer in each drawer. Insert the drawers into the unit.
9. Select zone 1, then AIR FRY, then set the temperature to 360 degrees F/ 180 degrees C with an 8-minute timer. To match zone 2 settings to zone 1, choose MATCH. To begin, select START/STOP.
10. Serve and enjoy!

Nutrition:

- (Per serving) Calories 489 | Fat 15.9g | Sodium 1402mg | Carbs 69.7g | Fiber 2.5g | Sugar 4g | Protein 16.9g

Spicy Chicken Tenders
Servings:2
Cooking Time:12
Ingredients:

- 2 large eggs, whisked
- 2 tablespoons lemon juice
- Salt and black pepper
- 1 pound of chicken tenders
- 1 cup Panko breadcrumbs
- 1/2 cup Italian bread crumb
- 1 teaspoon smoked paprika

- 1/4 teaspoon garlic powder
- 1/4 teaspoon onion powder
- 1/2 cup fresh grated parmesan cheese

Directions:

1. Take a bowl and whisk eggs in it and set aside for further use.
2. In a large bowl add lemon juice, paprika, salt, black pepper, garlic powder, onion powder
3. In a separate bowl mix Panko breadcrumbs, Italian bread crumbs, and parmesan cheese.
4. Dip the chicken tender in the spice mixture and coat the entire tender well.
5. Let the tenders sit for 1 hour.
6. Then dip each chicken tender in egg and then in bread crumbs.
7. Line both the basket of the air fryer with parchment paper.
8. Divide the tenders between the baskets.
9. Set zone 1 basket to air fry mode at 350 degrees F for 12 minutes.
10. Select the MATCH button for the zone 2 basket.
11. Once it's done, serve.

Nutrition:

- (Per serving) Calories 836| Fat 36g| Sodium1307 mg | Carbs 31.3g | Fiber 2.5g| Sugar3.3 g | Protein 95.3g

Vegetables And Sides Recipes

Brussels Sprouts
Servings:2
Cooking Time:20
Ingredients:

- 2 pounds Brussels sprouts
- 2 tablespoons avocado oil
- Salt and pepper, to taste
- 1 cup pine nuts, roasted

Directions:

1. Trim the bottom of Brussels sprouts.
2. Take a bowl and combine the avocado oil, salt, and black pepper.
3. Toss the Brussels sprouts well.
4. Divide it in both air fryer baskets.
5. For the zone 1 basket use AIR fry mode for 20 minutes at 390 degrees F.
6. Select the MATCH button for the zone 2 basket.
7. Once the Brussels sprouts get crisp and tender, take out and serve.

Nutrition:

- (Per serving) Calories 672| Fat 50g| Sodium 115mg | Carbs 51g | Fiber 20.2g | Sugar 12.3g | Protein 25g

Kale And Spinach Chips
Servings:2
Cooking Time:6
Ingredients:

- 2 cups spinach, torn in pieces and stem removed
- 2 cups kale, torn in pieces, stems removed
- 1 tablespoon of olive oil
- Sea salt, to taste
- 1/3 cup Parmesan cheese

Directions:

1. Take a bowl and add spinach to it.
2. Take another bowl and add kale to it.
3. Now, season both of them with olive oil, and sea salt.
4. Add kale to zone 1 basket and spinach to zone 2 basket.
5. Select the zone 1 air fry mode at 350 degrees F for 6 minutes.
6. Set zone 2 to AIR FRY mode at 350 for 5 minutes.
7. Once done, take out the crispy chips and sprinkle Parmesan cheese on top.
8. Serve and Enjoy.

Nutrition:

- (Per serving) Calories 166| Fat 11.1g| Sodium 355mg | Carbs 8.1g | Fiber1.7 g | Sugar 0.1g | Protein 8.2g

Air Fryer Vegetables
Servings: 2
Cooking Time: 15 Minutes
Ingredients:

- 1 courgette, diced
- 2 capsicums, diced
- 1 head broccoli, diced
- 1 red onion, diced
- Marinade
- 1 teaspoon smoked paprika
- 1 teaspoon garlic granules
- 1 teaspoon Herb de Provence
- Salt and black pepper, to taste
- 1½ tablespoon olive oil
- 2 tablespoons lemon juice

Directions:

1. Toss the veggies with the rest of the marinade ingredients in a bowl.
2. Spread the veggies in the air fryer baskets.
3. Return the air fryer basket 1 to Zone 1, and basket 2 to Zone 2 of the Ninja Foodi 2-Basket Air Fryer.
4. Choose the "Air Fry" mode for Zone 1 at 400 degrees F and 15 minutes of cooking time.
5. Select the "MATCH COOK" option to copy the settings for Zone 2.
6. Initiate cooking by pressing the START/PAUSE BUTTON.
7. Toss the veggies once cooked half way through.

8. Serve warm.

Nutrition:

- (Per serving) Calories 166 | Fat 3.2g |Sodium 437mg | Carbs 28.8g | Fiber 1.8g | Sugar 2.7g | Protein 5.8g

Beets With Orange Gremolata And Goat's Cheese

Servings: 12

Cooking Time: 45 Minutes

Ingredients:

- 3 medium fresh golden beets (about 1 pound)
- 3 medium fresh beets (about 1 pound)
- 2 tablespoons lime juice
- 2 tablespoons orange juice
- ½ teaspoon fine sea salt
- 1 tablespoon minced fresh parsley
- 1 tablespoon minced fresh sage
- 1 garlic clove, minced
- 1 teaspoon grated orange zest
- 3 tablespoons crumbled goat's cheese
- 2 tablespoons sunflower kernels

Directions:

1. Scrub the beets and trim the tops by 1 inch.
2. Place the beets on a double thickness of heavy-duty foil (about 24 x 12 inches). Fold the foil around the beets, sealing tightly.
3. Place a crisper plate in both drawers. Put the beets in a single layer in each drawer. Insert the drawers into the unit.
4. Select zone 1, then AIR FRY, then set the temperature to 360 degrees F/ 180 degrees C with a 45-minute timer. To match zone 2 settings to zone 1, choose MATCH. To begin, select START/STOP.
5. Remove the beets from the drawers after the timer has finished. Peel, halve, and slice them when they're cool enough to handle. Place them in a serving bowl.
6. Toss in the lime juice, orange juice, and salt to coat. Sprinkle the beets with the parsley, sage, garlic, and orange zest. The sunflower kernels and goat's cheese go on top.

Nutrition:

- (Per serving) Calories 481 | Fat 20g | Sodium 1162mg | Carbs 56g | Fiber 4g | Sugar 9g | Protein 19g

Balsamic-glazed Tofu With Roasted Butternut Squash

Servings:4

Cooking Time: 40 Minutes

Ingredients:

- FOR THE BALSAMIC TOFU
- 2 tablespoons balsamic vinegar
- 1 tablespoon maple syrup
- 1 teaspoon soy sauce

- 1 teaspoon Dijon mustard
- 1 (14-ounce) package firm tofu, drained and cut into large cubes
- 1 tablespoon canola oil
- FOR THE BUTTERNUT SQUASH
- 1 small butternut squash
- 1 tablespoon canola oil
- 1 teaspoon light brown sugar
- ¼ teaspoon kosher salt
- ¼ teaspoon freshly ground black pepper

Directions:

1. To prep the balsamic tofu: In a large bowl, whisk together the vinegar, maple syrup, soy sauce, and mustard. Add the tofu and stir to coat. Cover and marinate for at least 20 minutes (or up to overnight in the refrigerator).
2. To prep the butternut squash: Peel the squash and cut in half lengthwise. Remove and discard the seeds. Cut the squash crosswise into ½-inch-thick slices.
3. Brush the squash pieces with the oil, then sprinkle with the brown sugar, salt, and black pepper.
4. To cook the tofu and squash: Install a crisper plate in each of the two baskets. Place the tofu in the Zone 1 basket, drizzle with the oil, and insert the basket in the unit. Place the squash in the Zone 2 basket and insert the basket in the unit.
5. Select Zone 1, select AIR FRY, set the temperature to 400°F, and set the timer to 10 minutes.
6. Select Zone 2, select ROAST, set the temperature to 400°F, and set the timer to 40 minutes. Select SMART FINISH.
7. Press START/PAUSE to begin cooking.
8. When cooking is complete, the tofu will have begun to crisp and brown around the edges and the squash should be tender. Serve hot.

Nutrition:

- (Per serving) Calories: 253; Total fat: 11g; Saturated fat: 1g; Carbohydrates: 30g; Fiber: 4.5g; Protein: 11g; Sodium: 237mg

Zucchini With Stuffing

Servings:3

Cooking Time:20

Ingredients:

- 1 cup quinoa, rinsed
- 1 cup black olives
- 6 medium zucchinis, about 2 pounds
- 2 cups cannellini beans, drained
- 1 white onion, chopped
- ¼ cup almonds, chopped
- 4 cloves of garlic, chopped
- 4 tablespoons olive oil
- 1 cup of water
- 2 cups Parmesan cheese, for topping

Directions:

1. First wash the zucchini and cut it lengthwise.

2. Take a skillet and heat oil in it
3. Sauté the onion in olive oil for a few minutes.
4. Then add the quinoa and water and let it cook for 8 minutes with the lid on the top.
5. Transfer the quinoa to a bowl and add all remaining ingredients excluding zucchini and Parmesan cheese.
6. Scoop out the seeds of zucchinis.
7. Fill the cavity of zucchinis with bowl mixture.
8. Top it with a handful of Parmesan cheese.
9. Arrange 4 zucchinis in both air fryer baskets.
10. Select zone1 basket at AIR FRY for 20 minutes and adjusting the temperature to 390 degrees F.
11. Use the Match button to select the same setting for zone 2.
12. Serve and enjoy.

Nutrition:

- (Per serving) Calories 1171| Fat 48.6g| Sodium 1747mg | Carbs 132.4g | Fiber 42.1g | Sugar 11.5g | Protein 65.7g

Lemon Herb Cauliflower

Servings: 4
Cooking Time: 10 Minutes

Ingredients:

- 384g cauliflower florets
- 1 tsp lemon zest, grated
- 1 tbsp thyme, minced
- 60ml olive oil
- 1 tbsp rosemary, minced
- ¼ tsp red pepper flakes, crushed
- 30ml lemon juice
- 25g parsley, minced
- ½ tsp salt

Directions:

1. In a bowl, toss cauliflower florets with the remaining ingredients until well coated.
2. Insert a crisper plate in the Ninja Foodi air fryer baskets.
3. Add cauliflower florets into both baskets.
4. Select zone 1, then select “air fry” mode and set the temperature to 360 degrees F for 10 minutes. Press “match” and “start/stop” to begin.

Nutrition:

- (Per serving) Calories 166 | Fat 14.4g |Sodium 340mg | Carbs 9.5g | Fiber 4.6g | Sugar 3.8g | Protein 3.3g

Buffalo Seitan With Crispy Zucchini Noodles

Servings:4
Cooking Time: 12 Minutes

Ingredients:

- FOR THE BUFFALO SEITAN

- 1 (8-ounce) package precooked seitan strips
- 1 teaspoon garlic powder, divided
- ½ teaspoon onion powder
- ¼ teaspoon smoked paprika
- ¼ cup Louisiana-style hot sauce
- 2 tablespoons vegetable oil
- 1 tablespoon tomato paste
- ¼ teaspoon freshly ground black pepper
- FOR THE ZUCCHINI NOODLES
- 3 large egg whites
- 1¼ cups all-purpose flour
- 1 teaspoon kosher salt, divided
- 12 ounces seltzer water or club soda
- 5 ounces zucchini noodles
- Nonstick cooking spray

Directions:

1. To prep the Buffalo seitan: Season the seitan strips with ½ teaspoon of garlic powder, the onion powder, and smoked paprika.
2. In a large bowl, whisk together the hot sauce, oil, tomato paste, remaining ½ teaspoon of garlic powder, and the black pepper. Set the bowl of Buffalo sauce aside.
3. To prep the zucchini noodles: In a medium bowl, use a handheld mixer to beat the egg whites until stiff peaks form.
4. In a large bowl, combine the flour and ½ teaspoon of salt. Mix in the seltzer to form a thin batter. Fold in the beaten egg whites.
5. Add the zucchini to the batter and gently mix to coat.
6. To cook the seitan and zucchini noodles: Install a crisper plate in each of the two baskets. Place the seitan in the Zone 1 basket and insert the basket in the unit. Lift the noodles from the batter one at a time, letting the excess drip off, and place them in the Zone 2 basket. Insert the basket in the unit.
7. Select Zone 1, select BAKE, set the temperature to 370°F, and set the timer to 12 minutes.
8. Select Zone 2, select AIR FRY, set the temperature to 400°F, and set the timer to 12 minutes. Select SMART FINISH.
9. Press START/PAUSE to begin cooking.
10. When the Zone 1 timer reads 2 minutes, press START/PAUSE. Remove the basket and transfer the seitan to the bowl of Buffalo sauce. Turn to coat, then return the seitan to the basket. Reinsert the basket and press START/PAUSE to resume cooking.
11. When cooking is complete, the seitan should be warmed through and the zucchini noodles crisp and light golden brown.
12. Sprinkle the zucchini noodles with the remaining ½ teaspoon of salt. If desired, drizzle extra Buffalo sauce over the seitan. Serve hot.

Nutrition:

- (Per serving) Calories: 252; Total fat: 15g; Saturated fat: 1g; Carbohydrates: 22g; Fiber: 1.5g; Protein: 13g; Sodium: 740mg

Green Salad With Crispy Fried Goat Cheese And Baked Croutons
Servings:4
Cooking Time: 10 Minutes
Ingredients:

- FOR THE GOAT CHEESE
- 1 (4-ounce) log soft goat cheese
- ½ cup panko bread crumbs
- 2 tablespoons vegetable oil
- FOR THE CROUTONS
- 2 slices Italian-style sandwich bread
- 2 tablespoons vegetable oil
- 1 tablespoon poultry seasoning
- ½ teaspoon kosher salt
- ¼ teaspoon freshly ground black pepper
- FOR THE SALAD
- 8 cups green leaf lettuce leaves
- ½ cup store-bought balsamic vinaigrette

Directions:

1. To prep the goat cheese: Cut the goat cheese into 8 round slices.
2. Spread the panko on a plate. Gently press the cheese into the panko to coat on both sides. Drizzle with the oil.
3. To prep the croutons: Cut the bread into cubes and place them in a large bowl. Add the oil, poultry seasoning, salt, and black pepper. Mix well to coat the bread cubes evenly.
4. To cook the goat cheese and croutons: Install a crisper plate in each of the two baskets. Place the goat cheese in the Zone 1 basket and insert the basket in the unit. Place the croutons in the Zone 2 basket and insert the basket in the unit.
5. Select Zone 1, select AIR FRY, set the temperature to 400°F, and set the timer to 6 minutes.
6. Select Zone 2, select BAKE, set the temperature to 390°F, and set the timer to 10 minutes. Select SMART FINISH.
7. Press START/PAUSE to begin cooking.
8. When cooking is complete, the goat cheese will be golden brown and the croutons crisp.
9. Remove the Zone 1 basket. Let the goat cheese cool in the basket for 5 minutes; it will firm up as it cools.
10. To assemble the salad: In a large bowl, combine the lettuce, vinaigrette, and croutons. Toss well. Divide the salad among four plates. Top each plate with 2 pieces of goat cheese.

Nutrition:

- (Per serving) Calories: 578; Total fat: 40g; Saturated fat: 14g; Carbohydrates: 39g; Fiber: 3.5g; Protein: 24g; Sodium: 815mg

Green Beans With Baked Potatoes

Servings:2

Cooking Time:45

Ingredients:

- 2 cups of green beans
- 2 large potatoes, cubed
- 3 tablespoons of olive oil
- 1 teaspoon of seasoned salt
- ½ teaspoon chili powder
- 1/6 teaspoon garlic powder
- 1/4 teaspoon onion powder

Directions:

1. Take a large bowl and pour olive oil into it.
2. Now add all the seasoning in the olive oil and whisk it well.
3. Toss the green bean in it, then transfer it to zone 1 basket of the air fryer.
4. Now season the potatoes with the seasoning and add them to the zone 2 basket.
5. Now set the zone one basket to AIRFRY mode at 350 degrees F for 18 minutes.
6. Now hit 2 for the second basket and set it to AIR FRY mode at 350 degrees F, for 45 minutes.
7. Once the cooking cycle is complete, take out and serve it by transferring it to the serving plates.

Nutrition:

- (Per serving) Calories473 | Fat21.6g | Sodium796 mg | Carbs 66.6g | Fiber12.9 g | Sugar6 g | Protein8.4 g

Fresh Mix Veggies In Air Fryer

Servings:4

Cooking Time:12

Ingredients:

- 1 cup cauliflower florets
- 1 cup of carrots, peeled chopped
- 1 cup broccoli florets
- 2 tablespoons of avocado oil
- Salt, to taste
- ½ teaspoon of chili powder
- ½ teaspoon of garlic powder
- ½ teaspoon of herbs de Provence
- 1 cup parmesan cheese

Directions:

1. Take a bowl, and add all the veggies to it.
2. Toss and then season the veggies with salt, chili powder, garlic powder, and herbs de Provence.
3. Toss it all well and then drizzle avocado oil.
4. Make sure the ingredients are coated well.
5. Now distribute the veggies among both baskets of the air fryer.
6. Turn on the start button and set it to AIR FRY mode at 390 degrees for 10-12 minutes.
7. For the zone 2 basket setting, press the MATCH button.
8. After 8 minutes of cooking, select the pause button and then take out the baskets and sprinkle Parmesan cheese on top of the veggies.
9. Then let the cooking cycle complete for the next 3-4 minutes.
10. Once done, serve.

Nutrition:

- (Per serving) Calories161 | Fat 9.3g| Sodium434 mg | Carbs 7.7g | Fiber 2.4g | Sugar 2.5g | Protein 13.9

Veggie Burgers With "fried" Onion Rings

Servings:4

Cooking Time: 25 Minutes

Ingredients:

- FOR THE VEGGIE BURGERS
- 1 (15-ounce) can black beans, drained and rinsed
- ½ cup panko bread crumbs
- 1 large egg
- ¼ cup finely chopped red bell pepper
- ¼ cup frozen corn, thawed
- 1 tablespoon olive oil
- ½ teaspoon garlic powder
- ½ teaspoon ground cumin
- ¼ teaspoon smoked paprika
- Nonstick cooking spray
- 4 hamburger buns
- ¼ cup barbecue sauce, for serving
- FOR THE ONION RINGS
- 1 large sweet onion
- ½ cup all-purpose flour
- 2 large eggs
- 1 cup panko bread crumbs
- ½ teaspoon kosher salt
- Nonstick cooking spray

Directions:

1. To prep the veggie burgers: In a large bowl, mash the beans with a potato masher or a fork. Stir in the panko, egg, bell pepper, corn, oil, garlic powder, cumin, and smoked paprika. Mix well.
2. Shape the mixture into 4 patties. Spritz both sides of each patty with cooking spray.
3. To prep the onion rings: Cut the onion into ½-inch-thick rings.
4. Set up a breading station with three small shallow bowls. Place the flour in the first bowl. In the second bowl, beat the eggs. Place the panko and salt in the third bowl.
5. Bread the onions rings in this order: First, dip them into the flour, coating both sides. Then, dip into the beaten egg. Finally, coat them in the panko. Spritz each with cooking spray.
6. To cook the burgers and onion rings: Install a crisper plate in each of the two baskets. Place 2 veggie burgers in the Zone 1 basket. Place the onion rings in the Zone 2 basket and insert both baskets in the unit.
7. Select Zone 1, select AIR FRY, set the temperature to 390°F, and set the timer to 25 minutes.
8. Select Zone 2, select AIR FRY, set the temperature to 375°F, and set the timer to 10 minutes. Select SMART FINISH.
9. Press START/PAUSE to begin cooking.
10. When the Zone 1 timer reads 10 minutes, press START/PAUSE. Remove the basket and use a silicone spatula to flip the burgers. Reinsert the basket and press START/PAUSE to resume cooking.
11. When the Zone 1 timer reads 10 minutes, press START/PAUSE. Remove the basket and transfer the burgers to a plate. Place the 2 remaining burgers in the basket. Reinsert the basket and press START/PAUSE to resume cooking.
12. When both timers read 5 minutes, press START/PAUSE. Remove the Zone 1 basket and flip the burgers, then reinsert the basket. Remove the Zone 2 basket and shake vigorously to rearrange the onion rings and separate any that have stuck together. Reinsert the basket and press START/PAUSE to resume cooking.
13. When cooking is complete, the veggie burgers should be cooked through and the onion rings golden brown.
14. Place 1 burger on each bun. Top with barbecue sauce and serve with onion rings on the side.

Nutrition:

- (Per serving) Calories: 538; Total fat: 16g; Saturated fat: 2g; Carbohydrates: 83g; Fiber: 10g; Protein: 19g; Sodium: 914mg

Caprese Panini With Zucchini Chips
Servings:4
Cooking Time: 20 Minutes
Ingredients:

- FOR THE PANINI
- 4 tablespoons pesto
- 8 slices Italian-style sandwich bread
- 1 tomato, diced
- 6 ounces fresh mozzarella cheese, shredded
- ¼ cup mayonnaise
- FOR THE ZUCCHINI CHIPS
- ½ cup all-purpose flour
- 2 large eggs
- ¼ teaspoon freshly ground black pepper
- ⅛ teaspoon kosher salt
- ½ cup panko bread crumbs
- ¼ cup grated Parmesan cheese
- 1 teaspoon Italian seasoning
- 1 medium zucchini, cut into ¼-inch-thick rounds
- 2 tablespoons vegetable oil

Directions:

1. To prep the panini: Spread 1 tablespoon of pesto each on 4 slices of the bread. Layer the diced tomato and shredded mozzarella on the other 4 slices of bread. Top the tomato/cheese mixture with the pesto-coated bread, pesto-side down, to form 4 sandwiches.
2. Spread the outside of each sandwich (both bread slices) with a thin layer of the mayonnaise.
3. To prep the zucchini chips: Set up a breading station with three small shallow bowls. Place the flour in the first bowl. In the second bowl, beat together the eggs, salt, and black pepper. Place the panko, Parmesan, and Italian seasoning in the third bowl.
4. Bread the zucchini in this order: First, dip the slices into the flour, coating both sides. Then, dip into the beaten egg. Finally, coat in the panko mixture. Drizzle the zucchini on both sides with the oil.
5. To cook the panini and zucchini chips: Install a crisper plate in each of the two baskets. Place 2 sandwiches in the Zone 1 basket and insert the basket in the unit. Place half of the zucchini chips in a single layer in the Zone 2 basket and insert the basket in the unit.
6. Select Zone 1, select AIR FRY, set the temperature to 375°F, and set the timer to 20 minutes.
7. Select Zone 2, select AIR FRY, set the temperature to 400°F, and set the timer to 20 minutes. Select SMART FINISH.
8. Press START/PAUSE to begin cooking.
9. When the Zone 1 timer reads 15 minutes, press START/PAUSE. Remove the basket, and use silicone-tipped tongs or a spatula to flip the sandwiches. Reinsert the basket and press START/PAUSE to resume cooking.
10. When both timers read 10 minutes, press START/PAUSE. Remove the Zone 1 basket and transfer the sandwiches to a plate. Place the remaining 2 sandwiches into the basket and insert the basket in the unit. Remove the Zone 2 basket and transfer the zucchini chips to a serving plate. Place the remaining zucchini chips in the basket. Reinsert the basket and press START/PAUSE to resume cooking.

11. When the Zone 1 timer reads 5 minutes, press START/PAUSE. Remove the basket and flip the sandwiches. Reinsert the basket and press START/PAUSE to resume cooking.
12. When cooking is complete, the panini should be toasted and the zucchini chips golden brown and crisp.
13. Cut each panini in half. Serve hot with zucchini chips on the side.

Nutrition:

- (Per serving) Calories: 751; Total fat: 39g; Saturated fat: 9.5g; Carbohydrates: 77g; Fiber: 3.5g; Protein: 23g; Sodium: 1,086mg

Fried Patty Pan Squash

Servings: 6

Cooking Time: 15 Minutes

Ingredients:

- 5 cups small pattypan squash, halved
- 1 tablespoon olive oil
- 2 garlic cloves, minced
- ½ teaspoon salt
- ¼ teaspoon dried oregano
- ¼ teaspoon dried thyme
- ¼ teaspoon pepper
- 1 tablespoon minced parsley

Directions:

1. Rub the squash with oil, garlic and the rest of the ingredients.
2. Spread the squash in the air fryer baskets.
3. Return the air fryer basket 1 to Zone 1, and basket 2 to Zone 2 of the Ninja Foodi 2-Basket Air Fryer.
4. Choose the "Air Fry" mode for Zone 1 at 375 degrees F and 15 minutes of cooking time.
5. Select the "MATCH COOK" option to copy the settings for Zone 2.
6. Initiate cooking by pressing the START/PAUSE BUTTON.
7. Flip the squash once cooked halfway through.
8. Garnish with parsley.
9. Serve warm.

Nutrition:

- (Per serving) Calories 208 | Fat 5g |Sodium 1205mg | Carbs 34.1g | Fiber 7.8g | Sugar 2.5g | Protein 5.9g

Satay-style Tempeh With Corn Fritters

Servings:4

Cooking Time: 15 Minutes

Ingredients:

- FOR THE TEMPEH
- 1 (8-ounce) package tempeh
- 3 tablespoons fresh lemon juice, divided
- 2 tablespoons soy sauce, divided

- 2 garlic cloves, chopped
- ½ teaspoon ground turmeric
- 2 tablespoons vegetable oil
- ¾ cup canned full-fat coconut milk
- 4 tablespoons peanut butter
- 1 teaspoon light brown sugar
- ½ teaspoon red pepper flakes
- 1 scallion, chopped
- FOR THE CORN FRITTERS
- 2 cups frozen corn, thawed and drained
- 2 scallions, thinly sliced
- ¼ cup chopped fresh cilantro
- ¼ teaspoon kosher salt
- 2 large eggs
- ½ cup all-purpose flour
- 2 tablespoons vegetable oil

Directions:

1. To prep the tempeh: Slice the tempeh into ¼-inch-thick slabs.
2. In a large bowl, combine 2 tablespoons of lemon juice, 1 tablespoon of soy sauce, the garlic, turmeric, and oil.
3. Add the tempeh to the marinade and toss to coat the pieces. Let marinate for 15 minutes.
4. In a medium bowl, whisk together the coconut milk, peanut butter, remaining 1 tablespoon of lemon juice, remaining 1 tablespoon of soy sauce, brown sugar, red pepper flakes, and scallion. Set aside.
5. To prep the corn fritters: In a large bowl, combine the corn, scallions, cilantro, and salt. Mix in the eggs and flour until everything is well combined.
6. To cook the tempeh and fritters: Install a broil rack in the Zone 1 basket. Arrange the tempeh in a single layer on the rack and insert the basket in the unit. Install a crisper plate in the Zone 2 basket. Spoon 2 tablespoons of corn fritter batter into each corner of the basket and drizzle with oil. Flatten slightly with the back of the spoon and insert the basket in the unit.
7. Select Zone 1, select AIR BROIL, set the temperature to 400°F, and set the timer to 8 minutes.
8. Select Zone 2, select AIR FRY, set the temperature to 375°F, and set the timer to 15 minutes. Select SMART FINISH.
9. Press START/PAUSE to begin cooking.
10. When the Zone 2 timer reads 5 minutes, press START/PAUSE. Remove the basket and use silicone-tipped tongs or a spatula to flip the corn fritters. Reinsert the basket and press START/PAUSE to resume cooking.
11. When cooking is complete, the tempeh will be golden brown and the corn fritters set in the center and browned on the edges.
12. Serve the tempeh with the peanut sauce for dipping and the corn fritters on the side.

Nutrition:

- (Per serving) Calories: 578; Total fat: 40g; Saturated fat: 14g; Carbohydrates: 39g; Fiber: 3.5g; Protein: 24g; Sodium: 815mg

Jerk Tofu With Roasted Cabbage

Servings:4

Cooking Time: 20 Minutes

Ingredients:

- FOR THE JERK TOFU
- 1 (14-ounce) package extra-firm tofu, drained
- 1 tablespoon apple cider vinegar
- 1 tablespoon reduced-sodium soy sauce
- 2 tablespoons jerk seasoning
- Juice of 1 lime
- ½ teaspoon kosher salt
- 2 tablespoons olive oil
- FOR THE CABBAGE
- 1 (14-ounce) bag coleslaw mix
- 1 red bell pepper, thinly sliced
- 2 scallions, thinly sliced
- 2 tablespoons water
- 3 garlic cloves, minced
- ¼ teaspoon fresh thyme leaves
- ¼ teaspoon onion powder
- ¼ teaspoon kosher salt
- ¼ teaspoon freshly ground black pepper

Directions:

1. To prep the jerk tofu: Cut the tofu horizontally into 4 slabs.
2. In a shallow dish (big enough to hold the tofu slabs), whisk together the vinegar, soy sauce, jerk seasoning, lime juice, and salt.
3. Place the tofu in the marinade and turn to coat both sides. Cover and marinate for at least 15 minutes (or up to overnight in the refrigerator).
4. To prep the cabbage: In the Zone 2 basket, combine the coleslaw, bell pepper, scallions, water, garlic, thyme, onion powder, salt, and black pepper.
5. To cook the tofu and cabbage: Install a crisper plate in the Zone 1 basket and add the tofu in a single layer. Brush the tofu with the oil and insert the basket in the unit. Insert the Zone 2 basket in the unit.
6. Select Zone 1, select AIR FRY, set the temperature to 390°F, and set the timer to 15 minutes.
7. Select Zone 2, select ROAST, set the temperature to 330°F, and set the timer to 20 minutes. Select SMART FINISH.
8. Press START/PAUSE to begin cooking.
9. When both timers read 5 minutes, press START/PAUSE. Remove the Zone 1 basket and use silicone-tipped tongs to flip the tofu. Reinsert the basket in the unit. Remove the Zone 2 basket and stir the cabbage. Reinsert the basket and press START/PAUSE to resume cooking.
10. When cooking is complete, the tofu will be crispy and browned around the edges and the cabbage soft.
11. Transfer the tofu to four plates and serve with the cabbage on the side.

Nutrition:

- (Per serving) Calories: 220; Total fat: 12g; Saturated fat: 1.5g; Carbohydrates: 21g; Fiber: 5g; Protein: 12g; Sodium: 817mg

Potato And Parsnip Latkes With Baked Apples

Servings:4

Cooking Time: 20 Minutes

Ingredients:

- FOR THE LATKES
- 2 medium russet potatoes, peeled
- 1 large egg white
- 2 tablespoons all-purpose flour
- ¼ teaspoon garlic powder
- ¼ teaspoon kosher salt
- ¼ teaspoon freshly ground black pepper
- 1 medium parsnip, peeled and shredded
- 2 scallions, thinly sliced
- 2 tablespoons vegetable oil
- FOR THE BAKED APPLES
- 2 Golden Delicious apples, peeled and diced
- 2 tablespoons granulated sugar
- 2 teaspoons unsalted butter, cut into small pieces

Directions:

1. To prep the latkes: Grate the potatoes using the large holes of a box grater. Squeeze as much liquid out of the potatoes as you can into a large bowl. Set the potatoes aside in a separate bowl.
2. Let the potato liquid sit for 5 minutes, during which time the potato starch will settle to the bottom of the bowl. Pour off the water that has risen to the top, leaving the potato starch in the bowl.
3. Add the egg white, flour, salt, and black pepper to the potato starch to form a thick paste. Add the potatoes, parsnip, and scallions and mix well. Divide the mixture into 4 patties. Brush both sides of each patty with the oil.
4. To prep the baked apples: Place the apples in the Zone 2 basket. Sprinkle the sugar and butter over the top.
5. To cook the latkes and apples: Install a crisper plate in the Zone 1 basket. Place the latkes in the basket in a single layer, then insert the basket in the unit. Insert the Zone 2 basket in the unit.
6. Select Zone 1, select AIR FRY, set the temperature to 375°F, and set the timer to 15 minutes.
7. Select Zone 2, select BAKE, set the temperature to 330°F, and set the timer to 20 minutes. Select SMART FINISH.
8. Press START/PAUSE to begin cooking.
9. When both timers read 5 minutes, press START/PAUSE. Remove the Zone 1 basket and use silicone-tipped tongs or a spatula to flip the latkes. Reinsert the basket in the unit. Remove the Zone 2 basket and gently mash the apples with a fork or the back of a spoon. Reinsert the basket and press START/PAUSE to resume cooking.
10. When cooking is complete, the latkes should be golden brown and cooked through and the apples very soft.
11. Transfer the latkes to a plate and serve with apples on the side.

Nutrition:

- (Per serving) Calories: 257; Total fat: 9g; Saturated fat: 2g; Carbohydrates: 42g; Fiber: 5.5g; Protein: 4g; Sodium: 91mg

Garlic-rosemary Brussels Sprouts

Servings: 4

Cooking Time: 8 Minutes

Ingredients:

- 3 tablespoons olive oil
- 2 garlic cloves, minced
- ½ teaspoon salt
- ¼ teaspoon black pepper
- 455g Brussels sprouts, halved

- ½ cup panko bread crumbs
- 1-½ teaspoons rosemary, minced

Directions:

1. Toss the Brussels sprouts with crumbs and the rest of the ingredients in a bowl.
2. Divide the sprouts into the Ninja Foodi 2 Baskets Air Fryer baskets.
3. Return the air fryer basket 1 to Zone 1, and basket 2 to Zone 2 of the Ninja Foodi 2-Basket Air Fryer.
4. Choose the "Air Fry" mode for Zone 1 at 350 degrees F and 8 minutes of cooking time.
5. Select the "MATCH COOK" option to copy the settings for Zone 2.
6. Initiate cooking by pressing the START/PAUSE BUTTON.
7. Toss the Brussels sprouts once cooked halfway through.
8. Serve warm.

Nutrition:

- (Per serving) Calories 231 | Fat 9g |Sodium 271mg | Carbs 32.8g | Fiber 6.4g | Sugar 7g | Protein 6.3g

Air-fried Radishes

Servings: 6

Cooking Time: 15 Minutes

Ingredients:

- 1020g radishes, quartered
- 3 tablespoons olive oil
- 1 tablespoon fresh oregano, minced
- ¼ teaspoon salt
- ⅛ teaspoon black pepper

Directions:

1. Toss radishes with oil, black pepper, salt and oregano in a bowl.
2. Divide the radishes into the Ninja Foodi 2 Baskets Air Fryer baskets.
3. Return the air fryer basket 1 to Zone 1, and basket 2 to Zone 2 of the Ninja Foodi 2-Basket Air Fryer.
4. Choose the "Air Fry" mode for Zone 1 at 375 degrees F and 15 minutes of cooking time.
5. Select the "MATCH COOK" option to copy the settings for Zone 2.
6. Initiate cooking by pressing the START/PAUSE BUTTON.
7. Toss the radishes once cooked halfway through.
8. Serve.

Nutrition:

- (Per serving) Calories 270 | Fat 14.6g |Sodium 394mg | Carbs 31.3g | Fiber 7.5g | Sugar 9.7g | Protein 6.4g

Mixed Air Fry Veggies

Servings:4

Cooking Time:25

Ingredients:

- 2 cups of carrots, cubed

- 2 cups of potatoes, cubed
- 2 cups of shallots, cubed
- 2 cups zucchini, diced
- 2 cups yellow squash, cubed
- Salt and black pepper, to taste
- 1 tablespoon of Italian seasoning
- 2 tablespoons of ranch seasoning
- 4 tablespoons of olive oil

Directions:

1. Take a large bowl and add all the veggies to it.
2. Season the veggies with salt, pepper, Italian seasoning, ranch seasoning, and olive oil
3. Toss all the ingredients well.
4. Now divide this between two baskets of the air fryer.
5. Set zone 1 basket to AIRFRY mode at 360 degrees F for 25 minutes.
6. Select the Match button for the zone 2 basket.
7. Once it is cooked and done, serve, and enjoy.

Nutrition:

- (Per serving) Calories 275| Fat 15.3g| Sodium129 mg | Carbs 33g | Fiber3.8 g | Sugar5 g | Protein 4.4g

Curly Fries

Servings: 6

Cooking Time: 20 Minutes.

Ingredients:

- 2 spiralized zucchinis
- 1 cup flour
- 2 tablespoons paprika
- 1 teaspoon cayenne pepper
- 1 teaspoon garlic powder
- 1 teaspoon black pepper
- 1 teaspoon salt
- 2 eggs
- Olive oil or cooking spray

Directions:

1. Mix flour with paprika, cayenne pepper, garlic powder, black pepper, and salt in a bowl.
2. Beat eggs in another bowl and dip the zucchini in the eggs.
3. Coat the zucchini with the flour mixture and divide it into two crisper plates.
4. Spray the zucchini with cooking oil.
5. Return the crisper plate to the Ninja Foodi Dual Zone Air Fryer.
6. Choose the Air Fry mode for Zone 1 and set the temperature to 400 degrees F and the time to 20 minutes.
7. Select the "MATCH" button to copy the settings for Zone 2.
8. Initiate cooking by pressing the START/STOP button.
9. Toss the zucchini once cooked halfway through, then resume cooking.
10. Serve warm.

Nutrition:

- (Per serving) Calories 212 | Fat 11.8g |Sodium 321mg | Carbs 24.6g | Fiber 4.4g | Sugar 8g | Protein 7.3g

Stuffed Sweet Potatoes

Servings: 4

Cooking Time: 55 Minutes

Ingredients:

- 2 medium sweet potatoes
- 1 teaspoon olive oil
- 1 cup cooked chopped spinach, drained
- 1 cup shredded cheddar cheese, divided
- 2 cooked bacon strips, crumbled
- 1 green onion, chopped
- ¼ cup fresh cranberries, coarsely chopped
- ⅓ cup chopped pecans, toasted
- 2 tablespoons butter
- ¼ teaspoon kosher salt
- ¼ teaspoon pepper

Directions:

1. Brush the sweet potatoes with the oil.
2. Place a crisper plate in both drawers. Add one sweet potato to each drawer. Place the drawers in the unit.
3. Select zone 1, then AIR FRY, then set the temperature to 360 degrees F/ 180 degrees C with a 40-minute timer. To match zone 2 settings to zone 1, choose MATCH. To begin, select START/STOP.
4. Remove the sweet potatoes from the drawers after the timer has finished. Cut them in half lengthwise. Scoop out the pulp, leaving a ¼-inch thick shell.
5. Put the pulp in a large bowl and stir in the spinach, ¾ cup of cheese, bacon, onion, pecans, cranberries, butter, salt, and pepper.
6. Spoon the mixture into the potato shells, mounding the mixture slightly.
7. Place a crisper plate in each drawer. Put one filled potato into each drawer and insert them into the unit.
8. Select zone 1, then AIR FRY, then set the temperature to 360 degrees F/ 180 degrees C with a 10-minute timer. To match zone 2 settings to zone 1, choose MATCH. To begin, select START/STOP.
9. Sprinkle with the remaining ¼ cup of cheese. Cook using the same settings until the cheese is melted (about 1 to 2 minutes).

Nutrition:

- (Per serving) Calories 376 | Fat 25g | Sodium 489mg | Carbs 28g | Fiber 10g | Sugar 5g | Protein 12g

Healthy Air Fried Veggies

Servings: 4

Cooking Time: 15 Minutes

Ingredients:

- 52g onion, sliced
- 71g broccoli florets
- 116g radishes, sliced

- 15ml olive oil
- 100g Brussels sprouts, cut in half
- 325g cauliflower florets
- 1 tsp balsamic vinegar
- ½ tsp garlic powder
- Pepper
- Salt

Directions:

1. In a bowl, toss veggies with oil, vinegar, garlic powder, pepper, and salt.
2. Insert a crisper plate in the Ninja Foodi air fryer baskets.
3. Add veggies in both baskets.
4. Select zone 1 then select "air fry" mode and set the temperature to 380 degrees F for 15 minutes. Press "match" to match zone 2 settings to zone 1. Press "start/stop" to begin. Stir halfway through.

Nutrition:

- (Per serving) Calories 71 | Fat 3.8g |Sodium 72mg | Carbs 8.8g | Fiber 3.2g | Sugar 3.3g | Protein 2.5g

Buffalo Bites
Servings: 6
Cooking Time: 30 Minutes
Ingredients:

- For the bites:
- 1 small cauliflower head, cut into florets
- 2 tablespoons olive oil
- 3 tablespoons buffalo wing sauce
- 3 tablespoons butter, melted
- For the dip:
- 1½ cups 2% cottage cheese
- ¼ cup fat-free plain Greek yogurt
- ¼ cup crumbled blue cheese
- 1 sachet ranch salad dressing mix
- Celery sticks (optional)

Directions:

1. In a large bowl, combine the cauliflower and oil; toss to coat.
2. Place a crisper plate in each drawer. Put the coated cauliflower florets in each drawer in a single layer. Place the drawers in the unit.
3. Select zone 1, then AIR FRY, then set the temperature to 360 degrees F/ 180 degrees C with a 15-minute timer. To match zone 2 settings to zone 1, choose MATCH. To begin, select START/STOP.
4. Remove the cauliflower from the drawers after the timer has finished.
5. Combine the buffalo sauce and melted butter in a large mixing bowl. Put in the cauliflower and toss to coat. Place on a serving dish and serve.
6. Combine the dip ingredients in a small bowl. Serve with the cauliflower and celery sticks, if desired.

Nutrition:

- (Per serving) Calories 203 | Fat 13g | Sodium 1470mg | Carbs 13g | Fiber 4g | Sugar 1g | Protein 9g

Fried Avocado Tacos
Servings: 4
Cooking Time: 10 Minutes
Ingredients:

- For the sauce:
- 2 cups shredded fresh kale or coleslaw mix
- 1/4 cup minced fresh cilantro
- 1/4 cup plain Greek yogurt
- 2 tablespoons lime juice
- 1 teaspoon honey
- 1/4 teaspoon salt
- 1/4 teaspoon ground chipotle pepper
- 1/4 teaspoon pepper
- For the tacos:
- 1 large egg, beaten
- 1/4 cup cornmeal
- 1/2 teaspoon salt
- 1/2 teaspoon garlic powder
- 1/2 teaspoon ground chipotle pepper
- 2 medium avocados, peeled and sliced
- Cooking spray
- 8 flour tortillas or corn tortillas (6 inches), heated up
- 1 medium tomato, chopped
- Crumbled queso fresco (optional)

Directions:

1. Combine the first 8 ingredients in a bowl. Cover and refrigerate until serving.
2. Place the egg in a shallow bowl. In another shallow bowl, mix the cornmeal, salt, garlic powder, and chipotle pepper.
3. Dip the avocado slices in the egg, then into the cornmeal mixture, gently patting to help adhere.
4. Place a crisper plate in both drawers. Put the avocado slices in the drawers in a single layer. Insert the drawers into the unit.
5. Select zone 1, then AIR FRY, then set the temperature to 360 degrees F/ 180 degrees C with a 6-minute timer. To match zone 2 settings to zone 1, choose MATCH. To begin, select START/STOP.
6. Put the avocado slices, prepared sauce, tomato, and queso fresco in the tortillas and serve.

Nutrition:

- (Per serving) Calories 407 | Fat 21g | Sodium 738mg | Carbs 48g | Fiber 4g | Sugar 9g | Protein 9g

Stuffed Tomatoes
Servings:2
Cooking Time:8
Ingredients:

- 2 cups brown rice, cooked
- 1 cup of tofu, grilled and chopped
- 4 large red tomatoes
- 4 tablespoons basil, chopped
- 1/4 tablespoon olive oil
- Salt and black pepper, to taste
- 2 tablespoons of lemon juice
- 1 teaspoon of red chili powder
- ½ cup Parmesan cheese

Directions:

1. Take a large bowl and mix rice, tofu, basil, olive oil, salt, black pepper, lemon juice, and chili powder.
2. Take four large tomatoes and center core them.
3. Fill the cavity with the rice mixture.
4. Top it off with the cheese sprinkle.
5. Divide the tomatoes into two air fryer baskets.
6. turn on zone one basket and cook tomatoes at AIRFRY mode, for 8 minutes at 400 degrees F.
7. Select the MATCH button for zone two baskets, which cooks food by copying the setting across both zones.
8. Serve and enjoy.

Nutrition:

- (Per serving) Calories 1034| Fat 24.2g| Sodium 527mg | Carbs165 g | Fiber12.1 g | Sugar 1.2g | Protein 43.9g

Balsamic Vegetables
Servings: 4
Cooking Time: 13 Minutes
Ingredients:

- 125g asparagus, cut woody ends
- 88g mushrooms, halved
- 1 tbsp Dijon mustard
- 3 tbsp soy sauce
- 27g brown sugar
- 57ml balsamic vinegar
- 32g olive oil
- 1 zucchini, sliced
- 1 yellow squash, sliced
- 170g grape tomatoes
- Pepper
- Salt

Directions:

1. In a bowl, mix asparagus, tomatoes, oil, mustard, soy sauce, mushrooms, zucchini, squash, brown sugar, vinegar, pepper, and salt.
2. Cover the bowl and place it in the refrigerator for 45 minutes.
3. Insert a crisper plate in the Ninja Foodi air fryer baskets.
4. Add the vegetable mixture in both baskets.

5. Select zone 1, then select "air fry" mode and set the temperature to 390 degrees F for 12 minutes. Press "match" to match zone 2 settings to zone 1. Press "start/stop" to begin. Stir halfway through.

Nutrition:

- (Per serving) Calories 184 | Fat 13.3g |Sodium 778mg | Carbs 14.7g | Fiber 3.6g | Sugar 9.5g | Protein 5.5g

Garlic-herb Fried Squash

Servings: 4

Cooking Time: 15 Minutes

Ingredients:

- 5 cups halved small pattypan squash (about 1¼ pounds)
- 1 tablespoon olive oil
- 2 garlic cloves, minced
- ½ teaspoon salt
- ¼ teaspoon dried oregano
- ¼ teaspoon dried thyme
- ¼ teaspoon pepper
- 1 tablespoon minced fresh parsley, for serving

Directions:

1. Place the squash in a large bowl.
2. Mix the oil, garlic, salt, oregano, thyme, and pepper; drizzle over the squash. Toss to coat.
3. Place a crisper plate in both drawers. Put the squash in a single layer in each drawer. Insert the drawers into the unit.
4. Select zone 1, then AIR FRY, then set the temperature to 360 degrees F/ 180 degrees C with a 6-minute timer. To match zone 2 settings to zone 1, choose MATCH. To begin, select START/STOP.
5. Remove the squash from the drawers after the timer has finished. Sprinkle with the parsley.

Nutrition:

- (Per serving) Calories 58 | Fat 3g | Sodium 296mg | Carbs 6g | Fiber 2g | Sugar 3g | Protein 2g

Herb And Lemon Cauliflower

Servings: 4

Cooking Time: 10 Minutes

Ingredients:

- 1 cauliflower head, cut into florets
- 4 tablespoons olive oil
- ¼ cup fresh parsley
- 1 tablespoon fresh rosemary
- 1 tablespoon fresh thyme
- 1 teaspoon lemon zest, grated
- 2 tablespoons lemon juice
- ½ teaspoon salt
- ¼ teaspoon crushed red pepper flakes

Directions:

1. Toss cauliflower with oil, herbs and the rest of the ingredients in a bowl.
2. Divide the seasoned cauliflower in the air fryer baskets.
3. Return the air fryer basket 1 to Zone 1, and basket 2 to Zone 2 of the Ninja Foodi 2-Basket Air Fryer.
4. Choose the "Air Fry" mode for Zone 1 at 350 degrees F and 10 minutes of cooking time.
5. Select the "MATCH COOK" option to copy the settings for Zone 2.
6. Initiate cooking by pressing the START/PAUSE BUTTON.
7. Serve warm.

Nutrition:

- (Per serving) Calories 212 | Fat 11.8g |Sodium 321mg | Carbs 24.6g | Fiber 4.4g | Sugar 8g | Protein 7.3g

Spanakopita Rolls With Mediterranean Vegetable Salad

Servings:4

Cooking Time: 15 Minutes

Ingredients:

- FOR THE SPANAKOPITA ROLLS
- 1 (10-ounce) package chopped frozen spinach, thawed
- 4 ounces feta cheese, crumbled
- 2 large eggs
- 1 teaspoon dried oregano
- ½ teaspoon freshly ground black pepper
- 12 sheets phyllo dough, thawed
- Nonstick cooking spray
- FOR THE ROASTED VEGETABLES
- 1 medium eggplant, diced
- 1 small red onion, cut into 8 wedges
- 1 red bell pepper, sliced
- 2 tablespoons olive oil
- FOR THE SALAD
- 1 (15-ounce) can chickpeas, drained and rinsed
- ¼ cup chopped fresh parsley
- ¼ cup olive oil
- ¼ cup red wine vinegar
- 2 garlic cloves, minced
- ½ teaspoon dried oregano
- ¼ teaspoon kosher salt
- ¼ teaspoon freshly ground black pepper

Directions:

1. To prep the spanakopita rolls: Squeeze as much liquid from the spinach as you can and place the spinach in a large bowl. Add the feta, eggs, oregano, and black pepper. Mix well.
2. Lay one sheet of phyllo on a clean work surface and mist it with cooking spray. Place another sheet of phyllo directly on top of the first sheet and mist it with cooking spray. Repeat with a third sheet.

3. Spoon one-quarter of the spinach mixture along one short side of the phyllo. Fold the long sides in over the spinach, then roll up it like a burrito.
4. Repeat this process with the remaining phyllo sheets and spinach mixture to form 4 rolls.
5. To prep the vegetables: In a large bowl, combine the eggplant, onion, bell pepper, and oil. Mix well.
6. To cook the rolls and vegetables: Install a crisper plate in each of the two baskets. Place the spanakopita rolls seam-side down in the Zone 1 basket, and spritz the rolls with cooking spray. Place the vegetables in the Zone 2 basket and insert both baskets in the unit.
7. Select Zone 1, select AIR FRY, set the temperature to 375°F, and set the timer to 10 minutes.
8. Select Zone 2, select ROAST, set the temperature to 375°F, and set the timer to 15 minutes. Select SMART FINISH.
9. Press START/PAUSE to begin cooking.
10. When the Zone 1 timer reads 3 minutes, press START/PAUSE. Remove the basket and use silicone-tipped tongs or a spatula to flip the spanakopita rolls. Reinsert the basket and press START/PAUSE to resume cooking.
11. When cooking is complete, the rolls should be crisp and golden brown and the vegetables tender.
12. To assemble the salad: Transfer the roasted vegetables to a large bowl. Stir in the chickpeas and parsley.
13. In a small bowl, whisk together the oil, vinegar, garlic, oregano, salt, and black pepper. Pour the dressing over the vegetables and toss to coat. Serve warm.

Nutrition:

- (Per serving) Calories: 739; Total fat: 51g; Saturated fat: 8g; Carbohydrates: 67g; Fiber: 11g; Protein: 21g; Sodium: 806mg

Bacon Potato Patties

Servings: 2

Cooking Time: 15 Minutes

Ingredients:

- 1 egg
- 600g mashed potatoes
- 119g breadcrumbs
- 2 bacon slices, cooked & chopped
- 235g cheddar cheese, shredded
- 15g flour
- Pepper
- Salt

Directions:

1. In a bowl, mix mashed potatoes with remaining ingredients until well combined.
2. Make patties from potato mixture and place on a plate.
3. Place plate in the refrigerator for 10 minutes
4. Insert a crisper plate in the Ninja Foodi air fryer baskets.
5. Place the prepared patties in both baskets.
6. Select zone 1 then select "air fry" mode and set the temperature to 390 degrees F for 15 minutes. Press "match" to match zone 2 settings to zone 1. Press "start/stop" to begin. Turn halfway through.

Nutrition:

- (Per serving) Calories 702 | Fat 26.8g |Sodium 1405mg | Carbs 84.8g | Fiber 2.7g | Sugar 3.8g | Protein 30.5g

Breaded Summer Squash
Servings: 4
Cooking Time: 10 Minutes
Ingredients:

- 4 cups yellow summer squash, sliced
- 3 tablespoons olive oil
- ½ teaspoon salt
- ½ teaspoon pepper
- ⅛ teaspoon cayenne pepper
- ¾ cup panko bread crumbs
- ¾ cup grated Parmesan cheese

Directions:

1. Mix crumbs, cheese, cayenne pepper, black pepper, salt and oil in a bowl.
2. Coat the squash slices with the breadcrumb mixture.
3. Place these slices in the air fryer baskets.
4. Return the air fryer basket 1 to Zone 1, and basket 2 to Zone 2 of the Ninja Foodi 2-Basket Air Fryer.
5. Choose the "Air Fry" mode for Zone 1 at 350 degrees F and 10 minutes of cooking time.
6. Select the "MATCH COOK" option to copy the settings for Zone 2.
7. Initiate cooking by pressing the START/PAUSE BUTTON.
8. Flip the squash slices once cooked half way through.
9. Serve warm.

Nutrition:

- (Per serving) Calories 193 | Fat 1g |Sodium 395mg | Carbs 38.7g | Fiber 1.6g | Sugar 0.9g | Protein 6.6g

Fried Olives
Servings: 6
Cooking Time: 9 Minutes.
Ingredients:

- 2 cups blue cheese stuffed olives, drained
- ½ cup all-purpose flour
- 1 cup panko breadcrumbs
- ½ teaspoon garlic powder
- 1 pinch oregano
- 2 eggs

Directions:

1. Mix flour with oregano and garlic powder in a bowl and beat two eggs in another bowl.
2. Spread panko breadcrumbs in a bowl.
3. Coat all the olives with the flour mixture, dip in the eggs and then coat with the panko breadcrumbs.
4. As you coat the olives, place them in the two crisper plates in a single layer, then spray them with cooking oil.
5. Return the crisper plates to the Ninja Foodi Dual Zone Air Fryer.
6. Choose the Air Fry mode for Zone 1 and set the temperature to 375 degrees F and the time to 9 minutes.
7. Select the "MATCH" button to copy the settings for Zone 2.

8. Initiate cooking by pressing the START/STOP button.
9. Flip the olives once cooked halfway through, then resume cooking.
10. Serve.

Nutrition:

- (Per serving) Calories 166 | Fat 3.2g |Sodium 437mg | Carbs 28.8g | Fiber 1.8g | Sugar 2.7g | Protein 5.8g

Fried Asparagus

Servings: 4

Cooking Time: 6 Minutes

Ingredients:

- ¼ cup mayonnaise
- 4 teaspoons olive oil
- 1½ teaspoons grated lemon zest
- 1 garlic clove, minced
- ½ teaspoon pepper
- ¼ teaspoon seasoned salt
- 1-pound fresh asparagus, trimmed
- 2 tablespoons shredded parmesan cheese
- Lemon wedges (optional)

Directions:

1. In a large bowl, combine the first 6 ingredients.
2. Add the asparagus; toss to coat.
3. Put a crisper plate in both drawers. Put the asparagus in a single layer in each drawer. Top with the parmesan cheese. Place the drawers into the unit.
4. Select zone 1, then AIR FRY, then set the temperature to 375 degrees F/ 190 degrees C with a 6-minute timer. To match zone 2 settings to zone 1, choose MATCH. To begin, select START/STOP.
5. Remove the asparagus from the drawers after the timer has finished.

Nutrition:

- (Per serving) Calories 156 | Fat 15g | Sodium 214mg | Carbs 3g | Fiber 1g | Sugar 1g | Protein 2g

Acorn Squash Slices

Servings: 6

Cooking Time: 10 Minutes

Ingredients:

- 2 medium acorn squashes
- ⅔ cup packed brown sugar
- ½ cup butter, melted

Directions:

1. Cut the squash in half, remove the seeds and slice into ½ inch slices.

2. Place the squash slices in the air fryer baskets.
3. Drizzle brown sugar and butter over the squash slices.
4. Return the air fryer basket 1 to Zone 1, and basket 2 to Zone 2 of the Ninja Foodi 2-Basket Air Fryer.
5. Choose the "Air Fry" mode for Zone 1 and set the temperature to 350 degrees F and 10 minutes of cooking time.
6. Select the "MATCH COOK" option to copy the settings for Zone 2.
7. Initiate cooking by pressing the START/PAUSE BUTTON.
8. Flip the squash once cooked halfway through.
9. Serve.

Nutrition:

- (Per serving) Calories 206 | Fat 3.4g |Sodium 174mg | Carbs 35g | Fiber 9.4g | Sugar 5.9g | Protein 10.6g

Sweet Potatoes With Honey Butter

Servings: 4

Cooking Time: 40 Minutes.

Ingredients:

- 4 sweet potatoes, scrubbed
- 1 teaspoon oil
- Honey Butter
- 4 tablespoons unsalted butter
- 1 tablespoon Honey
- 2 teaspoons hot sauce
- ¼ teaspoon salt

Directions:

1. Rub the sweet potatoes with oil and place two potatoes in each crisper plate.
2. Return the crisper plate to the Ninja Foodi Dual Zone Air Fryer.
3. Choose the Air Fry mode for Zone 1 and set the temperature to 400 degrees F and the time to 40 minutes.
4. Select the "MATCH" button to copy the settings for Zone 2.
5. Initiate cooking by pressing the START/STOP button.
6. Flip the potatoes once cooked halfway through, then resume cooking.
7. Mix butter with hot sauce, honey, and salt in a bowl.
8. When the potatoes are done, cut a slit on top and make a well with a spoon
9. Pour the honey butter in each potato jacket.
10. Serve.

Nutrition:

- (Per serving) Calories 288 | Fat 6.9g |Sodium 761mg | Carbs 46g | Fiber 4g | Sugar 12g | Protein 9.6g

Beef, Pork, And Lamb Recipes

Bell Peppers With Sausages

Servings:4

Cooking Time:20

Ingredients:

- 6 beef or pork Italian sausages
- 4 bell peppers, whole
- Oil spray, for greasing
- 2 cups of cooked rice
- 1 cup of sour cream

Directions:

1. Put the bell pepper in the zone 1 basket and sausages in the zone 2 basket of the air fryer.
2. Set zone 1 to AIR FRY MODE for 10 minutes at 400 degrees F.
3. For zone 2 set it to 20 minutes at 375 degrees F.
4. Hit the smart finish button, so both finish at the same time.
5. After 5 minutes take out the sausage basket and break or mince it with a plastic spatula.
6. Then, let the cooking cycle finish.
7. Once done serve the minced meat with bell peppers and serve over cooked rice with a dollop of sour cream.

Nutrition:

- (Per serving) Calories1356 | Fat 81.2g| Sodium 3044 mg | Carbs 96g | Fiber 3.1g | Sugar 8.3g | Protein 57.2 g

Barbecue Ribs With Roasted Green Beans And Shallots

Servings:4

Cooking Time: 40 Minutes

Ingredients:

- FOR THE RIBS
- 1 tablespoon light brown sugar
- 1 tablespoon smoked paprika
- 1 tablespoon chili powder
- 2 teaspoons kosher salt
- 1 teaspoon freshly ground black pepper
- 1 teaspoon garlic powder
- ¼ teaspoon cayenne pepper (optional)
- 2 pounds pork ribs
- 1 cup barbecue sauce (your favorite), for serving
- FOR THE GREEN BEANS AND SHALLOTS
- 1 pound green beans, trimmed
- 2 shallots, sliced
- 1 tablespoon olive oil
- ¼ teaspoon kosher salt

Directions:

1. To prep the ribs: In a small bowl, combine the brown sugar, paprika, chili powder, salt, black pepper, garlic powder, and cayenne (if using).
2. Rub the spice blend all over both sides of the ribs.
3. To prep the green beans and shallots: In a large bowl, combine the green beans, shallots, and oil. Toss to coat. Season with the salt.

4. To cook the ribs and vegetables: Install a crisper plate in each of the two baskets. Place the ribs in the Zone 1 basket and insert the basket in the unit. Place the green beans in the Zone 2 basket and insert the basket in the unit.
5. Select Zone 1, select AIR FRY, set the temperature to 375°F, and set the time to 40 minutes.
6. Select Zone 2, select ROAST, set the temperature to 400°F, and set the time to 20 minutes. Select SMART FINISH.
7. Press START/PAUSE to begin cooking.
8. When the Zone 1 timer reads 10 minutes, press START/PAUSE. Increase the temperature of Zone 1 to 400°F. Press START/PAUSE to resume cooking.
9. When cooking is complete, an instant-read thermometer inserted into the ribs should read 170°F and the green beans should be tender-crisp. Serve topped with your favorite barbecue sauce.

Nutrition:

- (Per serving) Calories: 541; Total fat: 27g; Saturated fat: 9g; Carbohydrates: 48g; Fiber: 4.5g; Protein: 28g; Sodium: 1,291mg

Paprika Pork Chops

Servings: 4

Cooking Time: 12 Minutes

Ingredients:

- 4 bone-in pork chops (6–8 ounces each)
- 1½ tablespoons brown sugar
- 1¼ teaspoons kosher salt
- 1 teaspoon dried Italian seasoning
- 1 teaspoon smoked paprika
- ¼ teaspoon garlic powder
- ¼ teaspoon onion powder
- ¼ teaspoon black pepper
- 1 teaspoon sweet paprika
- 3 tablespoons butter, melted
- 2 tablespoons chopped fresh parsley
- Cooking spray

Directions:

1. In a small mixing bowl, combine the brown sugar, salt, Italian seasoning, smoked paprika, garlic powder, onion powder, black pepper, and sweet paprika. Mix thoroughly.
2. Brush the pork chops on both sides with the melted butter.
3. Rub the spice mixture all over the meat on both sides.
4. Install a crisper plate in both drawers. Place half the chops in the zone 1 drawer and half in zone 2's, then insert the drawers into the unit.
5. Select zone 1, select AIR FRY, set temperature to 390 degrees F/ 200 degrees C, and set time to 12 minutes. Select MATCH to match zone 2 settings to zone 1. Press the START/STOP button to begin cooking.
6. When the time reaches 10 minutes, press START/STOP to pause the unit. Remove the drawers and flip the chops. Re-insert the drawers into the unit and press START/STOP to resume cooking.
7. Serve and enjoy!

Nutrition:

- (Per serving) Calories 338 | Fat 21.2g | Sodium 1503mg | Carbs 5.1g | Fiber 0.3g | Sugar 4.6g | Protein 29.3g

Steak Fajitas With Onions And Peppers
Servings: 6
Cooking Time: 15 Minutes
Ingredients:

- 1 pound steak
- 1 green bell pepper, sliced
- 1 yellow bell pepper, sliced
- 1 red bell pepper, sliced
- ½ cup sliced white onions
- 1 packet gluten-free fajita seasoning
- Olive oil spray

Directions:

1. Thinly slice the steak against the grain. These should be about ¼-inch slices.
2. Mix the steak with the peppers and onions.
3. Evenly coat with the fajita seasoning.
4. Install a crisper plate in both drawers. Place half the steak mixture in the zone 1 drawer and half in zone 2's, then insert the drawers into the unit.
5. Select zone 1, select AIR FRY, set temperature to 390 degrees F/ 200 degrees C, and set time to 15 minutes. Select MATCH to match zone 2 settings to zone 1. Press the START/STOP button to begin cooking.
6. When the time reaches 10 minutes, press START/STOP to pause the unit. Remove the drawers and flip the steak strips. Re-insert the drawers into the unit and press START/STOP to resume cooking.
7. Serve in warm tortillas.

Nutrition:

- (Per serving) Calories 305 | Fat 17g | Sodium 418mg | Carbs 15g | Fiber 2g | Sugar 4g | Protein 22g

Curry-crusted Lamb Chops With Baked Brown Sugar Acorn Squash
Servings:4
Cooking Time: 20 Minutes
Ingredients:

- FOR THE LAMB CHOPS
- 4 lamb loin chops (4 ounces each)
- 1 tablespoon olive oil
- 2 teaspoons curry powder
- ¼ teaspoon kosher salt
- FOR THE ACORN SQUASH
- 2 small acorn squash
- 4 teaspoons dark brown sugar
- 2 teaspoons salted butter
- ⅛ teaspoon kosher salt

Directions:

1. To prep the lamb chops: Brush both sides of the lamb chops with the oil and season with the curry powder and salt.

2. To prep the acorn squash: Cut the squash in half through the stem end and remove the seeds. Place 1 teaspoon of brown sugar and ½ teaspoon of butter into the well of each squash half.
3. To cook the lamb and squash: Install a crisper plate in each of the two baskets. Place the lamb chops in the Zone 1 basket and insert the basket in the unit. Place the squash cut-side up in the Zone 2 basket and insert the basket in the unit.
4. Select Zone 1, select AIR FRY, set the temperature to 400°F, and set the timer to 15 minutes.
5. Select Zone 2, select BAKE, set the temperature to 400°F, and set the time to 20 minutes. Select SMART FINISH.
6. Press START/PAUSE to begin cooking.
7. When both timers read 5 minutes, press START/PAUSE. Remove the Zone 1 basket and use a pair of silicone-tipped tongs to flip the lamb chops. Reinsert the basket in the unit. Remove the Zone 2 basket and spoon the melted butter and sugar over the top edges of the squash. Reinsert the basket and press START/PAUSE to resume cooking.
8. When cooking is complete, the lamb should be cooked to your liking and the squash soft when pierced with a fork.
9. Remove the lamb chops from the basket and let rest for 5 minutes. Season the acorn squash with salt before serving.

Nutrition:

- (Per serving) Calories: 328; Total fat: 19g; Saturated fat: 7.5g; Carbohydrates: 23g; Fiber: 3g; Protein: 16g; Sodium: 172mg

Pigs In A Blanket With Spinach-artichoke Stuffed Mushrooms

Servings:4

Cooking Time: 15 Minutes

Ingredients:

- FOR THE PIGS IN A BLANKET
- Half an 8-ounce tube refrigerated crescent roll dough
- 4 hot dogs
- ½ teaspoon everything bagel seasoning (optional)
- FOR THE STUFFED MUSHROOMS
- 1 cup frozen chopped spinach, thawed and drained
- 1 (14-ounce) can artichoke hearts, drained and chopped
- 2 ounces (¼ cup) cream cheese, at room temperature
- ¼ cup grated Parmesan cheese
- ½ teaspoon garlic powder
- 1 (8-ounce) package whole cremini mushrooms, stems removed

Directions:

1. To prep the pigs in a blanket: Unroll the crescent roll dough. It will be scored into 4 triangular pieces, but leave them in place and pinch together at the seams to form 1 large square of dough. Cut the dough into 4 strips.
2. Wrap one strip of dough around each hot dog, starting with a short end of the strips and wrapping in a spiral motion around the hot dog. If desired, sprinkle each pig in a blanket with everything bagel seasoning.
3. To prep the stuffed mushrooms: In a medium bowl, combine the spinach, artichoke hearts, cream cheese, Parmesan, and garlic powder. Stuff about 1 tablespoon of filling into each mushroom cap.
4. To cook the pigs in a blanket and mushrooms: Install a crisper plate in each of the two baskets. Place the pigs in a blanket in the Zone 1 basket and insert the basket in the unit. Place the mushrooms in the Zone 2 basket and insert the basket in the unit.
5. Select Zone 1, select AIR FRY, set the temperature to 370°F, and set the time to 8 minutes.
6. Select Zone 2, select BAKE, set the temperature to 370°F, and set the time to 15 minutes. Select SMART FINISH.

7. Press START/PAUSE to begin cooking.
8. When cooking is complete, the crescent roll dough should be cooked through and golden brown, and the mushrooms should be tender.

Nutrition:

- (Per serving) Calories: 371; Total fat: 25g; Saturated fat: 11g; Carbohydrates: 22g; Fiber: 2.5g; Protein: 14g; Sodium: 1,059mg

Beef Ribs Ii
Servings:2
Cooking Time:1
Ingredients:

- ¼ cup olive oil
- 4 garlic cloves, minced
- ½ cup white wine vinegar
- ¼ cup soy sauce, reduced-sodium
- ¼ cup Worcestershire sauce
- 1 lemon juice
- Salt and black pepper, to taste
- 2 tablespoons of Italian seasoning
- 1 teaspoon of smoked paprika
- 2 tablespoons of mustard
- ½ cup maple syrup
- Meat Ingredients:
- Oil spray, for greasing
- 8 beef ribs lean

Directions:

1. Take a large bowl and add all the ingredients under marinade ingredients.
2. Put the marinade in a zip lock bag and add ribs to it.
3. Let it sit for 4 hours.
4. Now take out the basket of air fryer and grease the baskets with oil spray.
5. Now dived the ribs among two baskets.
6. Set it to AIR fry mode at 220 degrees F for 30 minutes.
7. Select Pause and take out the baskets.
8. Afterward, flip the ribs and cook for 30 minutes at 250 degrees F.
9. Once done, serve the juicy and tender ribs.
10. Enjoy.

Nutrition:

- (Per serving) Calories 1927| Fat116g| Sodium 1394mg | Carbs 35.2g | Fiber 1.3g| Sugar29 g | Protein 172.3g

Italian Sausages With Peppers, Potatoes, And Onions
Servings:4

Cooking Time: 22 Minutes

Ingredients:

- FOR THE PEPPERS, POTATOES, AND ONIONS
- 2 Yukon Gold potatoes, cut into ¼-inch slices
- 1 red bell pepper, sliced
- 1 yellow onion, sliced
- ¼ cup canned tomato sauce
- 1 tablespoon olive oil
- 1 teaspoon minced garlic
- ½ teaspoon dried oregano
- ¼ teaspoon kosher salt
- FOR THE SAUSAGES
- 4 links Italian sausage

Directions:

1. To prep the peppers, potatoes, and onions: In a large bowl, combine the potatoes, pepper, onion, tomato sauce, oil, garlic, oregano, and salt. Mix to combine.
2. To cook the sausage and vegetables: Install a crisper plate in each of the two baskets. Place the sausages in the Zone 1 basket and insert the basket in the unit. Place the potato mixture in the Zone 2 basket and insert the basket in the unit.
3. Select Zone 1, select AIR FRY, set the temperature to 390°F, and set the time to 22 minutes.
4. Select Zone 2, select ROAST, set the temperature to 375°F, and set the time to 20 minutes. Select SMART FINISH.
5. Press START/PAUSE to begin cooking.
6. When cooking is complete, the sausages will be cooked through and the vegetables tender.
7. Slice the sausages into rounds, then mix them into the potato and pepper mixture. Serve.

Nutrition:

- (Per serving) Calories: 335; Total fat: 22g; Saturated fat: 6.5g; Carbohydrates: 21g; Fiber: 2g; Protein: 15g; Sodium: 658mg

Gochujang Brisket

Servings: 6

Cooking Time: 55 Minutes.

Ingredients:

- ½ tablespoons sweet paprika
- ½ teaspoon toasted sesame oil
- 2 lbs. beef brisket, cut into 4 pieces
- Salt, to taste
- ⅛ cup Gochujang, Korean chili paste
- Black pepper, to taste
- 1 small onion, diced
- 2 garlic cloves, minced
- 1 teaspoon Asian fish sauce
- 1 ½ tablespoons peanut oil, as needed
- ½ tablespoon fresh ginger, grated
- ¼ teaspoon red chili flakes
- ½ cup of water

- 1 tablespoon ketchup
- 1 tablespoon soy sauce

Directions:

1. Thoroughly rub the beef brisket with olive oil, paprika, chili flakes, black pepper, and salt.
2. Cut the brisket in half, then divide the beef in the two crisper plate.
3. Return the crisper plate to the Ninja Foodi Dual Zone Air Fryer.
4. Choose the Air Fry mode for Zone 1 and set the temperature to 390 degrees F and the time to 35 minutes.
5. Select the "MATCH" button to copy the settings for Zone 2.
6. Initiate cooking by pressing the START/STOP button.
7. Flip the brisket halfway through, and resume cooking.
8. Meanwhile, heat oil in a skillet and add ginger, onion, and garlic.
9. Sauté for 5 minutes, then add all the remaining ingredients.
10. Cook the mixture for 15 minutes approximately until well thoroughly mixed.
11. Serve the brisket with this sauce on top.

Nutrition:

- (Per serving) Calories 374 | Fat 25g |Sodium 275mg | Carbs 7.3g | Fiber 0g | Sugar 6g | Protein 12.3g

Pork Chops With Apples

Servings: 2

Cooking Time: 15 Minutes

Ingredients:

- ½ small red cabbage, sliced
- 1 apple, sliced
- 1 sweet onion, sliced
- 2 tablespoons oil
- ½ teaspoon cumin
- ½ teaspoon paprika
- Salt and black pepper, to taste
- 2 boneless pork chops (1" thick)

Directions:

1. Toss pork chops with apple and the rest of the ingredients in a bowl.
2. Divide the mixture in the air fryer baskets.
3. Return the air fryer basket 1 to Zone 1, and basket 2 to Zone 2 of the Ninja Foodi 2-Basket Air Fryer.
4. Choose the "Air Fry" mode for Zone 1 and set the temperature to 400 degrees F and 15 minutes of cooking time.
5. Select the "MATCH COOK" option to copy the settings for Zone 2.
6. Initiate cooking by pressing the START/PAUSE BUTTON.
7. Serve warm.

Nutrition:

- (Per serving) Calories 374 | Fat 25g |Sodium 275mg | Carbs 7.3g | Fiber 0g | Sugar 6g | Protein 12.3g

Rosemary And Garlic Lamb Chops
Servings: 4
Cooking Time: 15 Minutes
Ingredients:
- 8 lamb chops
- 3 tablespoons olive oil
- 2 tablespoons chopped fresh rosemary
- 1 teaspoon garlic powder or 3 cloves garlic, minced
- 1 teaspoon salt, or to taste
- ½ teaspoon black pepper, or to taste

Directions:
1. Dry the lamb chops with a paper towel.
2. Combine the olive oil, rosemary, garlic, salt, and pepper in a large mixing bowl. Toss the lamb in the marinade gently to coat it. Cover and set aside to marinate for 1 hour or up to overnight.
3. Install a crisper plate in both drawers. Place half the lamb chops in the zone 1 drawer and half in zone 2's, then insert the drawers into the unit.
4. Select zone 1, select AIR FRY, set temperature to 390 degrees F/ 200 degrees C, and set time to 15 minutes. Select MATCH to match zone 2 settings to zone 1. Press the START/STOP button to begin cooking.
5. When the time reaches 10 minutes, press START/STOP to pause the unit. Remove the drawers and flip the chops. Re-insert the drawers into the unit and press START/STOP to resume cooking.
6. Serve and enjoy!

Nutrition:
- (Per serving) Calories 427 | Fat 34g | Sodium 668mg | Carbs 1g | Fiber 1g | Sugar 1g | Protein 31g

Breaded Pork Chops
Servings: 4
Cooking Time: 10 Minutes
Ingredients:
- 4 boneless, center-cut pork chops, 1-inch thick
- 1 teaspoon Cajun seasoning
- 1½ cups cheese and garlic-flavored croutons
- 2 eggs
- Cooking spray

Directions:
1. Season both sides of the pork chops with the Cajun seasoning on a platter.
2. In a small food processor, pulse the croutons until finely chopped; transfer to a shallow plate.
3. In a separate shallow bowl, lightly beat the eggs.
4. Dip the pork chops in the egg, allowing any excess to drip off. Then place the chops in the crouton crumbs. Coat the chops in cooking spray.
5. Install a crisper plate in both drawers. Place half the pork chops in the zone 1 drawer and half in zone 2's, then insert the drawers into the unit.
6. Select zone 1, select ROAST, set temperature to 390 degrees F/ 200 degrees C, and set time to 10 minutes. Select MATCH to match zone 2 settings to zone 1. Press the START/STOP button to begin cooking.

7. When the time reaches 6 minutes, press START/STOP to pause the unit. Remove the drawers and flip the chops. Reinsert the drawers into the unit and press START/STOP to resume cooking.
8. When cooking is complete, serve and enjoy!

Nutrition:

- (Per serving) Calories 394 | Fat 18.1g | Sodium 428mg | Carbs 10g | Fiber 0.8g | Sugar 0.9g | Protein 44.7g

Lamb Chops With Dijon Garlic

Servings: 4

Cooking Time: 22 Minutes

Ingredients:

- 2 teaspoons Dijon mustard
- 2 teaspoons olive oil
- 1 teaspoon soy sauce
- 1 teaspoon garlic, minced
- 1 teaspoon cumin powder
- 1 teaspoon cayenne pepper
- 1 teaspoon Italian spice blend (optional)
- ¼ teaspoon salt
- 8 lamb chops

Directions:

1. Combine the Dijon mustard, olive oil, soy sauce, garlic, cumin powder, cayenne pepper, Italian spice blend (optional), and salt in a medium mixing bowl.
2. Put the marinade in a large Ziploc bag. Add the lamb chops. Seal the bag tightly after pressing out the air. Coat the lamb in the marinade by shaking the bag and pressing the chops into the mixture. Place in the fridge for at least 30 minutes, or up to overnight, to marinate.
3. Install a crisper plate in both drawers. Place half the lamb chops in the zone 1 drawer and half in zone 2's, then insert the drawers into the unit.
4. Select zone 1, select AIR FRY, set temperature to 390 degrees F/ 200 degrees C, and set time to 22 minutes. Select MATCH to match zone 2 settings to zone 1. Press the START/STOP button to begin cooking.
5. When the time reaches 11 minutes, press START/STOP to pause the unit. Remove the drawers and flip the lamb chops. Re-insert the drawers into the unit and press START/STOP to resume cooking.
6. Serve and enjoy!

Nutrition:

- (Per serving) Calories 343 | Fat 15.1g | Sodium 380mg | Carbs 0.9 g | Fiber 0.3g | Sugar 0.1g | Protein 48.9g

Juicy Pork Chops

Servings: 4

Cooking Time: 15 Minutes

Ingredients:

- 450g pork chops
- ¼ tsp garlic powder

- 15ml olive oil
- ¼ tsp smoked paprika
- Pepper
- Salt

Directions:

1. In a small bowl, mix the garlic powder, paprika, pepper, and salt.
2. Brush the pork chops with oil and rub with spice mixture.
3. Insert a crisper plate in the Ninja Foodi air fryer baskets.
4. Place the pork chops in both baskets.
5. Select zone 1, then select "bake" mode and set the temperature to 410 degrees F for 15 minutes. Press "match" to match zone 2 settings to zone 1. Press "start/stop" to begin. Turn halfway through.

Nutrition:

- (Per serving) Calories 394 | Fat 31.7g |Sodium 118mg | Carbs 0.2g | Fiber 0.1g | Sugar 0.1g | Protein 25.5g

Garlic-rosemary Pork Loin With Scalloped Potatoes And Cauliflower

Servings:6

Cooking Time: 50 Minutes

Ingredients:

- FOR THE PORK LOIN
- 2 pounds pork loin roast
- 2 tablespoons vegetable oil
- 2 teaspoons dried thyme
- 2 teaspoons dried crushed rosemary
- 1 teaspoon minced garlic
- ¾ teaspoon kosher salt
- FOR THE SCALLOPED POTATOES AND CAULIFLOWER
- 1 teaspoon vegetable oil
- ¾ pound Yukon Gold potatoes, peeled and very thinly sliced
- 1½ cups cauliflower florets
- ¼ teaspoon kosher salt
- ¼ teaspoon freshly ground black pepper
- 1 tablespoon very cold unsalted butter, grated
- 3 tablespoons all-purpose flour
- 1 cup whole milk
- 1 cup shredded Gruyère cheese

Directions:

1. To prep the pork loin: Coat the pork with the oil. Season with thyme, rosemary, garlic, and salt.
2. To prep the potatoes and cauliflower: Brush the bottom and sides of the Zone 2 basket with the oil. Add one-third of the potatoes to the bottom of the basket and arrange in a single layer. Top with ½ cup of cauliflower florets. Sprinkle a third of the salt and black pepper on top. Scatter one-third of the butter on top and sprinkle on 1 tablespoon of flour. Repeat this step twice more for a total of three layers.
3. Pour the milk over the layered potatoes and cauliflower; it should just cover the top layer. Top with the Gruyère.

4. To cook the pork and scalloped vegetables: Install a crisper plate in the Zone 1 basket. Place the pork loin in the basket and insert the basket in the unit. Insert the Zone 2 basket in the unit.
5. Select Zone 1, select AIR FRY, set the temperature to 390°F, and set the time to 50 minutes.
6. Select Zone 2, select BAKE, set the temperature to 350°F, and set the time to 45 minutes. Select SMART FINISH.
7. Press START/PAUSE to begin cooking.
8. When cooking is complete, the pork will be cooked through (an instant-read thermometer should read 145°F) and the potatoes and cauliflower will be tender.
9. Let the pork rest for at least 15 minutes before slicing and serving with the scalloped vegetables.

Nutrition:

- (Per serving) Calories: 439; Total fat: 25g; Saturated fat: 10g; Carbohydrates: 17g; Fiber: 1.5g; Protein: 37g; Sodium: 431mg

Chipotle Beef

Servings: 4

Cooking Time: 18 Minutes.

Ingredients:

- 1 lb. beef steak, cut into chunks
- 1 large egg
- ½ cup parmesan cheese, grated
- ½ cup pork panko
- ½ teaspoon seasoned salt
- Chipotle Ranch Dip
- ¼ cup mayonnaise
- ¼ cup sour cream
- 1 teaspoon chipotle paste
- ½ teaspoon ranch dressing mix
- ¼ medium lime, juiced

Directions:

1. Mix all the ingredients for chipotle ranch dip in a bowl.
2. Keep it in the refrigerator for 30 minutes.
3. Mix pork panko with salt and parmesan.
4. Beat egg in one bowl and spread the panko mixture in another flat bowl.
5. Dip the steak chunks in the egg first, then coat them with panko mixture.
6. Spread them in the two crisper plates and spray them with cooking oil.
7. Return the crisper plate to the Ninja Foodi Dual Zone Air Fryer.
8. Choose the Air Fry mode for Zone 1 and set the temperature to 390 degrees F and the time to 18 minutes.
9. Select the "MATCH" button to copy the settings for Zone 2.
10. Initiate cooking by pressing the START/STOP button.
11. Serve with chipotle ranch and salt and pepper on top. Enjoy.

Nutrition:

- (Per serving) Calories 310 | Fat 17g |Sodium 271mg | Carbs 4.3g | Fiber 0.9g | Sugar 2.1g | Protein 35g

Beef And Bean Taquitos With Mexican Rice
Servings:4
Cooking Time: 15 Minutes
Ingredients:

- FOR THE TAQUITOS
- ½ pound ground beef (85 percent lean)
- 1 tablespoon taco seasoning
- 8 (6-inch) soft white corn tortillas
- Nonstick cooking spray
- ¾ cup canned refried beans
- ½ cup shredded Mexican blend cheese (optional)
- FOR THE MEXICAN RICE
- 1 cup dried instant white rice (not microwavable)
- 1½ cups chicken broth
- ¼ cup jarred salsa
- 2 tablespoons canned tomato sauce
- 1 tablespoon vegetable oil
- ½ teaspoon kosher salt

Directions:

1. To prep the taquitos: In a large bowl, mix the ground beef and taco seasoning until well combined.
2. Mist both sides of each tortilla lightly with cooking spray.
3. To prep the Mexican rice: In the Zone 2 basket, combine the rice, broth, salsa, tomato sauce, oil, and salt. Stir well to ensure all of the rice is submerged in the liquid.
4. To cook the taquitos and rice: Install a crisper plate in the Zone 1 basket. Place the seasoned beef in the basket and insert the basket in the unit. Insert the Zone 2 basket in the unit.
5. Select Zone 1, select AIR FRY, set the temperature to 390°F, and set the time to 15 minutes.
6. Select Zone 2, select BAKE, set the temperature to 350°F, and set the time to 10 minutes. Select SMART FINISH.
7. Press START/PAUSE to begin cooking.
8. When the Zone 1 timer reads 10 minutes, press START/PAUSE. Remove the basket and transfer the beef to a medium bowl. Add the refried beans and cheese (if using) and combine well. Spoon 2 tablespoons of the filling onto each tortilla and roll tightly. Place the taquitos in the Zone 1 basket seam-side down. Reinsert the basket in the unit and press START/PAUSE to resume cooking.
9. When cooking is complete, the taquitos should be crisp and golden brown and the rice cooked through. Serve hot.

Nutrition:

- (Per serving) Calories: 431; Total fat: 18g; Saturated fat: 4g; Carbohydrates: 52g; Fiber: 5.5g; Protein: 18g; Sodium: 923mg

Pork Chops And Potatoes
Servings: 3
Cooking Time: 12 Minutes
Ingredients:

- 455g red potatoes
- Olive oil
- Salt and pepper
- 1 teaspoon garlic powder

- 1 teaspoon fresh rosemary, chopped
- 2 tablespoons brown sugar
- 1 tablespoon soy sauce
- 1 tablespoon Worcestershire sauce
- 1 teaspoon lemon juice
- 3 small pork chops

Directions:

1. Mix potatoes and pork chops with remaining ingredients in a bowl.
2. Divide the ingredients in the air fryer baskets.
3. Return the air fryer basket 1 to Zone 1, and basket 2 to Zone 2 of the Ninja Foodi 2-Basket Air Fryer.
4. Choose the "Air Fry" mode for Zone 1 at 400 degrees F and 12 minutes of cooking time.
5. Select the "MATCH COOK" option to copy the settings for Zone 2.
6. Initiate cooking by pressing the START/PAUSE BUTTON.
7. Flip the chops and toss potatoes once cooked halfway through.
8. Serve warm.

Nutrition:

- (Per serving) Calories 352 | Fat 9.1g |Sodium 1294mg | Carbs 3.9g | Fiber 1g | Sugar 1g | Protein 61g

Pork Chops

Servings:2

Cooking Time:17

Ingredients:

- 1 tablespoon of rosemary, chopped
- Salt and black pepper, to taste
- 2 garlic cloves
- 1-inch ginger
- 2 tablespoons of olive oil
- 8 pork chops

Directions:

1. Take a blender and pulse together rosemary, salt, pepper, garlic cloves, ginger, and olive oil.
2. Rub this marinade over pork chops and let it rest for 1 hour.
3. Then divide it amongst air fryer baskets and set it to AIR FRY mode for 17 minutes at 375 degrees F.
4. Once the cooking cycle is done, take out and serve hot.

Nutrition:

- (Per serving) Calories 1154| Fat 93.8g| Sodium 225mg | Carbs 2.1g | Fiber0.8 g| Sugar 0g | Protein 72.2g

Steak In Air Fry

Servings:1

Cooking Time:20

Ingredients:

- 2 teaspoons of canola oil
- 1 tablespoon of Montreal steaks seasoning
- 1 pound of beef steak

Directions:

1. The first step is to season the steak on both sides with canola oil and then rub a generous amount of steak seasoning all over.
2. We are using the AIR BROIL feature of the ninja air fryer and it works with one basket.
3. Put the steak in the basket and set it to AIR BROIL at 450 degrees F for 20 -22 minutes.
4. After 7 minutes, hit pause and take out the basket to flip the steak, and cover it with foil on top, for the remaining 14 minutes.
5. Once done, serve the medium-rare steak and enjoy it by resting for 10 minutes.
6. Serve by cutting in slices.
7. Enjoy.

Nutrition:

- (Per serving) Calories 935| Fat 37.2g| Sodium 1419mg | Carbs 0g | Fiber 0g| Sugar 0g | Protein137.5 g

Balsamic Steak Tips With Roasted Asparagus And Mushroom Medley

Servings:4

Cooking Time: 25 Minutes

Ingredients:

- FOR THE STEAK TIPS
- 1½ pounds sirloin tips
- ½ cup olive oil
- ¼ cup balsamic vinegar
- ¼ cup packed light brown sugar
- 1 tablespoon reduced-sodium soy sauce
- 1 teaspoon finely chopped fresh rosemary
- 1 teaspoon minced garlic
- FOR THE ASPARAGUS AND MUSHROOMS
- 6 ounces sliced cremini mushrooms
- 1 small red onion, sliced
- 1 tablespoon olive oil
- 1 pound asparagus, tough ends trimmed
- ⅛ teaspoon kosher salt

Directions:

1. To prep the steak tips: In a large bowl, combine the sirloin tips, oil, vinegar, brown sugar, soy sauce, rosemary, and garlic. Mix well to coat the steak.
2. To prep the mushrooms: In a large bowl, combine the mushrooms, onion, and oil.
3. To cook the steak and vegetables: Install a crisper plate in each of the two baskets. Shake any excess marinade from the steak tips, place the steak in the Zone 1 basket, and insert the basket in the unit. Place the mushrooms and onions in the Zone 2 basket and insert the basket in the unit.
4. Select Zone 1, select AIR FRY, set the temperature to 400°F, and set the time to 12 minutes.
5. Select Zone 2, select ROAST, set the temperature to 400°F, and set the time to 25 minutes. Select SMART FINISH.

6. Press START/PAUSE to begin cooking.
7. When the Zone 2 timer reads 10 minutes, press START/PAUSE. Remove the basket, add the asparagus to the mushrooms and onion, and sprinkle with salt. Reinsert the basket and press START/PAUSE to resume cooking.
8. When cooking is complete, the beef should be cooked to your liking and the asparagus crisp-tender. Serve warm.

Nutrition:

- (Per serving) Calories: 524; Total fat: 33g; Saturated fat: 2.5g; Carbohydrates: 16g; Fiber: 3g; Protein: 41g; Sodium: 192mg

Cheesesteak Taquitos

Servings: 8

Cooking Time: 12 Minutes

Ingredients:

- 1 pack soft corn tortillas
- 136g beef steak strips
- 2 green peppers, sliced
- 1 white onion, chopped
- 1 pkg dry Italian dressing mix
- 10 slices Provolone cheese
- Cooking spray or olive oil

Directions:

1. Mix beef with cooking oil, peppers, onion, and dressing mix in a bowl.
2. Divide the strips in the air fryer baskets.
3. Return the air fryer basket 1 to Zone 1, and basket 2 to Zone 2 of the Ninja Foodi 2-Basket Air Fryer.
4. Choose the "Air Fry" mode for Zone 1 at 375 degrees F and 12 minutes of cooking time.
5. Select the "MATCH COOK" option to copy the settings for Zone 2.
6. Initiate cooking by pressing the START/PAUSE BUTTON.
7. Flip the strips once cooked halfway through.
8. Divide the beef strips in the tortillas and top the beef with a beef slice.
9. Roll the tortillas and serve.

Nutrition:

- (Per serving) Calories 410 | Fat 17.8g |Sodium 619mg | Carbs 21g | Fiber 1.4g | Sugar 1.8g | Protein 38.4g

Yogurt Lamb Chops

Servings:2

Cooking Time:20

Ingredients:

- 1½ cups plain Greek yogurt
- 1 lemon, juice only
- 1 teaspoon ground cumin
- 1 teaspoon ground coriander
- ¾teaspoon ground turmeric

- ¼ teaspoon ground allspice
- 10 rib lamb chops (1–1¼ inches thick cut)
- 2 tablespoons olive oil, divided

Directions:

1. Take a bowl and add lamb chop along with listed ingredients.
2. Rub the lamb chops well.
3. and let it marinate in the refrigerator for 1 hour.
4. Afterward takeout the lamb chops from the refrigerator.
5. Layer parchment paper on top of the baskets of the air fryer.
6. Divide it between ninja air fryer baskets.
7. Set the time for zone 1 to 20 minutes at 400 degrees F.
8. Select the MATCH button for the zone 2 basket.
9. Hit start and then wait for the chop to be cooked.
10. Once the cooking is done, the cool sign will appear on display.
11. Take out the lamb chops and let the chops serve on plates.

Nutrition:

- (Per serving) Calories1973 | Fat90 g| Sodium228 mg | Carbs 109.2g | Fiber 1g | Sugar 77.5g | Protein 184g

Sausage Meatballs

Servings: 24

Cooking Time: 10 Minutes

Ingredients:

- 1 egg, lightly beaten
- 900g pork sausage
- 29g breadcrumbs
- 100g pimientos, drained & diced
- 1 tsp curry powder
- 1 tbsp garlic, minced
- 30ml olive oil
- 1 tbsp fresh rosemary, minced
- 25g parsley, minced
- Pepper
- Salt

Directions:

1. In a bowl, add pork sausage and remaining ingredients and mix until well combined.
2. Insert a crisper plate in the Ninja Foodi air fryer baskets.
3. Make small balls from the meat mixture and place them in both baskets.
4. Select zone 1 then select “air fry” mode and set the temperature to 390 degrees F for 10 minutes. Press “match” to match zone 2 settings to zone 1. Press “start/stop” to begin.

Nutrition:

- (Per serving) Calories 153 | Fat 12.2g |Sodium 303mg | Carbs 2.6g | Fiber 0.4g | Sugar 1.1g | Protein 8g

Roast Beef With Yorkshire Pudding
Servings:6
Cooking Time: 40 Minutes
Ingredients:

- FOR THE ROAST BEEF
- 3-pound beef roast, trimmed
- 1 tablespoon vegetable oil
- ½ teaspoon kosher salt
- ½ teaspoon freshly ground black pepper
- ½ teaspoon garlic powder
- ½ teaspoon onion powder
- ½ teaspoon dried thyme
- FOR THE YORKSHIRE PUDDING
- 3 large eggs
- ¾ cup whole milk
- 2 tablespoons beef broth
- ¾ cup all-purpose flour
- ½ teaspoon kosher salt
- 2 teaspoons unsalted butter

Directions:

1. To prep the roast beef: If necessary, trim the beef roast to fit in the Zone 1 basket. Rub the beef with the oil.
2. In a small bowl, combine the salt, black pepper, garlic powder, onion powder, and thyme. Rub the spice mixture all over the beef roast.
3. To prep the Yorkshire pudding: In a large bowl, whisk the eggs, milk, and beef broth until well combined. Whisk in the flour and salt to form a thin batter.
4. To cook the beef and Yorkshire pudding: Install a crisper plate in the Zone 1 basket. Place the beef roast in the basket and insert the basket in the unit. Place the butter in the Zone 2 basket and insert the basket in the unit.
5. Select Zone 1, select AIR FRY, set the temperature to 375°F, and set the time to 40 minutes for a medium-rare roast (set to 50 minutes for medium or 60 minutes for well done).
6. Select Zone 2, select BAKE, set the temperature to 400°F, and set the time to 20 minutes. Select SMART FINISH.
7. Press START/PAUSE to begin cooking.
8. When the Zone 2 timer reads 18 minutes, press START/PAUSE. Remove the basket and pour the batter into it. Reinsert the basket and press START/PAUSE to resume cooking.
9. When cooking is complete, the beef should be cooked to your liking and the Yorkshire pudding should be fluffy on the edges and set in the center.
10. Remove the beef from the basket and let rest for at least 15 minutes before slicing.
11. Cut the Yorkshire pudding into 6 servings and serve the sliced beef on top.

Nutrition:

- (Per serving) Calories: 517; Total fat: 26g; Saturated fat: 9.5g; Carbohydrates: 13g; Fiber: 0.5g; Protein: 52g; Sodium: 354mg

Korean Bbq Beef
Servings: 6
Cooking Time: 30 Minutes

Ingredients:

- For the meat:
- 1 pound flank steak or thinly sliced steak
- ¼ cup corn starch
- Coconut oil spray
- For the sauce:
- ½ cup soy sauce or gluten-free soy sauce
- ½ cup brown sugar
- 2 tablespoons white wine vinegar
- 1 clove garlic, crushed
- 1 tablespoon hot chili sauce
- 1 teaspoon ground ginger
- ½ teaspoon sesame seeds
- 1 tablespoon corn starch
- 1 tablespoon water

Directions:

1. To begin, prepare the steak. Thinly slice it in that toss it in the corn starch to be coated thoroughly. Spray the tops with some coconut oil.
2. Spray the crisping plates and drawers with the coconut oil.
3. Place the crisping plates into the drawers. Place the steak strips into each drawer. Insert both drawers into the unit.
4. Select zone 1, Select AIR FRY, set the temperature to 375 degrees F/ 190 degrees C, and set time to 30 minutes. Select MATCH to match zone 2 settings with zone 1. Press the START/STOP button to begin cooking.
5. While the steak is cooking, add the sauce ingredients EXCEPT for the corn starch and water to a medium saucepan.
6. Warm it up to a low boil, then whisk in the corn starch and water.
7. Carefully remove the steak and pour the sauce over. Mix well.

Nutrition:

- (Per serving) Calories 500 | Fat 19.8g | Sodium 680mg | Carbs 50.1g | Fiber 4.1g | Sugar 0g | Protein 27.9g

Italian-style Meatballs With Garlicky Roasted Broccoli

Servings:4

Cooking Time: 15 Minutes

Ingredients:

- FOR THE MEATBALLS
- 1 large egg
- ¼ cup Italian-style bread crumbs
- 1 pound ground beef (85 percent lean)
- ¼ cup grated Parmesan cheese
- ¼ teaspoon kosher salt
- Nonstick cooking spray
- 2 cups marinara sauce
- FOR THE ROASTED BROCCOLI
- 4 cups broccoli florets
- 1 tablespoon olive oil
- ¼ teaspoon kosher salt
- ¼ teaspoon freshly ground pepper

- ¼ teaspoon red pepper flakes
- 1 tablespoon minced garlic

Directions:

1. To prep the meatballs: In a large bowl, beat the egg. Mix in the bread crumbs and let sit for 5 minutes.
2. Add the beef, Parmesan, and salt and mix until just combined. Form the meatball mixture into 8 meatballs, about 1 inch in diameter. Mist with cooking spray.
3. To prep the broccoli: In a large bowl, combine the broccoli, olive oil, salt, black pepper, and red pepper flakes. Toss to coat the broccoli evenly.
4. To cook the meatballs and broccoli: Install a crisper plate in the Zone 1 basket. Place the meatballs in the basket and insert the basket in the unit. Place the broccoli in the Zone 2 basket, sprinkle the garlic over the broccoli, and insert the basket in the unit.
5. Select Zone 1, select AIR FRY, set the temperature to 400°F, and set the time to 12 minutes.
6. Select Zone 2, select ROAST, set the temperature to 390°F, and set the time to 15 minutes. Select SMART FINISH.
7. Press START/PAUSE to begin cooking.
8. When the Zone 1 timer reads 5 minutes, press START/PAUSE. Remove the basket and pour the marinara sauce over the meatballs. Reinsert the basket and press START/PAUSE to resume cooking.
9. When cooking is complete, the meatballs should be cooked through and the broccoli will have begun to brown on the edges.

Nutrition:

- (Per serving) Calories: 493; Total fat: 33g; Saturated fat: 9g; Carbohydrates: 24g; Fiber: 3g; Protein: 31g; Sodium: 926mg

Parmesan Pork Chops

Servings: 4

Cooking Time: 15 Minutes.

Ingredients:

- 4 boneless pork chops
- 2 tablespoons olive oil
- ½ cup freshly grated Parmesan
- 1 teaspoon salt
- 1 teaspoon paprika
- 1 teaspoon garlic powder
- 1 teaspoon onion powder
- ½ teaspoon black pepper

Directions:

1. Pat dry the pork chops with a paper towel and rub them with olive oil.
2. Mix parmesan with spices in a medium bowl.
3. Rub the pork chops with Parmesan mixture.
4. Place 2 seasoned pork chops in each of the two crisper plate
5. Return the crisper plate to the Ninja Foodi Dual Zone Air Fryer.
6. Choose the Air Fry mode for Zone 1 and set the temperature to 390 degrees F and the time to 15 minutes.
7. Select the "MATCH" button to copy the settings for Zone 2.
8. Initiate cooking by pressing the START/STOP button.
9. Flip the pork chops when cooked halfway through, then resume cooking.

10. Serve warm.

Nutrition:

- (Per serving) Calories 396 | Fat 23.2g |Sodium 622mg | Carbs 0.7g | Fiber 0g | Sugar 0g | Protein 45.6g

Pork Katsu With Seasoned Rice
Servings:4
Cooking Time: 15 Minutes
Ingredients:

- FOR THE PORK KATSU
- 4 thin-sliced boneless pork chops (4 ounces each)
- 2 tablespoons all-purpose flour
- 2 large eggs
- 1 cup panko bread crumbs
- ¼ teaspoon kosher salt
- ¼ teaspoon freshly ground black pepper
- 1 teaspoon vegetable oil
- 3 tablespoons ketchup
- 3 tablespoons Worcestershire sauce
- 1 tablespoon oyster sauce
- ⅛ teaspoon granulated sugar
- FOR THE RICE
- 2 cups dried instant rice (not microwavable)
- 2½ cups water
- 1 tablespoon sesame oil
- 1 teaspoon soy sauce
- 1 tablespoon toasted sesame seeds
- 3 scallions, sliced

Directions:

1. To prep the pork katsu: Place the pork chops between two slices of plastic wrap. Using a meat mallet or rolling pin, pound the pork into ½-inch-thick cutlets.
2. Set up a breading station with three small shallow bowls. Place the flour in the first bowl. In the second bowl, whisk the eggs. Combine the panko, salt, and black pepper in the third bowl.
3. Bread the cutlets in this order: First, dip them in the flour, coating both sides. Then, dip them into the beaten egg. Finally, coat them in panko, gently pressing the bread crumbs to adhere to the pork. Drizzle both sides of the cutlets with the oil.
4. To prep the rice: In the Zone 2 basket, combine the rice, water, sesame oil, and soy sauce. Stir well to ensure all of the rice is submerged in the liquid.
5. To cook the pork and rice: Install a crisper plate in the Zone 1 basket. Place the pork in the basket and insert the basket in the unit. Insert the Zone 2 basket in the unit.
6. Select Zone 1, select AIR FRY, set the temperature to 390°F, and set the time to 15 minutes.
7. Select Zone 2, select BAKE, set the temperature to 350°F, and set the time to 10 minutes. Select SMART FINISH.
8. Press START/PAUSE to begin cooking.
9. When the Zone 1 timer reads 10 minutes, press START/PAUSE. Remove the basket and use silicone-tipped tongs to flip the pork. Reinsert the basket and press START/PAUSE to resume cooking.
10. When cooking is complete, the pork should be crisp and cooked through and the rice tender.

11. Stir the sesame seeds and scallions into the rice. For the sauce to go with the pork, in a small bowl, whisk together the ketchup, Worcestershire sauce, oyster sauce, and sugar. Drizzle the sauce over the pork and serve with the hot rice.

Nutrition:

- (Per serving) Calories: 563; Total fat: 20g; Saturated fat: 5.5g; Carbohydrates: 62g; Fiber: 1g; Protein: 34g; Sodium: 665mg

Meatloaf

Servings: 6

Cooking Time: 25 Minutes

Ingredients:

- For the meatloaf:
- 2 pounds ground beef
- 2 eggs, beaten
- 2 cups old-fashioned oats, regular or gluten-free
- ½ cup evaporated milk
- ½ cup chopped onion
- ½ teaspoon garlic salt
- For the sauce:
- 1 cup ketchup
- ¾ cup brown sugar, packed
- ¼ cup chopped onion
- ½ teaspoon liquid smoke
- ¼ teaspoon garlic powder
- Olive oil cooking spray

Directions:

1. In a large bowl, combine all the meatloaf ingredients.
2. Spray 2 sheets of foil with olive oil cooking spray.
3. Form the meatloaf mixture into a loaf shape, cut in half, and place each half on one piece of foil.
4. Roll the foil up a bit on the sides. Allow it to be slightly open.
5. Put all the sauce ingredients in a saucepan and whisk until combined on medium-low heat. This should only take 1–2 minutes
6. Install a crisper plate in both drawers. Place half the meatloaf in the zone 1 drawer and half in zone 2's, then insert the drawers into the unit.
7. Select zone 1, select AIR FRY, set temperature to 390 degrees F/ 200 degrees C, and set time to 25 minutes. Select MATCH to match zone 2 settings to zone 1. Press the START/STOP button to begin cooking.
8. When the time reaches 20 minutes, press START/STOP to pause the unit. Remove the drawers and coat the meatloaf with the sauce using a brush. Re-insert the drawers into the unit and press START/STOP to resume cooking.
9. Carefully remove and serve.

Nutrition:

- (Per serving) Calories 727 | Fat 34g | Sodium 688mg | Carbs 57g | Fiber 3g | Sugar 34g | Protein 49g

Steak Bites With Cowboy Butter
Servings: 4
Cooking Time: 15 Minutes
Ingredients:

- 455g steak sirloin
- Cooking spray
- Cowboy butter sauce
- 1 stick salted butter melted
- 1 tablespoon lemon zest
- 1 tablespoon lemon juice
- ½ teaspoon garlic powder
- ¼ teaspoon red pepper flakes
- ½ teaspoon sea salt
- ½ teaspoon black pepper
- ½ tablespoon Dijon mustard
- ½ teaspoon Worcestershire sauce
- 1 tablespoon parsley freshly chopped

Directions:

1. Mix all the cowboy butter ingredients in a bowl.
2. Stir in steak cubes and mix well.
3. Cover and marinate in the refrigerator for 1 hour.
4. Divide the steak cubes in the air fryer baskets then use cooking spray.
5. Return the air fryer basket 1 to Zone 1, and basket 2 to Zone 2 of the Ninja Foodi 2-Basket Air Fryer.
6. Choose the "Air Fry" mode for Zone 1 at 400 degrees F and 15 minutes of cooking time.
7. Select the "MATCH COOK" option to copy the settings for Zone 2.
8. Initiate cooking by pressing the START/PAUSE BUTTON.
9. Serve warm.

Nutrition:

- (Per serving) Calories 264 | Fat 17g |Sodium 129mg | Carbs 0.9g | Fiber 0.3g | Sugar 0g | Protein 27g

Pork With Green Beans And Potatoes
Servings: 4
Cooking Time: 15 Minutes.
Ingredients:

- ¼ cup Dijon mustard
- 2 tablespoons brown sugar
- 1 teaspoon dried parsley flake
- ½ teaspoon dried thyme
- ¼ teaspoons salt
- ¼ teaspoons black pepper
- 1 ¼ lbs. pork tenderloin
- ¾ lb. small potatoes halved
- 1 (12-oz) package green beans, trimmed

- 1 tablespoon olive oil
- Salt and black pepper ground to taste

Directions:

1. Preheat your Air Fryer Machine to 400 degrees F.
2. Add mustard, parsley, brown sugar, salt, black pepper, and thyme in a large bowl, then mix well.
3. Add tenderloin to the spice mixture and coat well.
4. Toss potatoes with olive oil, salt, black pepper, and green beans in another bowl.
5. Place the prepared tenderloin in the crisper plate.
6. Return this crisper plate to the Zone 1 of the Ninja Foodi Dual Zone Air Fryer.
7. Choose the Air Fry mode for Zone 1 and set the temperature to 390 degrees F and the time to 15 minutes.
8. Add potatoes and green beans to the Zone 2.
9. Choose the Air Fry mode for Zone 2 with 350 degrees F and the time to 10 minutes.
10. Press the SYNC button to sync the finish time for both Zones.
11. Initiate cooking by pressing the START/STOP button.
12. Serve the tenderloin with Air Fried potatoes

Nutrition:

- (Per serving) Calories 400 | Fat 32g |Sodium 721mg | Carbs 2.6g | Fiber 0g | Sugar 0g | Protein 27.4g

Lamb Shank With Mushroom Sauce

Servings: 4

Cooking Time: 35 Minutes.

Ingredients:

- 20 mushrooms, chopped
- 2 red bell pepper, chopped
- 2 red onion, chopped
- 1 cup red wine
- 4 leeks, chopped
- 6 tablespoons balsamic vinegar
- 2 teaspoons black pepper
- 2 teaspoons salt
- 3 tablespoons fresh rosemary
- 6 garlic cloves
- 4 lamb shanks
- 3 tablespoons olive oil

Directions:

1. Season the lamb shanks with salt, pepper, rosemary, and 1 teaspoon of olive oil.
2. Set half of the shanks in each of the crisper plate.
3. Return the crisper plate to the Ninja Foodi Dual Zone Air Fryer.
4. Choose the Air Fry mode for Zone 1 and set the temperature to 390 degrees F and the time to 25 minutes.
5. Select the "MATCH" button to copy the settings for Zone 2.
6. Initiate cooking by pressing the START/STOP button.
7. Flip the shanks halfway through, and resume cooking.
8. Meanwhile, add and heat the remaining olive oil in a skillet.
9. Add onion and garlic to sauté for 5 minutes.

10. Add in mushrooms and cook for 5 minutes.
11. Add red wine and cook until it is absorbed
12. Stir all the remaining vegetables along with black pepper and salt.
13. Cook until vegetables are al dente.
14. Serve the air fried shanks with sautéed vegetable fry.

Nutrition:

- (Per serving) Calories 352 | Fat 9.1g |Sodium 1294mg | Carbs 3.9g | Fiber 1g | Sugar 1g | Protein 61g

Garlic Butter Steaks

Servings: 2

Cooking Time: 25 Minutes

Ingredients:

- 2 (6 ounces each) sirloin steaks or ribeyes
- 2 tablespoons unsalted butter
- 1 clove garlic, crushed
- ½ teaspoon dried parsley
- ½ teaspoon dried rosemary
- Salt and pepper, to taste

Directions:

1. Season the steaks with salt and pepper and set them to rest for about 2 hours before cooking.
2. Put the butter in a bowl. Add the garlic, parsley, and rosemary. Allow the butter to soften.
3. Whip together with a fork or spoon once the butter has softened.
4. When you're ready to cook, install a crisper plate in both drawers. Place the sirloin steaks in a single layer in each drawer. Insert the drawers into the unit.
5. Select zone 1, select AIR FRY, set temperature to 360 degrees F/ 180 degrees C, and set time to 10 minutes. Select MATCH to match zone 2 settings to zone 1. Select START/STOP to begin.
6. Once done, serve with the garlic butter.

Nutrition:

- (Per serving) Calories 519 | Fat 36g | Sodium 245mg | Carbs 1g | Fiber 0g | Sugar 0g | Protein 46g

Turkey And Beef Meatballs

Servings: 6

Cooking Time: 24 Minutes.

Ingredients:

- 1 medium shallot, minced
- 2 tablespoons olive oil
- 3 garlic cloves, minced
- ¼ cup panko crumbs
- 2 tablespoons whole milk
- ⅔ lb. lean ground beef
- ⅓ lb. bulk turkey sausage

- 1 large egg, lightly beaten
- 1/4 cup parsley, chopped
- 1 tablespoon fresh thyme, chopped
- 1 tablespoon fresh rosemary, chopped
- 1 tablespoon Dijon mustard
- 1/2 teaspoon salt

Directions:

1. Preheat your oven to 400 degrees F. Place a medium non-stick pan over medium-high heat.
2. Add oil and shallot, then sauté for 2 minutes.
3. Toss in the garlic and cook for 1 minute.
4. Remove this pan from the heat.
5. Whisk panko with milk in a large bowl and leave it for 5 minutes.
6. Add cooked shallot mixture and mix well.
7. Stir in egg, parsley, turkey sausage, beef, thyme, rosemary, salt, and mustard.
8. Mix well, then divide the mixture into 1 1/2-inch balls.
9. Divide these balls into the two crisper plates and spray them with cooking oil.
10. Return the crisper plates to the Ninja Foodi Dual Zone Air Fryer.
11. Choose the Air Fry mode for Zone 1 and set the temperature to 400 degrees F and the time to 21 minutes.
12. Select the "MATCH" button to copy the settings for Zone 2.
13. Initiate cooking by pressing the START/STOP button.
14. Serve warm.

Nutrition:

- (Per serving) Calories 551 | Fat 31g |Sodium 1329mg | Carbs 1.5g | Fiber 0.8g | Sugar 0.4g | Protein 64g

Strip Steaks With Hasselback Potatoes

Servings:4

Cooking Time: 30 Minutes

Ingredients:

- FOR THE STRIP STEAK
- 2 boneless strip steaks (8 ounces each)
- 2 teaspoons vegetable oil
- 1 tablespoon steak seasoning
- FOR THE HASSELBACK POTATOES
- 4 russet potatoes
- 1 tablespoon vegetable oil
- 1 teaspoon kosher salt
- 1 tablespoon salted butter, at room temperature
- 2 teaspoons minced garlic
- 2 teaspoons minced fresh parsley

Directions:

1. To prep the strip steak: Brush both sides of the steaks with the oil and season with the steak seasoning.
2. To prep the Hasselback potatoes: Set a potato on a work surface and lay the handles of two wooden spoons lengthwise on either side of the potato. Make crosswise slits along the potato, spacing them 1/8 inch apart, being

careful to not cut the potato completely through (the spoon handles will prevent you from cutting all the way through). Repeat with the remaining potatoes.

3. Rub the potatoes with the oil and season with salt.
4. In a small bowl, mix the butter, garlic, and parsley until smooth.
5. To cook the steak and potatoes: Install a crisper plate in each of the two baskets. Place the steaks in the Zone 1 basket and insert the basket in the unit. Place the potatoes in the Zone 2 basket and insert the basket in the unit.
6. Select Zone 1, select AIR FRY, set the temperature to 375°F, and set the time to 20 minutes.
7. Select Zone 2, select BAKE, set the temperature to 375°F, and set the time to 30 minutes. Select SMART FINISH.
8. Press START/PAUSE to begin cooking.
9. When both timers read 6 minutes, press START/PAUSE. Remove the Zone 1 basket and use silicone-tipped tongs to flip the steaks. Reinsert the basket in the unit. Remove the Zone 2 basket and spread the herb butter into the potatoes, being sure to work the butter in between the slices. Reinsert the basket and press START/PAUSE to resume cooking.
10. When cooking is complete, the steak should be cooked to your liking and the potato soft when pierced with a fork.
11. Remove the steaks from the basket and let rest for 5 minutes before slicing.

Nutrition:

- (Per serving) Calories: 361; Total fat: 15g; Saturated fat: 5g; Carbohydrates: 31g; Fiber: 2g; Protein: 25g; Sodium: 694mg

Poultry Recipes

Delicious Chicken Skewers

Servings: 4
Cooking Time: 15 Minutes

Ingredients:

- 900g chicken thighs, cut into cubes
- 45ml fresh lime juice
- 59ml coconut milk
- 2 tbsp Thai red curry
- 35ml maple syrup
- 120ml tamari soy sauce

Directions:

1. Add chicken and remaining ingredients into the bowl and mix well.
2. Cover the bowl and place in the refrigerator for 2 hours.
3. Thread the marinated chicken onto the soaked skewers.
4. Insert a crisper plate in the Ninja Foodi air fryer baskets.
5. Place the chicken skewers in both baskets.
6. Select zone 1 then select "air fry" mode and set the temperature to 360 degrees F for 15 minutes. Press "match" to match zone 2 settings to zone 1. Press "start/stop" to begin.

Nutrition:

- (Per serving) Calories 526 | Fat 20.5g |Sodium 2210mg | Carbs 12.9g | Fiber 0.6g | Sugar 10g | Protein 69.7g

Cajun Chicken With Vegetables
Servings: 6
Cooking Time: 20 Minutes
Ingredients:

- 450g chicken breast, boneless & diced
- 1 tbsp Cajun seasoning
- 400g grape tomatoes
- 1/8 tsp dried thyme
- 1/8 tsp dried oregano
- 1 tsp smoked paprika
- 1 zucchini, diced
- 30ml olive oil
- 1 bell pepper, diced
- 1 tsp onion powder
- 1 1/2 tsp garlic powder
- Pepper
- Salt

Directions:

1. In a bowl, toss chicken with vegetables, oil, herb, spices, and salt until well coated.
2. Insert a crisper plate in the Ninja Foodi air fryer baskets.
3. Add chicken and vegetable mixture to both baskets.
4. Select zone 1, then select "air fry" mode and set the temperature to 390 degrees F for 20 minutes. Press "match" to match zone 2 settings to zone 1. Press "start/stop" to begin.

Nutrition:

- (Per serving) Calories 153 | Fat 6.9g |Sodium 98mg | Carbs 6g | Fiber 1.6g | Sugar 3.5g | Protein 17.4g

Air Fried Chicken Legs
Servings: 4
Cooking Time: 10 Minutes
Ingredients:

- 8 chicken legs
- 2 tablespoons olive oil
- 1 teaspoon salt
- 1 teaspoon black pepper
- 1 teaspoon smoked paprika
- 1 teaspoon garlic powder
- 1 teaspoon dried parsley

Directions:

1. Mix chicken with oil, herbs and spices in a bowl.
2. Divide the chicken legs in the air fryer baskets.
3. Return the air fryer basket 1 to Zone 1, and basket 2 to Zone 2 of the Ninja Foodi 2-Basket Air Fryer.
4. Choose the "Air Fry" mode for Zone 1 at 400 degrees F and 10 minutes of cooking time.
5. Select the "MATCH COOK" option to copy the settings for Zone 2.

6. Initiate cooking by pressing the START/PAUSE BUTTON.
7. Flip the chicken once cooked halfway through.
8. Serve warm.

Nutrition:

- (Per serving) Calories 220 | Fat 13g |Sodium 542mg | Carbs 0.9g | Fiber 0.3g | Sugar 0.2g | Protein 25.6g

Goat Cheese–stuffed Chicken Breast With Broiled Zucchini And Cherry Tomatoes

Servings:4

Cooking Time: 25 Minutes

Ingredients:

- FOR THE STUFFED CHICKEN BREASTS
- 2 ounces soft goat cheese
- 1 tablespoon minced fresh parsley
- ½ teaspoon minced garlic
- 4 boneless, skinless chicken breasts (6 ounces each)
- 1 tablespoon vegetable oil
- ½ teaspoon Italian seasoning
- ½ teaspoon kosher salt
- ½ teaspoon freshly ground black pepper
- FOR THE ZUCCHINI AND TOMATOES
- 1 pound zucchini, diced
- 1 cup cherry tomatoes, halved
- 1 tablespoon vegetable oil
- ½ teaspoon kosher salt
- ¼ teaspoon freshly ground black pepper

Directions:

1. To prep the stuffed chicken breasts: In a small bowl, combine the goat cheese, parsley, and garlic. Mix well.
2. Cut a deep slit into the fatter side of each chicken breast to create a pocket (taking care to not go all the way through). Stuff each breast with the goat cheese mixture. Use a toothpick to secure the opening of the chicken, if needed.
3. Brush the outside of the chicken breasts with the oil and season with the Italian seasoning, salt, and black pepper.
4. To prep the zucchini and tomatoes: In a large bowl, combine the zucchini, tomatoes, and oil. Mix to coat. Season with salt and black pepper.
5. To cook the chicken and vegetables: Install a crisper plate in each of the two baskets. Insert a broil rack in the Zone 2 basket over the crisper plate. Place the chicken in the Zone 1 basket and insert the basket in the unit. Place the vegetables on the broiler rack in the Zone 2 basket and insert the basket in the unit.
6. Select Zone 1, select AIR FRY, set the temperature to 390°F, and set the time to 25 minutes.
7. Select Zone 2, select AIR BROIL, set the temperature to 450°F, and set the time to 10 minutes. Select SMART FINISH.
8. Press START/PAUSE to begin cooking.
9. When cooking is complete, the chicken will be golden brown and cooked through (an instant-read thermometer should read 165°F) and the zucchini will be soft and slightly charred. Serve hot.

Nutrition:

- (Per serving) Calories: 330; Total fat: 15g; Saturated fat: 4g; Carbohydrates: 5g; Fiber: 1.5g; Protein: 42g; Sodium: 409mg

Chicken Tenders And Curly Fries
Servings: 4
Cooking Time: 35 Minutes
Ingredients:

- 1-pound frozen chicken tenders
- 1-pound frozen curly French fries
- Dipping sauces of your choice

Directions:

1. Place a crisper plate in each drawer. In the zone 1 drawer, place the chicken tenders, then place the drawer into the unit.
2. Fill the zone 2 drawer with the curly French fries, then place the drawer in the unit.
3. Select zone 1, then AIR FRY, and set the temperature to 390 degrees F/ 200 degrees C with a 22-minute timer. Select zone 2, then AIR FRY, and set the temperature to 400 degrees F/ 200 degrees C with a 30-minute timer. Select SYNC. To begin cooking, press the START/STOP button.
4. Press START/STOP to pause the device when the zone 1 and 2 times reach 8 minutes. Shake the drawers for 10 seconds after removing them from the unit. To resume cooking, re-insert the drawers into the unit and press START/STOP.
5. Enjoy!

Nutrition:

- (Per serving) Calories 500 | Fat 19.8g | Sodium 680mg | Carbs 50.1g | Fiber 4.1g | Sugar 0g | Protein 27.9g

Chicken Drumettes
Servings: 5
Cooking Time: 52 Minutes.
Ingredients:

- 10 large chicken drumettes
- Cooking spray
- ¼ cup of rice vinegar
- 3 tablespoons honey
- 2 tablespoons unsalted chicken stock
- 1 tablespoon soy sauce
- 1 tablespoon toasted sesame oil
- ⅜ teaspoons crushed red pepper
- 1 garlic clove, chopped
- 2 tablespoons chopped unsalted roasted peanuts
- 1 tablespoon chopped fresh chives

Directions:

1. Spread the chicken in the two crisper plates in an even layer and spray cooking spray on top.

2. Return the crisper plate to the Ninja Foodi Dual Zone Air Fryer.
3. Choose the Air Fry mode for Zone 1 and set the temperature to 390 degrees F and the time to 47 minutes.
4. Select the "MATCH" button to copy the settings for Zone 2.
5. Initiate cooking by pressing the START/STOP button.
6. Flip the chicken drumettes once cooked halfway through, then resume cooking.
7. During this time, mix soy sauce, honey, stock, vinegar, garlic, and crushed red pepper in a suitable saucepan and place it over medium-high heat to cook on a simmer.
8. Cook this sauce for 6 minutes with occasional stirring, then pour it into a medium-sized bowl.
9. Add air fried drumettes and toss well to coat with the honey sauce.
10. Garnish with chives and peanuts.
11. Serve warm and fresh.

Nutrition:

- (Per serving) Calories 268 | Fat 10.4g |Sodium 411mg | Carbs 0.4g | Fiber 0.1g | Sugar 0.1g | Protein 40.6g

Chicken Bites

Servings: 4

Cooking Time: 20 Minutes

Ingredients:

- 900g chicken thighs, cut into chunks
- ¼ tsp white pepper
- ½ tsp onion powder
- 30ml olive oil
- 59ml fresh lemon juice
- ½ tsp garlic powder
- Pepper
- Salt

Directions:

1. Add chicken chunks and remaining ingredients into the bowl and mix well.
2. Cover the bowl and place it in the refrigerator overnight.
3. Insert a crisper plate in the Ninja Foodi air fryer baskets.
4. Place the marinated chicken in both baskets.
5. Select zone 1 then select "air fry" mode and set the temperature to 380 degrees F for 20 minutes. Press "match" to match zone 2 settings to zone 1. Press "start/stop" to begin.

Nutrition:

- (Per serving) Calories 497 | Fat 23.9g |Sodium 237mg | Carbs 0.9g | Fiber 0.2g | Sugar 0.5g | Protein 65.8g

Bacon-wrapped Chicken

Servings: 2

Cooking Time: 28 Minutes.

Ingredients:

- Butter:

- ½ stick butter softened
- ½ garlic clove, minced
- ¼ teaspoon dried thyme
- ¼ teaspoon dried basil
- ⅛ teaspoon coarse salt
- 1 pinch black pepper, ground
- ⅓ lb. thick-cut bacon
- 1 ½ lbs. boneless skinless chicken thighs
- 2 teaspoons garlic, minced

Directions:

1. Mix garlic softened butter with thyme, salt, basil, and black pepper in a bowl.
2. Add butter mixture on a piece of wax paper and roll it up tightly to make a butter log.
3. Place the log in the refrigerator for 2 hours.
4. Spray one bacon strip on a piece of wax paper.
5. Place each chicken thigh on top of one bacon strip and rub it with garlic.
6. Make a slit in the chicken thigh and add a teaspoon of butter to the chicken.
7. Wrap the bacon around the chicken thigh.
8. Repeat those same steps with all the chicken thighs.
9. Place the bacon-wrapped chicken thighs in the two crisper plates.
10. Return the crisper plates to the Ninja Foodi Dual Zone Air Fryer.
11. Choose the Air Fry mode for Zone 1 and set the temperature to 390 degrees F and the time to 28 minutes.
12. Select the "MATCH" button to copy the settings for Zone 2.
13. Initiate cooking by pressing the START/STOP button.
14. Flip the chicken once cooked halfway through, and resume cooking.
15. Serve warm.

Nutrition:

- (Per serving) Calories 380 | Fat 29g |Sodium 821mg | Carbs 34.6g | Fiber 0g | Sugar 0g | Protein 30g

Maple-mustard Glazed Turkey Tenderloin With Apple And Sage Stuffing

Servings:4

Cooking Time: 35 Minutes

Ingredients:

- FOR THE TURKEY TENDERLOIN
- 2 tablespoons maple syrup
- 1 tablespoon unsalted butter, at room temperature
- 1 tablespoon Dijon mustard
- ½ teaspoon kosher salt
- ½ teaspoon freshly ground black pepper
- 1½ pounds turkey tenderloin
- FOR THE STUFFING
- 6 ounces seasoned stuffing mix
- 1½ cups chicken broth
- 1 apple, peeled, cored, and diced
- 1 tablespoon chopped fresh sage
- 2 teaspoons unsalted butter, cut into several pieces

Directions:

1. To prep the turkey tenderloin: In a small bowl, mix the maple syrup, butter, mustard, salt, and black pepper until smooth. Spread the maple mixture over the entire turkey tenderloin.
2. To prep the stuffing: In the Zone 2 basket, combine the stuffing mix and chicken broth. Stir well to ensure the bread is fully moistened. Stir in the apple and sage. Scatter the butter on top.
3. To cook the turkey and stuffing: Install a crisper plate in the Zone 1 basket. Place the turkey tenderloin in the basket and insert the basket in the unit. Insert the Zone 2 basket in the unit.
4. Select Zone 1, select AIR FRY, set the temperature to 390°F, and set the time to 35 minutes.
5. Select Zone 2, select BAKE, set the temperature to 340°F, and set the time to 20 minutes. Select SMART FINISH.
6. Press START/PAUSE to begin cooking.
7. When the Zone 2 timer reads 10 minutes, press START/PAUSE. Remove the basket and stir the stuffing. Reinsert the basket and press START/PAUSE to resume cooking.
8. When cooking is complete, the turkey will be cooked through (an instant-read thermometer should read 165°F) and the stuffing will have absorbed all the liquid and be slightly crisp on top. Serve warm.

Nutrition:

- (Per serving) Calories: 455; Total fat: 10g; Saturated fat: 3g; Carbohydrates: 42g; Fiber: 2.5g; Protein: 46g; Sodium: 1,230mg

Italian Chicken & Potatoes

Servings: 4

Cooking Time: 24 Minutes

Ingredients:

- 450g chicken breast, boneless & diced
- 30ml olive oil
- ½ tsp lemon zest
- 2 tbsp fresh lemon juice
- 450g baby potatoes, quartered
- 1 tbsp Greek seasoning
- Pepper
- Salt

Directions:

1. Toss potatoes with ½ tablespoon Greek seasoning, 1 tablespoon oil, lemon zest, lemon juice, pepper, and salt in a bowl.
2. Insert a crisper plate in the Ninja Foodi air fryer baskets.
3. Add potatoes into the zone 1 basket.
4. In a bowl, toss chicken with the remaining oil and seasoning.
5. Add the chicken into the zone 2 basket.
6. Select zone 1, then select "air fry" mode and set the temperature to 390 degrees F for 12 minutes. Press "match" to match zone 2 settings to zone 1. Press "start/stop" to begin.

Nutrition:

- (Per serving) Calories 262 | Fat 10.1g |Sodium 227mg | Carbs 15.5g | Fiber 2.9g | Sugar 0.2g | Protein 27.2g

Thai Curry Chicken Kabobs
Servings: 4
Cooking Time: 15 Minutes
Ingredients:

- 900g skinless chicken thighs
- 120ml Tamari
- 60ml coconut milk
- 3 tablespoons lime juice
- 3 tablespoons maple syrup
- 2 tablespoons Thai red curry

Directions:

1. Mix red curry paste, honey, lime juice, coconut milk, soy sauce in a bowl.
2. Add this sauce and chicken to a Ziplock bag.
3. Seal the bag and shake it to coat well.
4. Refrigerate the chicken for 2 hours then thread the chicken over wooden skewers.
5. Divide the skewers in the air fryer baskets.
6. Return the air fryer basket 1 to Zone 1, and basket 2 to Zone 2 of the Ninja Foodi 2-Basket Air Fryer.
7. Choose the "Air Fry" mode for Zone 1 at 350 degrees F and 15 minutes of cooking time.
8. Select the "MATCH COOK" option to copy the settings for Zone 2.
9. Initiate cooking by pressing the START/PAUSE BUTTON.
10. Flip the skewers once cooked halfway through.
11. Serve warm.

Nutrition:

- (Per serving) Calories 353 | Fat 5g |Sodium 818mg | Carbs 53.2g | Fiber 4.4g | Sugar 8g | Protein 17.3g

Bbq Cheddar-stuffed Chicken Breasts
Servings: 2
Cooking Time: 25 Minutes
Ingredients:

- 3 strips cooked bacon, divided
- 2 ounces cheddar cheese, cubed, divided
- 1/4 cup BBQ sauce, divided
- 2 (4-ounces) skinless, boneless chicken breasts
- Salt and ground black pepper, to taste

Directions:

1. In a mixing bowl, combine the cooked bacon, cheddar cheese, and 1 tablespoon BBQ sauce.
2. Make a horizontal 1-inch cut at the top of each chicken breast with a long, sharp knife, producing a little interior pouch. Fill each breast with an equal amount of the bacon-cheese mixture. Wrap the remaining bacon strips around each chicken breast. Coat the chicken breasts with the leftover BBQ sauce and lay them in a baking dish.
3. Install a crisper plate in both drawers. Place half the chicken breasts in zone 1 and half in zone 2, then insert the drawers into the unit.

4. Select zone 1, select AIR FRY, set temperature to 390 degrees F/ 200 degrees C, and set time to 22 minutes. Select MATCH to match zone 2 settings to zone 1. Press the START/STOP button to begin cooking.
5. When the time reaches 11 minutes, press START/STOP to pause the unit. Remove the drawers and flip the chicken. Re-insert drawers into the unit and press START/STOP to resume cooking.
6. When cooking is complete, remove the chicken breasts.

Nutrition:

- (Per serving) Calories 379 | Fat 12.8g | Sodium 906mg | Carbs 11.1g | Fiber 0.4g | Sugar 8.3g | Protein 37.7g

Turkey Burger Patties
Servings: 4
Cooking Time: 14 Minutes
Ingredients:

- 1 egg white
- 453g ground turkey
- 30ml Worcestershire sauce
- ½ tsp dried basil
- ½ tsp dried oregano
- Pepper
- Salt

Directions:

1. In a bowl, mix ground turkey with remaining ingredients until well combined.
2. Insert a crisper plate in the Ninja Foodi air fryer baskets.
3. Make patties from the turkey mixture and place them in both baskets.
4. Select zone 1, then select "air fry" mode and set the temperature to 360 degrees F for 14 minutes. Press "match" to match zone 2 settings to zone 1. Press "start/stop" to begin.

Nutrition:

- (Per serving) Calories 234 | Fat 12.5g |Sodium 251mg | Carbs 1.7g | Fiber 0.1g | Sugar 1.6g | Protein 32g

Lemon Chicken Thighs
Servings: 4
Cooking Time: 25 Minutes
Ingredients:

- ¼ cup butter, softened
- 3 garlic cloves, minced
- 2 teaspoons minced fresh rosemary or ½ teaspoon crushed dried rosemary
- 1 teaspoon minced fresh thyme or ¼ teaspoon dried thyme
- 1 teaspoon grated lemon zest
- 1 tablespoon lemon juice
- 4 bone-in chicken thighs (about 1½ pounds)
- 1/8 teaspoon salt
- 1/8 teaspoon pepper

Directions:

1. Combine the butter, garlic, rosemary, thyme, lemon zest, and lemon juice in a small bowl.
2. Under the skin of each chicken thigh, spread 1 teaspoon of the butter mixture. Apply the remaining butter to each thigh's skin. Season to taste with salt and pepper.
3. Install a crisper plate in both drawers. Place half the chicken tenders in the zone 1 drawer and half in zone 2's, then insert the drawers into the unit.
4. Select zone 1, select AIR FRY, set temperature to 390 degrees F/ 200 degrees C, and set time to 22 minutes. Select MATCH to match zone 2 settings to zone 1. Press the START/STOP button to begin cooking.
5. When the time reaches 11 minutes, press START/STOP to pause the unit. Remove the drawers and flip the chicken. Re-insert the drawers into the unit and press START/STOP to resume cooking.
6. When cooking is complete, remove the chicken and serve.

Nutrition:

- (Per serving) Calories 329 | Fat 26g | Sodium 253mg | Carbs 1g | Fiber 0g | Sugar 0g | Protein 23g

Sesame Ginger Chicken

Servings: 4

Cooking Time: 30 Minutes

Ingredients:

- 4 ounces green beans
- 1 tablespoon canola oil
- 1½ pounds boneless, skinless chicken breasts
- ⅓ cup prepared sesame-ginger sauce
- Kosher salt, to taste
- Black pepper, to taste

Directions:

1. Toss the green beans with a teaspoon of salt and pepper in a medium mixing bowl.
2. Place a crisper plate in each drawer. Place the green beans in the zone 1 drawer and insert it into the unit. Place the chicken breasts in the zone 2 drawer and place it inside the unit.
3. Select zone 1, then AIR FRY, and set the temperature to 390 degrees F/ 200 degrees C with a 10-minute timer. Select zone 2, then AIR FRY, and set the temperature to 390 degrees F/ 200 degrees C with an 18-minute timer. Select SYNC. To begin cooking, press the START/STOP button.
4. Press START/STOP to pause the unit when the zone 2 timer reaches 9 minutes. Remove the chicken from the drawer and toss it in the sesame ginger sauce. To resume cooking, re-insert the drawer into the unit and press START/STOP.
5. When cooking is complete, serve the chicken breasts and green beans straight away.

Nutrition:

- (Per serving) Calories 143 | Fat 7g | Sodium 638mg | Carbs 11.6g | Fiber 1.4g | Sugar 8.5g | Protein 11.1g

Bang-bang Chicken

Servings: 2

Cooking Time: 20 Minutes.

Ingredients:

- 1 cup mayonnaise
- ½ cup sweet chili sauce
- 2 tablespoons Sriracha sauce
- ⅓ cup flour
- 1 lb. boneless chicken breast, diced
- 1 ½ cups panko bread crumbs
- 2 green onions, chopped

Directions:

1. Mix mayonnaise with Sriracha and sweet chili sauce in a large bowl.
2. Keep ¾ cup of the mixture aside.
3. Add flour, chicken, breadcrumbs, and remaining mayo mixture to a resealable plastic bag.
4. Zip the bag and shake well to coat.
5. Divide the chicken in the two crisper plates in a single layer.
6. Return the crisper plate to the Ninja Foodi Dual Zone Air Fryer.
7. Choose the Air Fry mode for Zone 1 and set the temperature to 390 degrees F and the time to 20 minutes.
8. Select the "MATCH" button to copy the settings for Zone 2.
9. Initiate cooking by pressing the START/STOP button.
10. Flip the chicken once cooked halfway through.
11. Top the chicken with reserved mayo sauce.
12. Garnish with green onions and serve warm.

Nutrition:

- (Per serving) Calories 374 | Fat 13g |Sodium 552mg | Carbs 25g | Fiber 1.2g | Sugar 1.2g | Protein 37.7g

Yummy Chicken Breasts

Servings:2

Cooking Time:25

Ingredients:

- 4 large chicken breasts, 6 ounces each
- 2 tablespoons of oil bay seasoning
- 1 tablespoon Montreal chicken seasoning
- 1 teaspoon of thyme
- 1/2 teaspoon of paprika
- Salt, to taste
- oil spray, for greasing

Directions:

1. Season the chicken breast pieces with the listed seasoning and let them rest for 40 minutes.
2. Grease both sides of the chicken breast pieces with oil spray.
3. Divide the chicken breast piece between both baskets.
4. Set zone 1 to AIRFRY mode at 400 degrees F, for 15 minutes.
5. Select the MATCH button for another basket.
6. Select pause and take out the baskets and flip the chicken breast pieces, after 15 minutes.
7. Select the zones to 400 degrees F for 10 more minutes using the MATCH cook button.

8. Once it's done serve.

Nutrition:

- (Per serving) Calories 711| Fat 27.7g| Sodium 895mg | Carbs 1.6g | Fiber 0.4g | Sugar 0.1g | Protein 106.3g

Cornish Hen

Servings: 4

Cooking Time: 35 Minutes

Ingredients:

- 2 Cornish hens
- 2 tablespoons olive oil
- 2 teaspoons salt
- 1½ teaspoons Italian seasoning
- 1 teaspoon garlic powder
- 1 teaspoon paprika
- ½ teaspoon black pepper
- ½ teaspoon lemon zest

Directions:

1. Mix Italian seasoning with lemon zest, juice, black pepper, paprika, and garlic powder in a bowl.
2. Rub each hen with the seasoning mixture.
3. Tuck the hen wings in and place one in each air fryer basket.
4. Return the air fryer basket 1 to Zone 1, and basket 2 to Zone 2 of the Ninja Foodi 2-Basket Air Fryer.
5. Choose the "Air Fry" mode for Zone 1 and set the temperature to 375 degrees F and 35 minutes of cooking time.
6. Select the "MATCH COOK" option to copy the settings for Zone 2.
7. Initiate cooking by pressing the START/PAUSE BUTTON.
8. Flip the hens once cooked halfway through.
9. Serve warm.

Nutrition:

- (Per serving) Calories 223 | Fat 11.7g |Sodium 721mg | Carbs 13.6g | Fiber 0.7g | Sugar 8g | Protein 15.7g

Easy Chicken Thighs

Servings: 8

Cooking Time: 12 Minutes

Ingredients:

- 900g chicken thighs, boneless & skinless
- 2 tsp chilli powder
- 2 tsp olive oil
- 1 tsp garlic powder
- 1 tsp ground cumin
- Pepper
- Salt

Directions:

1. In a bowl, mix chicken with remaining ingredients until well coated.
2. Insert a crisper plate in the Ninja Foodi air fryer baskets.
3. Place chicken thighs in both baskets.
4. Select zone 1 then select "air fry" mode and set the temperature to 390 degrees F for 12 minutes. Press "match" to match zone 2 settings to zone 1. Press "start/stop" to begin. Turn halfway through.

Nutrition:

- (Per serving) Calories 230 | Fat 9.7g |Sodium 124mg | Carbs 0.7g | Fiber 0.3g | Sugar 0.2g | Protein 33g

Chicken Ranch Wraps

Servings: 4

Cooking Time: 22 Minutes

Ingredients:

- 1½ ounces breaded chicken breast tenders
- 4 (12-inch) whole-wheat tortilla wraps
- 2 heads romaine lettuce, chopped
- ½ cup shredded mozzarella cheese
- 4 tablespoons ranch dressing

Directions:

1. Place a crisper plate in each drawer. Place half of the chicken tenders in one drawer and half in the other. Insert the drawers into the unit.
2. Select zone 1, then AIR FRY, and set the temperature to 390 degrees F/ 200 degrees C with a 22-minute timer. To match zone 2 settings to zone 1, choose MATCH. To begin cooking, press the START/STOP button.
3. To pause the unit, press START/STOP when the timer reaches 11 minutes. Remove the drawers from the unit and flip the tenders over. To resume cooking, re-insert the drawers into the device and press START/STOP.
4. Remove the chicken from the drawers when they're done cooking and chop them up.
5. Divide the chopped chicken between warmed-up wraps. Top with some lettuce, cheese, and ranch dressing. Wrap and serve.

Nutrition:

- (Per serving) Calories 212 | Fat 7.8g | Sodium 567mg | Carbs 9.1g | Fiber 34.4g | Sugar 9.7g | Protein 10.6g

Coconut Chicken Tenders With Broiled Utica Greens

Servings:4

Cooking Time: 25 Minutes

Ingredients:

- FOR THE CHICKEN TENDERS
- 2 tablespoons all-purpose flour
- 2 large eggs
- 1 cup unsweetened shredded coconut
- ¾ cup panko bread crumbs
- ½ teaspoon kosher salt

- 1½ pounds chicken tenders
- Nonstick cooking spray
- FOR THE UTICA GREENS
- 12 ounces frozen chopped escarole or Swiss chard, thawed and drained
- ¼ cup diced prosciutto
- 2 tablespoons chopped pickled cherry peppers
- ½ teaspoon garlic powder
- ½ teaspoon onion powder
- ¼ teaspoon kosher salt
- ¼ cup Italian-style bread crumbs
- ¼ cup grated Romano cheese
- Nonstick cooking spray

Directions:

1. To prep the chicken tenders: Set up a breading station with three small shallow bowls. Place the flour in the first bowl. In the second bowl, beat the eggs. Combine the coconut, bread crumbs, and salt in the third bowl.
2. Bread the chicken tenders in this order: First, coat them in the flour. Then, dip into the beaten egg. Finally, coat them in the coconut breading, gently pressing the breading into the chicken to help it adhere. Mist both sides of each tender with cooking spray.
3. To prep the Utica greens: In the Zone 2 basket, mix the greens, prosciutto, cherry peppers, garlic powder, onion powder, and salt. Scatter the bread crumbs and Romano cheese over the top. Spritz the greens with cooking spray.
4. To cook the chicken and greens: Install a crisper plate in the Zone 1 basket. Place the chicken tenders in the basket in a single layer and insert the basket in the unit. Insert the Zone 2 basket in the unit.
5. Select Zone 1, select AIR FRY, set the temperature to 390°F, and set the time to 25 minutes.
6. Select Zone 2, select AIR BROIL, set the temperature to 450°F, and set the time to 10 minutes. Select SMART FINISH.
7. Press START/PAUSE to begin cooking.
8. When cooking is complete, the chicken will be crispy and cooked through (an instant-read thermometer should read 165°F) and the greens should be warmed through and toasted on top. Serve warm.

Nutrition:

- (Per serving) Calories: 527; Total fat: 26g; Saturated fat: 11g; Carbohydrates: 24g; Fiber: 6.5g; Protein: 50g; Sodium: 886mg

Veggie Stuffed Chicken Breasts

Servings: 2

Cooking Time: 10 Minutes.

Ingredients:

- 4 teaspoons chili powder
- 4 teaspoons ground cumin
- 1 skinless, boneless chicken breast
- 2 teaspoons chipotle flakes
- 2 teaspoons Mexican oregano
- Salt and black pepper, to taste
- ½ red bell pepper, julienned
- ½ onion, julienned
- 1 fresh jalapeno pepper, julienned

- 2 teaspoons corn oil
- ½ lime, juiced

Directions:

1. Slice the chicken breast in half horizontally.
2. Pound each chicken breast with a mallet into ¼ inch thickness.
3. Rub the pounded chicken breast with black pepper, salt, oregano, chipotle flakes, cumin, and chili powder.
4. Add ½ of bell pepper, jalapeno, and onion on top of each chicken breast piece.
5. Roll the chicken to wrap the filling inside and insert toothpicks to seal.
6. Place the rolls in crisper plate and spray them with cooking oil.
7. Return the crisper plate to the Ninja Foodi Dual Zone Air Fryer.
8. Choose the Air Fry mode for Zone 1 and set the temperature to 360 degrees F and the time to 10 minutes.
9. Initiate cooking by pressing the START/STOP button.
10. Serve warm.

Nutrition:

- (Per serving) Calories 351 | Fat 11g |Sodium 150mg | Carbs 3.3g | Fiber 0.2g | Sugar 1g | Protein 33.2g

Whole Chicken

Servings: 8

Cooking Time: 20 Minutes

Ingredients:

- 1 whole chicken (about 2.8 pounds), cut in half
- 4 tablespoons olive oil
- 2 teaspoons paprika
- 1 teaspoon garlic powder
- 1 teaspoon onion powder
- Salt and pepper, to taste

Directions:

1. Mix the olive oil, paprika, garlic powder, and onion powder together in a bowl.
2. Place the chicken halves, breast side up, on a plate. Spread a teaspoon or two of the oil mix all over the halves using either your hands or a brush. Season with salt and pepper.
3. Flip the chicken halves over and repeat on the other side. You'll want to reserve a little of the oil mix for later, but other than that, use it liberally.
4. Install a crisper plate in both drawers. Place one half of the chicken in the zone 1 drawer and the other half in the zone 2 drawer, then insert the drawers into the unit.
5. Select zone 1, select AIR FRY, set temperature to 390 degrees F/ 200 degrees C, and set time to 20 minutes. Select MATCH to match zone 2 settings to zone 1. Press the START/STOP button to begin cooking.
6. When cooking is done, check the internal temperature of the chicken. It should read 165°F. If the chicken isn't done, add more cooking time.

Nutrition:

- (Per serving) Calories 131 | Fat 8g | Sodium 51mg | Carbs 0g | Fiber 0g | Sugar 0g | Protein 14g

Chicken Parmesan
Servings: 4
Cooking Time: 20 Minutes
Ingredients:

- 2 large eggs
- ½ cup seasoned breadcrumbs
- ⅓ cup grated parmesan cheese
- ¼ teaspoon pepper
- 4 boneless, skinless chicken breast halves (6 ounces each)
- 1 cup pasta sauce
- 1 cup shredded mozzarella cheese
- Chopped fresh basil (optional)

Directions:

1. Lightly beat the eggs in a small bowl.
2. Combine the breadcrumbs, parmesan cheese, and pepper in a shallow bowl.
3. After dipping the chicken in the egg, coat it in the crumb mixture.
4. Install a crisper plate in both drawers. Place half the chicken breasts in the zone 1 drawer and half in zone 2's, then insert the drawers into the unit.
5. Select zone 1, select AIR FRY, set temperature to 390 degrees F/ 200 degrees C, and set time to 20 minutes. Select MATCH to match zone 2 settings to zone 1. Press the START/STOP button to begin cooking.
6. When the time reaches 10 minutes, press START/STOP to pause the unit. Remove the drawers and flip the chicken. Re-insert the drawers into the unit and press START/STOP to resume cooking.
7. When cooking is complete, remove the chicken.

Nutrition:

- (Per serving) Calories 293 | Fat 15.8g | Sodium 203mg | Carbs 11.1g | Fiber 2.4g | Sugar 8.7g | Protein 29g

Chicken Vegetable Skewers
Servings: 6
Cooking Time: 15 Minutes
Ingredients:

- 900g chicken breasts, cubed
- 1 bell pepper, chopped
- 51g Swerve
- 1 tsp ginger, grated
- 350g zucchini, chopped
- 8 mushrooms, sliced
- ½ medium onion, chopped
- 6 garlic cloves, crushed
- 120ml soy sauce

Directions:

1. Add chicken and the remaining ingredients to a zip-lock bag. Seal the bag and place it in the refrigerator overnight.
2. Thread the marinated chicken, zucchini, mushrooms, onion, and bell pepper onto the skewers.

3. Insert a crisper plate in the Ninja Foodi air fryer baskets.
4. Place skewers in both baskets.
5. Select zone 1 then select "air fry" mode and set the temperature to 380 degrees F for 15 minutes. Press "match" to match zone 2 settings to zone 1. Press "start/stop" to begin.

Nutrition:

- (Per serving) Calories 329 | Fat 11.5g |Sodium 1335mg | Carbs 8.6g | Fiber 1.4g | Sugar 2.9g | Protein 46.8g

Juicy Duck Breast
Servings: 1
Cooking Time: 20 Minutes
Ingredients:

- ½ duck breast
- Salt and black pepper, to taste
- 2 tablespoons plum sauce

Directions:

1. Rub the duck breast with black pepper and salt.
2. Place the duck breast in air fryer basket 1 and add plum sauce on top.
3. Return the basket to the Ninja Foodi 2 Baskets Air Fryer.
4. Choose the "Air Fry" mode for Zone 1 and set the temperature to 400 degrees F and 20 minutes of cooking time.
5. Initiate cooking by pressing the START/PAUSE BUTTON.
6. Flip the duck breast once cooked halfway through.
7. Serve warm.

Nutrition:

- (Per serving) Calories 379 | Fat 19g |Sodium 184mg | Carbs 12.3g | Fiber 0.6g | Sugar 2g | Protein 37.7g

Chicken Leg Piece
Servings:1
Cooking Time:25
Ingredients:

- 1 teaspoon of onion powder
- 1 teaspoon of paprika powder
- 1 teaspoon of garlic powder
- Salt and black pepper, to taste
- 1 tablespoon of Italian seasoning
- 1 teaspoon of celery seeds
- 2 eggs, whisked
- 1/3 cup buttermilk
- 1 cup of corn flour
- 1 pound of chicken leg

Directions:

1. Take a bowl and whisk egg along with pepper, salt, and buttermilk.
2. Set it aside for further use.
3. Mix all the spices in a small separate bowl.
4. Dredge the chicken in egg wash then dredge it in seasoning.
5. Coat the chicken legs with oil spray.
6. At the end dust it with the corn flour.
7. Divide the leg pieces into two zones.
8. Set zone 1 basket to 400 degrees F, for 25 minutes.
9. Select MATCH for zone 2 basket.
10. Let the air fryer do the magic.
11. Once it's done, serve and enjoy.

Nutrition:

- (Per serving) Calories 1511| Fat 52.3g| Sodium615 mg | Carbs 100g | Fiber 9.2g | Sugar 8.1g | Protein 154.2g

Chicken Thighs With Brussels Sprouts

Servings:2

Cooking Time:30

Ingredients:

- 2 tablespoons of honey
- 4 tablespoons of Dijon mustard
- Salt and black pepper, to tat
- 4 tablespoons of olive oil
- 1-1/2 cup Brussels sprouts
- 8 chicken thighs, skinless

Directions:

1. Take a bowl and add chicken thighs to it.
2. Add honey, Dijon mustard, salt, pepper, and 2 tablespoons of olive oil to the thighs.
3. Coat the chicken well and marinate it for 1 hour.
4. Now when start cooking season the Brussels sprouts with salt and black pepper along with remaining olive oil.
5. Put the chicken in the zone 1 basket.
6. Put the Brussels sprouts into the zone 2 basket.
7. Select ROAST function for chicken and set time to 30 minutes at 390 degrees F.
8. Select AIR FRY function for Brussels sprouts and set the timer to 20 at 400 degrees F.
9. Once done, serve and enjoy.

Nutrition:

- (Per serving) Calories1454 | Fat 72.2g| Sodium 869mg | Carbs 23g | Fiber 2.7g | Sugar 19g | Protein 172g

Turkey Meatloaf With Veggie Medley

Servings:4

Cooking Time: 30 Minutes

Ingredients:

- FOR THE MEATLOAF
- 1 large egg
- ¼ cup ketchup
- 2 teaspoons Worcestershire sauce
- ½ cup Italian-style bread crumbs
- 1 teaspoon kosher salt
- 1 pound ground turkey (93 percent lean)
- 1 tablespoon vegetable oil
- FOR THE VEGGIE MEDLEY
- 2 carrots, thinly sliced
- 8 ounces green beans, trimmed (about 2 cups)
- 2 cups broccoli florets
- 1 red bell pepper, sliced into strips
- 2 tablespoons vegetable oil
- ½ teaspoon kosher salt
- ½ teaspoon freshly ground black pepper

Directions:

1. To prep the meatloaf: In a large bowl, whisk the egg. Stir in the ketchup, Worcestershire sauce, bread crumbs, and salt. Let sit for 5 minutes to allow the bread crumbs to absorb some moisture.
2. Gently mix in the turkey until just incorporated. Form the mixture into a loaf. Brush with the oil.
3. To prep the veggie medley: In a large bowl, combine the carrots, green beans, broccoli, bell pepper, oil, salt, and black pepper. Mix well to coat the vegetables with the oil.
4. To cook the meatloaf and veggie medley: Install a crisper plate in each of the two baskets. Place the meatloaf in the Zone 1 basket and insert the basket in the unit. Place the vegetables in the Zone 2 basket and insert the basket in the unit.
5. Select Zone 1, select ROAST, set the temperature to 350°F, and set the time to 30 minutes.
6. Select Zone 2, select AIR FRY, set the temperature to 390°F, and set the time to 20 minutes. Select SMART FINISH.
7. Press START/PAUSE to begin cooking.
8. When cooking is complete, the meatloaf will be cooked through (an instant-read thermometer should read165°F) and the vegetables will be tender and roasted.

Nutrition:

- (Per serving) Calories: 394; Total fat: 20g; Saturated fat: 4.5g; Carbohydrates: 25g; Fiber: 4.5g; Protein: 28g; Sodium: 952mg

Buttermilk Fried Chicken
Servings: 6
Cooking Time: 30 Minutes
Ingredients:

- 1½ pounds boneless, skinless chicken thighs
- 2 cups buttermilk
- 1 cup all-purpose flour
- 1 tablespoon seasoned salt
- ½ tablespoon ground black pepper
- 1 cup panko breadcrumbs

- Cooking spray

Directions:

1. Place the chicken thighs in a shallow baking dish. Cover with the buttermilk. Refrigerate for 4 hours or overnight.
2. In a large gallon-sized resealable bag, combine the flour, seasoned salt, and pepper.
3. Remove the chicken from the buttermilk but don't discard the mixture.
4. Add the chicken to the bag and shake well to coat.
5. Dip the thighs in the buttermilk again, then coat in the panko breadcrumbs.
6. Install a crisper plate in each drawer. Place half the chicken thighs in the zone 1 drawer and half in zone 2's, then insert the drawers into the unit.
7. Select zone 1, select AIR FRY, set temperature to 390 degrees F/ 200 degrees C, and set time to 30 minutes. Select MATCH to match zone 2 settings to zone 1. Press the START/STOP button to begin cooking.
8. When the time reaches 15 minutes, press START/STOP to pause the unit. Remove the drawers and flip the chicken. Re-insert the drawers into the unit and press START/STOP to resume cooking.
9. When cooking is complete, remove the chicken.

Nutrition:

- (Per serving) Calories 335 | Fat 12.8g | Sodium 687mg | Carbs 33.1g | Fiber 0.4g | Sugar 4g | Protein 24.5g

Chicken Cordon Bleu

Servings: 4

Cooking Time: 20 Minutes

Ingredients:

- 4 boneless, skinless chicken breast halves (4 ounces each)
- ¼ teaspoon salt
- ¼ teaspoon pepper
- 4 slices deli ham
- 2 slices aged Swiss cheese, halved
- 1 cup panko breadcrumbs
- Cooking spray
- For the sauce:
- 1 tablespoon all-purpose flour
- ½ cup 2% milk
- ¼ cup dry white wine
- 3 tablespoons finely shredded Swiss cheese
- 1/8 teaspoon salt
- Dash pepper

Directions:

1. Season both sides of the chicken breast halves with salt and pepper. You may need to thin the breasts with a mallet.
2. Place 1 slice of ham and half slice of cheese on top of each chicken breast half.
3. Roll the breast up and use toothpicks to secure it.
4. Sprinkle the breadcrumbs on top and spray lightly with the cooking oil.
5. Insert a crisper plate into each drawer. Divide the chicken between each drawer and insert the drawers into the unit.
6. Select zone 1, select AIR FRY, set temperature to 390 degrees F/ 200 degrees C, and set time to 7 minutes. Select MATCH to match zone 2 settings to zone 1. Press the START/STOP button to begin cooking.

7. When the time reaches 5 minutes, press START/STOP to pause the unit. Remove the drawers and flip the chicken. Re-insert the drawers into the unit and press START/STOP to resume cooking.
8. To make the sauce, mix the flour, wine, and milk together in a small pot until smooth. Bring to a boil over high heat, stirring frequently, for 1–2 minutes, or until the sauce has thickened.
9. Reduce the heat to medium. Add the cheese. Cook and stir for 2–3 minutes, or until the cheese has melted and the sauce has thickened and bubbled. Add salt and pepper to taste. Keep the sauce heated at a low temperature until ready to serve.

Nutrition:

- (Per serving) Calories 272 | Fat 8g | Sodium 519mg | Carbs 14g | Fiber 2g | Sugar 1g | Protein 32g

Jamaican Fried Chicken

Servings: 6

Cooking Time: 25 Minutes

Ingredients:

- 6-8 chicken thighs
- Egg Marinade:
- 2 teaspoons of hot sauce
- 1 teaspoon of ground ginger
- 1 teaspoon of ground onion
- 1 teaspoon of black pepper
- 1 teaspoon of ground garlic
- 237ml of almond milk
- 1 tablespoon of lemon juice
- 1 large egg
- Breading:
- 2 cups of ground almonds
- ⅓ cup of tapioca starch
- 1 tablespoon of paprika
- 1 tablespoon of thyme
- 1 tablespoon of parsley
- 1 teaspoon of garlic powder
- 1 teaspoon of onion powder
- ½ teaspoon of cayenne pepper
- 1 teaspoon of pink salt
- Spray on cooking oil olive oil spray

Directions:

1. Mix egg marinade ingredients in a large bowl and add chicken thighs.
2. Stir well to coat then cover and refrigerate for 30 minutes.
3. Meanwhile, mix all the breading ingredients in a shallow bowl.
4. Remove the chicken from the egg marinade and coat with the breading mixture.
5. Place the coated chicken thighs in the air fryer baskets.
6. Return the air fryer basket 1 to Zone 1, and basket 2 to Zone 2 of the Ninja Foodi 2-Basket Air Fryer.
7. Choose the “Air Fry” mode for Zone 1 and set the temperature to 375 degrees F and 25 minutes of cooking time.
8. Select the “MATCH COOK” option to copy the settings for Zone 2.
9. Initiate cooking by pressing the START/PAUSE BUTTON.

10. Flip the chicken thighs once cooked halfway through.
11. Serve.

Nutrition:

- (Per serving) Calories 268 | Fat 10.4g |Sodium 411mg | Carbs 0.4g | Fiber 0.1g | Sugar 0.1g | Protein 40.6g

Chicken Potatoes

Servings: 4

Cooking Time: 22 Minutes.

Ingredients:

- 15 ounces canned potatoes drained
- 1 teaspoon olive oil
- 1 teaspoon Lawry's seasoned salt
- ⅛ teaspoons black pepper optional
- 8 ounces boneless chicken breast cubed
- ¼ teaspoon paprika
- ⅜ cup cheddar, shredded
- 4 bacon slices, cooked, cut into strips

Directions:

1. Dice the chicken into small pieces and toss them with olive oil and spices.
2. Drain and dice the potato pieces into smaller cubes.
3. Add potato to the chicken and mix well to coat.
4. Spread the mixture in the two crisper plates in a single layer.
5. Return the crisper plates to the Ninja Foodi Dual Zone Air Fryer.
6. Choose the Air Fry mode for Zone 1 and set the temperature to 390 degrees F and the time to 22 minutes.
7. Select the "MATCH" button to copy the settings for Zone 2.
8. Initiate cooking by pressing the START/STOP button.
9. Top the chicken and potatoes with cheese and bacon.
10. Return the crisper plates to the Ninja Foodi Dual Zone Air Fryer.
11. Select the Max Crisp mode for Zone 1 and set the temperature to 300 degrees F and the time to 5 minutes.
12. Initiate cooking by pressing the START/STOP button.
13. Repeat the same step for Zone 2 to broil the potatoes and chicken in the right drawer.
14. Enjoy with dried herbs on top.

Nutrition:

- (Per serving) Calories 346 | Fat 16.1g |Sodium 882mg | Carbs 1.3g | Fiber 0.5g | Sugar 0.5g | Protein 48.2g

Cornish Hen With Baked Potatoes

Servings:2

Cooking Time:45

Ingredients:

- Salt, to taste
- 1 large potato

- 1 tablespoon of avocado oil
- 1.5 pounds of Cornish hen, skinless and whole
- 2-3 teaspoons of poultry seasoning, dry rub

Directions:

1. Take a fork and pierce the large potato.
2. Rub the potato with avocado oil and salt.
3. Now put the potatoes in the first basket.
4. Now pick the Cornish hen and season the hen with poultry seasoning (dry rub) and salt.
5. Remember to coat the whole Cornish hen well.
6. Put the potato in zone 1 basket.
7. Now place the hen into zone 2 baskets.
8. Now hit 1 for the first basket and set it to AIR FRY mode at 350 degrees F, for 45 minutes.
9. For the second basket hit 2 and set the time to 45 minutes at 350 degrees F.
10. To start cooking, hit the smart finish button and press hit start.
11. Once the cooking cycle complete, turn off the air fryer and take out the potatoes and Cornish hen from both air fryer baskets.
12. Serve hot and enjoy.

Nutrition:

- (Per serving) Calories 612 | Fat14.3 g| Sodium 304mg | Carbs33.4 g | Fiber 4.5 g | Sugar 1.5g | Protein 83.2 g

Asian Chicken

Servings: 4

Cooking Time: 12 Minutes

Ingredients:

- 8 chicken thighs, boneless
- 4 garlic cloves, minced
- 85g honey
- 120ml soy sauce
- 1 tsp dried oregano
- 2 tbsp parsley, chopped
- 1 tbsp ketchup

Directions:

1. Add chicken and remaining ingredients in a bowl and mix until well coated. Cover and place in the refrigerator for 6 hours.
2. Insert a crisper plate in the Ninja Foodi air fryer baskets.
3. Remove the chicken from the marinade and place them in both baskets.
4. Select zone 1 then select "air fry" mode and set the temperature to 390 degrees F for 12 minutes. Press "match" to match zone 2 settings to zone 1. Press "start/stop" to begin.

Nutrition:

- (Per serving) Calories 646 | Fat 21.7g |Sodium 2092mg | Carbs 22.2g | Fiber 0.6g | Sugar 18.9g | Protein 86.9g

Honey-cajun Chicken Thighs
Servings: 6
Cooking Time: 25 Minutes
Ingredients:

- ½ cup buttermilk
- 1 teaspoon hot sauce
- 1½ pounds skinless, boneless chicken thighs
- ¼ cup all-purpose flour
- ⅓ cup tapioca flour
- 2 ½ teaspoons Cajun seasoning
- ½ teaspoon garlic salt
- ½ teaspoon honey powder
- ¼ teaspoon ground paprika
- ⅛ teaspoon cayenne pepper
- 4 teaspoons honey

Directions:

1. In a resealable plastic bag, combine the buttermilk and hot sauce. Marinate the chicken thighs in the bag for 30 minutes.
2. Combine the flour, tapioca flour, Cajun spice, garlic salt, honey powder, paprika, and cayenne pepper in a small mixing bowl.
3. Remove the thighs from the buttermilk mixture and dredge them in the flour. Remove any excess flour by shaking it off.
4. Install a crisper plate in both drawers. Place half the chicken thighs in the zone 1 drawer and half in zone 2's, then insert the drawers into the unit.
5. Select zone 1, select AIR FRY, set temperature to 390 degrees F/ 200 degrees C, and set time to 25 minutes. Select MATCH to match zone 2 settings to zone 1. Press the START/STOP button to begin cooking.
6. When the time reaches 11 minutes, press START/STOP to pause the unit. Remove the drawers and flip the chicken. Re-insert the drawers into the unit and press START/STOP to resume cooking.
7. When cooking is complete, remove the chicken and serve.

Nutrition:

- (Per serving) Calories 243 | Fat 11.8g | Sodium 203mg | Carbs 16.1g | Fiber 0.4g | Sugar 5.1g | Protein 19g

Fish And Seafood Recipes

Crumb-topped Sole
Servings: 4
Cooking Time: 7 Minutes
Ingredients:

- 3 tablespoons mayonnaise
- 3 tablespoons Parmesan cheese, grated
- 2 teaspoons mustard seeds
- ¼ teaspoon black pepper
- 4 (170g) sole fillets

- 1 cup soft bread crumbs
- 1 green onion, chopped
- ½ teaspoon ground mustard
- 2 teaspoons butter, melted
- Cooking spray

Directions:

1. Mix mayonnaise with black pepper, mustard seeds, and 2 tablespoons cheese in a bowl.
2. Place 2 sole fillets in each air fryer basket and top them with mayo mixture.
3. Mix breadcrumbs with rest of the ingredients in a bowl.
4. Drizzle this mixture over the sole fillets.
5. Return the air fryer basket 1 to Zone 1, and basket 2 to Zone 2 of the Ninja Foodi 2-Basket Air Fryer.
6. Choose the "Air Fry" mode for Zone 1 and set the temperature to 375 degrees F and 7 minutes of cooking time.
7. Select the "MATCH COOK" option to copy the settings for Zone 2.
8. Initiate cooking by pressing the START/PAUSE BUTTON.
9. Serve warm.

Nutrition:

- (Per serving) Calories 308 | Fat 24g |Sodium 715mg | Carbs 0.8g | Fiber 0.1g | Sugar 0.1g | Protein 21.9g

"fried" Fish With Seasoned Potato Wedges

Servings:4

Cooking Time: 30 Minutes

Ingredients:

- FOR THE FISH
- 4 cod fillets (6 ounces each)
- 4 tablespoons all-purpose flour, divided
- ¼ cup cornstarch
- 1 teaspoon baking powder
- ¼ teaspoon kosher salt
- ⅓ cup lager-style beer or sparkling water
- Tartar sauce, cocktail sauce, or malt vinegar, for serving (optional)
- FOR THE POTATOES
- 4 russet potatoes
- 2 tablespoons vegetable oil
- ½ teaspoon paprika
- ½ teaspoon kosher salt
- ¼ teaspoon garlic powder
- ¼ teaspoon freshly ground black pepper

Directions:

1. To prep the fish: Pat the fish dry with a paper towel and coat lightly with 2 tablespoons of flour.
2. In a shallow dish, combine the remaining 2 tablespoons of flour, the cornstarch, baking powder, and salt. Stir in the beer to form a thick batter.
3. Dip the fish in the batter to coat both sides, then let rest on a cutting board for 10 minutes.
4. To prep the potatoes: Cut each potato in half lengthwise, then cut each half into 4 wedges.

5. In a large bowl, combine the potatoes and oil. Toss well to fully coat the potatoes. Add the paprika, salt, garlic powder, and black pepper and toss well to coat.
6. To cook the fish and potato wedges: Install a crisper plate in each of the two baskets. Place a piece of parchment paper or aluminum foil over the plate in the Zone 1 basket. Place the fish in the basket and insert the basket in the unit. Place the potato wedges in a single layer in the Zone 2 basket and insert the basket in the unit.
7. Select Zone 1, select AIR FRY, set the temperature to 400°F, and set the timer to 13 minutes.
8. Select Zone 2, select AIR FRY, set the temperature to 400°F, and set the timer to 30 minutes. Select SMART FINISH.
9. Press START/PAUSE to begin cooking.
10. When the Zone 1 timer reads 5 minutes, press START/PAUSE. Remove the basket and use a silicone spatula to carefully flip the fish over. Reinsert the basket and press START/PAUSE to resume cooking.
11. When cooking is complete, the fish should be cooked through and the potatoes crispy outside and tender inside. Serve hot with tartar sauce, cocktail sauce, or malt vinegar (if using).

Nutrition:

- (Per serving) Calories: 360; Total fat: 8g; Saturated fat: 1g; Carbohydrates: 40g; Fiber: 2g; Protein: 30g; Sodium: 302mg

Salmon With Green Beans

Servings:1

Cooking Time:18

Ingredients:

- 1 salmon fillet, 2 inches thick
- 2 teaspoons of olive oil
- 2 teaspoons of smoked paprika
- Salt and black pepper, to taste
- 1 cup green beans
- Oil spray, for greasing

Directions:

1. Grease the green beans with oil spray and add them to zone 1 basket.
2. Now rub the salmon fillet with olive oil, smoked paprika, salt, and black pepper.
3. Put the salmon fillets in the zone 2 basket.
4. Now set the zone one basket to AIRFRY mode at 350 degrees F for 18 minutes.
5. Set the Zone 2 basket to 390 degrees F for 16-18 minutes
6. Hit the smart finish button.
7. Once done, take out the salmon and green beans and transfer them to the serving plates and enjoy.

Nutrition:

- (Per serving) Calories 367| Fat22 g| Sodium 87mg | Carbs 10.2g | Fiber 5.3g | Sugar 2g | Protein 37.2g

Pretzel-crusted Catfish

Servings: 4

Cooking Time: 12 Minutes

Ingredients:

- 4 catfish fillets
- ½ teaspoon salt
- ½ teaspoon black pepper
- 2 large eggs
- ⅓ cup Dijon mustard
- 2 tablespoons 2% milk
- ½ cup all-purpose flour
- 4 cups miniature pretzels, crushed
- Cooking spray
- Lemon slices

Directions:

1. Rub the catfish with black pepper and salt.
2. Beat eggs with milk and mustard in a bowl.
3. Spread pretzels and flour in two separate bowls.
4. Coat the catfish with flour then dip in the egg mixture and coat with the pretzels.
5. Place two fish fillets in each air fryer basket.
6. Return the air fryer basket 1 to Zone 1, and basket 2 to Zone 2 of the Ninja Foodi 2-Basket Air Fryer.
7. Choose the "Air Fry" mode for Zone 1 at 325 degrees F and 12 minutes of cooking time.
8. Select the "MATCH COOK" option to copy the settings for Zone 2.
9. Initiate cooking by pressing the START/PAUSE BUTTON.
10. Serve warm.

Nutrition:

- (Per serving) Calories 196 | Fat 7.1g |Sodium 492mg | Carbs 21.6g | Fiber 2.9g | Sugar 0.8g | Protein 13.4g

Lemon Pepper Fish Fillets

Servings: 4

Cooking Time: 10 Minutes

Ingredients:

- 4 tilapia fillets
- 30ml olive oil
- 2 tbsp lemon zest
- ⅛ tsp paprika
- 1 tsp garlic, minced
- 1 ½ tsp ground peppercorns
- Pepper
- Salt

Directions:

1. In a small bowl, mix oil, peppercorns, paprika, garlic, lemon zest, pepper, and salt.
2. Brush the fish fillets with oil mixture.
3. Insert a crisper plate in the Ninja Foodi air fryer baskets.
4. Place fish fillets in both baskets.
5. Select zone 1 then select "air fry" mode and set the temperature to 390 degrees F for 10 minutes. Press "match" to match zone 2 settings to zone 1. Press "start/stop" to begin.

Nutrition:

- (Per serving) Calories 203 | Fat 9g |Sodium 99mg | Carbs 0.9g | Fiber 0.2g | Sugar 0.2g | Protein 32.1g

Two-way Salmon

Servings:2

Cooking Time:18

Ingredients:

- 2 salmon fillets, 8 ounces each
- 2 tablespoons of Cajun seasoning
- 2 tablespoons of jerk seasoning
- 1 lemon cut in half
- oil spray, for greasing

Directions:

1. First, drizzle lemon juice over the salmon and wash it with tap water.
2. Rinse and pat dry the fillets with a paper towel.
3. Now rub 0 fillet with Cajun seasoning and grease it with oil spray.
4. Take the second fillet and rub it with jerk seasoning.
5. Grease the second fillet of salmon with oil spray.
6. now put the salmon fillets in both the baskets.
7. Set the Zone 1 basket to 390 degrees F for 16-18 minutes
8. Select MATCH button for zone 2 basket.
9. hit the start button to start cooking.
10. Once the cooking is done, serve the fish hot with mayonnaise.

Nutrition:

- (Per serving) Calories 238| Fat 11.8g| Sodium 488mg | Carbs 9g | Fiber 0g | Sugar8 g | Protein 35g

Fried Tilapia

Servings: 4

Cooking Time: 20 Minutes

Ingredients:

- 4 fresh tilapia fillets, approximately 6 ounces each
- 2 teaspoons olive oil
- 2 teaspoons chopped fresh chives
- 2 teaspoons chopped fresh parsley
- 1 teaspoon minced garlic
- Freshly ground pepper, to taste
- Salt to taste

Directions:

1. Pat the tilapia fillets dry with a paper towel.
2. Stir together the olive oil, chives, parsley, garlic, salt, and pepper in a small bowl.
3. Brush the mixture over the top of the tilapia fillets.

4. Place a crisper plate in each drawer. Add the fillets in a single layer to each drawer. Insert the drawers into the unit.
5. Select zone 1, then AIR FRY, then set the temperature to 360 degrees F/ 180 degrees C with a 20-minute timer. To match zone 2 settings to zone 1, choose MATCH. To begin, select START/STOP.
6. Remove the tilapia fillets from the drawers after the timer has finished.

Nutrition:

- (Per serving) Calories 140 | Fat 5.7g | Sodium 125mg | Carbs 1.5g | Fiber 0.4g | Sugar 0g | Protein 21.7g

Salmon With Coconut

Servings:2

Cooking Time:15

Ingredients:

- Oil spray, for greasing
- 2 salmon fillets, 6ounces each
- Salt and ground black pepper, to taste
- 1 tablespoon butter, for frying
- 1 tablespoon red curry paste
- 1 cup of coconut cream
- 2 tablespoons fresh cilantro, chopped
- 1 cup of cauliflower florets
- ½ cup Parmesan cheese, hard

Directions:

1. Take a bowl and mix salt, black pepper, butter, red curry paste, coconut cream in a bowl and marinate the salmon in it.
2. Oil sprays the cauliflower florets and then seasons it with salt and freshly ground black pepper.
3. Put the florets in the zone 1 basket.
4. Layer the parchment paper over the zone 2 baskets, and then place the salmon fillet on it.
5. Set the zone 2 basket to AIR FRY mod at 15 minutes for4 00 degrees F
6. Hit the smart finish button to finish it at the same time.
7. Once the time for cooking is over, serve the salmon with cauliflower floret with Parmesan cheese drizzle on top.

Nutrition:

- (Per serving) Calories 774 | Fat 59g| Sodium 1223mg | Carbs 12.2g | Fiber 3.9g | Sugar5.9 g | Protein53.5 g

Stuffed Mushrooms With Crab

Servings: 4

Cooking Time: 18 Minutes

Ingredients:

- 907g baby bella mushrooms
- cooking spray
- 2 teaspoons tony chachere's salt blend
- ¼ red onion, diced
- 2 celery ribs, diced

- 227g lump crab
- ½ cup seasoned bread crumbs
- 1 large egg
- ½ cup parmesan cheese, shredded
- 1 teaspoon oregano
- 1 teaspoon hot sauce

Directions:

1. Mix all the ingredients except the mushrooms in a bowl.
2. Divide the crab filling into the mushroom caps.
3. Place the caps in the air fryer baskets.
4. Return the air fryer basket 1 to Zone 1, and basket 2 to Zone 2 of the Ninja Foodi 2-Basket Air Fryer.
5. Choose the "Air Fry" mode for Zone 1 at 400 degrees F and 18 minutes of cooking time.
6. Select the "MATCH COOK" option to copy the settings for Zone 2.
7. Initiate cooking by pressing the START/PAUSE BUTTON.
8. Serve warm.

Nutrition:

- (Per serving) Calories 399 | Fat 16g |Sodium 537mg | Carbs 28g | Fiber 3g | Sugar 10g | Protein 35g

Tuna Patties

Servings: 6

Cooking Time: 10 Minutes

Ingredients:

- For the tuna patties:
- 1 tablespoon extra-virgin olive oil
- 1 tablespoon butter
- ½ cup chopped onion
- ½ red bell pepper, chopped
- 1 teaspoon minced garlic
- 2 (7-ounce) cans or 3 (5-ounce) cans albacore tuna fish in water, drained
- 1 tablespoon lime juice
- 1 celery stalk, chopped
- ¼ cup chopped fresh parsley
- 3 tablespoons grated parmesan cheese
- ½ teaspoon dried oregano
- ¼ teaspoon salt
- Black pepper, to taste
- 1 teaspoon sriracha
- ½ cup panko crumbs
- 2 whisked eggs
- For the crumb coating:
- ½ cup panko crumbs
- ¼ cup parmesan cheese
- Non-stick spray

Directions:

1. In a skillet, heat the oil and butter over medium-high heat.
2. Sauté the onions, red bell pepper, and garlic for 5 to 7 minutes.
3. Drain the tuna from the cans thoroughly. Put the tuna in a large mixing bowl. Add the lime juice.
4. Add the sautéed vegetables to the mixing bowl.
5. Add the celery, parsley, and cheese. Combine well.
6. Add the oregano, salt, and pepper to taste. Mix well.
7. Add a dash of sriracha for a spicy kick and mix well.
8. Add the panko crumbs and mix well.
9. Mix in the eggs until the mixture is well combined. You can add an extra egg if necessary, but the tuna is usually wet enough that it isn't required. Form 6 patties from the mixture.
10. Refrigerate for 30 to 60 minutes (or even overnight).
11. Remove from refrigerator and coat with a mixture of the ½ cup of panko crumbs and ¼ cup of parmesan cheese.
12. Spray the tops of the coated patties with some non-stick cooking spray.
13. Place a crisper place in each drawer. Put 3 patties in each drawer. Insert the drawers into the unit.
14. Select zone 1, then AIR FRY, then set the temperature to 390 degrees F/ 200 degrees C with a 10-minute timer. To match zone 2 settings to zone 1, choose MATCH. To begin, select START/STOP.
15. Remove and garnish with chopped parsley.

Nutrition:

- (Per serving) Calories 381 | Fat 16g | Sodium 1007mg | Carbs 23g | Fiber 2g | Sugar 4g | Protein 38g

Salmon With Fennel Salad

Servings: 4

Cooking Time: 17 Minutes.

Ingredients:

- 2 teaspoons fresh parsley, chopped
- 1 teaspoon fresh thyme, chopped
- 1 teaspoon salt
- 4 (6-oz) skinless center-cut salmon fillets
- 2 tablespoons olive oil
- 4 cups fennel, sliced
- ⅔ cup Greek yogurt
- 1 garlic clove, grated
- 2 tablespoons orange juice
- 1 teaspoon lemon juice
- 2 tablespoons fresh dill, chopped

Directions:

1. Preheat your Ninja Foodi Dual Zone Air Fryer to 200 degrees F.
2. Mix ½ teaspoon of salt, thyme, and parsley in a small bowl.
3. Brush the salmon with oil first, then rub liberally rub the herb mixture.
4. Place 2 salmon fillets in each of the crisper plate.
5. Return the crisper plate to the Ninja Foodi Dual Zone Air Fryer.
6. Choose the Air Fry mode for Zone 1 and set the temperature to 390 degrees F and the time to 17 minutes.
7. Select the "MATCH" button to copy the settings for Zone 2.
8. Initiate cooking by pressing the START/STOP button.
9. Meanwhile, mix fennel with garlic, yogurt, lemon juice, orange juice, remaining salt, and dill in a mixing bowl.

10. Serve the air fried salmon fillets with fennel salad.
11. Enjoy.

Nutrition:

- (Per serving) Calories 305 | Fat 15g |Sodium 482mg | Carbs 17g | Fiber 3g | Sugar 2g | Protein 35g

Honey Teriyaki Salmon

Servings: 3

Cooking Time: 12 Minutes

Ingredients:

- 8 tablespoon teriyaki sauce
- 3 tablespoons honey
- 2 cubes frozen garlic
- 2 tablespoons olive oil
- 3 pieces wild salmon

Directions:

1. Mix teriyaki sauce, honey, garlic and oil in a large bowl.
2. Add salmon to this sauce and mix well to coat.
3. Cover and refrigerate the salmon for 20 minutes.
4. Place the salmon pieces in one air fryer basket.
5. Return the air fryer basket 1 to Zone 1 of the Ninja Foodi 2-Basket Air Fryer.
6. Choose the "Air Fry" mode for Zone 1 and set the temperature to 350 degrees F and 12 minutes of cooking time.
7. Initiate cooking by pressing the START/PAUSE BUTTON.
8. Flip the pieces once cooked halfway through.
9. Serve warm.

Nutrition:

- (Per serving) Calories 260 | Fat 16g |Sodium 585mg | Carbs 3.1g | Fiber 1.3g | Sugar 0.2g | Protein 25.5g

Salmon With Broccoli And Cheese

Servings:2

Cooking Time:18

Ingredients:

- 2 cups of broccoli
- ½ cup of butter, melted
- Salt and pepper, to taste
- Oil spray, for greasing
- 1 cup of grated cheddar cheese
- 1 pound of salmon, fillets

Directions:

1. Take a bowl and add broccoli to it.

2. Add salt and black pepper and spray it with oil.
3. Put the broccoli in the air fryer zone 1 backset.
4. Now rub the salmon fillets with salt, black pepper, and butter.
5. Put it into zone 2 baskets.
6. Set zone 1 to air fry mode for 5 minters at 400 degrees F.
7. Set zone 2 to air fry mode for 18 minutes at 390 degrees F.
8. Hit start to start the cooking.
9. Once done, serve and by placing it on serving plates.
10. Put the grated cheese on top of the salmon and serve.

Nutrition:

- (Per serving) Calories 966 | Fat 79.1 g| Sodium 808 mg | Carbs 6.8 g | Fiber 2.4g | Sugar 1.9g | Protein 61.2 g

Fish Tacos

Servings: 5

Cooking Time: 30 Minutes

Ingredients:

- 1 pound firm white fish such as cod, haddock, pollock, halibut, or walleye
- ¾ cup gluten-free flour blend
- 3 eggs
- 1 cup gluten-free panko breadcrumbs
- 1 teaspoon garlic powder
- 1 teaspoon onion powder
- 1 teaspoon cumin
- 1 teaspoon lemon pepper
- 1 teaspoon red chili flakes
- 1 teaspoon kosher salt, divided
- 1 teaspoon pepper, divided
- Cooking oil spray
- 1 package corn tortillas
- Toppings such as tomatoes, avocado, cabbage, radishes, jalapenos, salsa, or hot sauce (optional)

Directions:

1. Dry the fish with paper towels. (Make sure to thaw the fish if it's frozen.) Depending on the size of the fillets, cut the fish in half or thirds.
2. On both sides of the fish pieces, liberally season with salt and pepper.
3. Put the flour in a dish.
4. In a separate bowl, crack the eggs and whisk them together until well blended.
5. Put the panko breadcrumbs in another bowl. Add the garlic powder, onion powder, cumin, lemon pepper, and red chili flakes. Add salt and pepper to taste. Stir until everything is well blended.
6. Each piece of fish should be dipped in the flour, then the eggs, and finally in the breadcrumb mixture. Make sure that each piece is completely coated.
7. Put a crisper plate in each drawer. Arrange the fish pieces in a single layer in each drawer. Insert the drawers into the unit.
8. Select zone 1, then AIR FRY, then set the temperature to 360 degrees F/ 180 degrees C with a 20-minute timer. To match zone 2 settings to zone 1, choose MATCH. To begin, select START/STOP.
9. Remove the fish from the drawers after the timer has finished. Place the crispy fish on warmed tortillas.

Nutrition:

- (Per serving) Calories 534 | Fat 18g | Sodium 679mg | Carbs 63g | Fiber 8g | Sugar 3g | Protein 27g

Blackened Mahimahi With Honey-roasted Carrots

Servings:4

Cooking Time: 30 Minutes

Ingredients:

- FOR THE MAHIMAHI
- 4 mahimahi fillets (4 ounces each)
- 1 tablespoon olive oil
- 1 tablespoon blackening seasoning
- Lemon wedges, for serving
- FOR THE CARROTS
- 1 pound carrots, peeled and cut into ½-inch rounds
- 2 teaspoons vegetable oil
- ½ teaspoon kosher salt
- ¼ teaspoon freshly ground black pepper
- 1 tablespoon salted butter, cut into small pieces
- 1 tablespoon honey
- 2 tablespoons chopped fresh parsley

Directions:

1. To prep the mahimahi: Brush both sides of the fish with the oil and sprinkle with the blackening seasoning.
2. To prep the carrots: In a large bowl, combine the carrots, oil, salt, and black pepper. Stir well to coat the carrots with the oil.
3. To cook the mahimahi and carrots: Install a crisper plate in each of the two baskets. Place the fish in the Zone 1 basket and insert the basket in the unit. Place the carrots in the Zone 2 basket and insert the basket in the unit.
4. Select Zone 1, select AIR FRY, set the temperature to 380°F, and set the timer to 14 minutes.
5. Select Zone 2, select ROAST, set the temperature to 400°F, and set the timer to 30 minutes. Select SMART FINISH.
6. Press START/PAUSE to begin cooking.
7. When the Zone 2 timer reads 15 minutes, press START/PAUSE. Remove the basket and scatter the butter over the carrots, then drizzle them with the honey. Reinsert the basket and press START/PAUSE to resume cooking.
8. When cooking is complete, the fish should be cooked through and the carrots soft.
9. Stir the parsley into the carrots. Serve the fish with lemon wedges.

Nutrition:

- (Per serving) Calories: 235; Total fat: 9.5g; Saturated fat: 3g; Carbohydrates: 15g; Fiber: 3g; Protein: 22g; Sodium: 672mg

Bacon-wrapped Shrimp

Servings: 8

Cooking Time: 10 Minutes

Ingredients:

- 24 jumbo raw shrimp, deveined with tail on, fresh or thawed from frozen

- 8 slices bacon, cut into thirds
- 1 tablespoon olive oil
- 1 teaspoon paprika
- 1–2 cloves minced garlic
- 1 tablespoon finely chopped fresh parsley

Directions:

1. Combine the olive oil, paprika, garlic, and parsley in a small bowl.
2. If necessary, peel the raw shrimp, leaving the tails on.
3. Add the shrimp to the oil mixture. Toss to coat well.
4. Wrap a piece of bacon around the middle of each shrimp and place seam-side down on a small baking dish.
5. Refrigerate for 30 minutes before cooking.
6. Place a crisper plate in each drawer. Put the shrimp in a single layer in each drawer. Insert the drawers into the unit.
7. Select zone 1, then AIR FRY, then set the temperature to 360 degrees F/ 180 degrees C with a 10-minute timer. To match zone 2 settings to zone 1, choose MATCH. To begin, select START/STOP.
8. Remove the shrimp from the drawers when the cooking time is over.

Nutrition:

- (Per serving) Calories 479 | Fat 15.7g | Sodium 949mg | Carbs 0.6g | Fiber 0.1g | Sugar 0g | Protein 76.1g

Garlic Butter Salmon

Servings: 4

Cooking Time: 10 Minutes

Ingredients:

- 4 (6-ounce) boneless, skin-on salmon fillets (preferably wild-caught)
- 4 tablespoons butter, melted
- 2 teaspoons garlic, minced
- 2 teaspoons fresh Italian parsley, chopped (or ¼ teaspoon dried)
- Salt and pepper to taste

Directions:

1. Season the fresh salmon with salt and pepper.
2. Mix together the melted butter, garlic, and parsley in a bowl.
3. Baste the salmon fillets with the garlic butter mixture.
4. Place a crisper plate in each drawer. Put 2 fillets in each drawer. Put the drawers inside the unit.
5. Select zone 1, then AIR FRY, then set the temperature to 360 degrees F/ 180 degrees C with a 10-minute timer. To match zone 2 settings to zone 1, choose MATCH. To begin, select START/STOP.
6. Remove the salmon from the drawers after the timer has finished.

Nutrition:

- (Per serving) Calories 338 | Fat 26g | Sodium 309mg | Carbs 1g | Fiber 0g | Sugar 0g | Protein 25g

Beer Battered Fish Fillet
Servings:2
Cooking Time:14
Ingredients:

- 1 cup all-purpose flour
- 4 tablespoons cornstarch
- 1 teaspoon baking soda
- 8 ounces beer
- 2 egg beaten
- ½ cup all-purpose flour
- 1 teaspoon smoked paprika
- 1 teaspoon salt
- 1/4 teaspoon freshly ground black pepper
- ¼ teaspoon of cayenne pepper
- 2 cod fillets, 1½-inches thick, cut into 4 pieces
- Oil spray, for greasing

Directions:

1. Take a large bowl and combine flour, baking soda, corn starch, and salt
2. In a separate bowl beat eggs along with the beer.
3. In a shallow dish mix paprika, salt, pepper, and cayenne pepper.
4. Dry the codfish fillets with a paper towel.
5. Dip the fish into the eggs and coat it with seasoned flour.
6. Then dip it in the seasoning.
7. Grease the fillet with oil spray.
8. Divide the fillet between both zones.
9. Set zone 1 to AIR FRY mode at 400 degrees F for 14 minutes.
10. Select MACTH button for zone 2 basket.
11. Press start and let the AIR fry do its magic.
12. Once cooking is done, serve the fish.
13. Enjoy it hot.

Nutrition:

- (Per serving) Calories 1691| Fat 6.1g| Sodium 3976mg | Carbs105.1 g | Fiber 3.4g | Sugar15.6 g | Protein 270g

Crispy Catfish
Servings: 4
Cooking Time: 17 Minutes.
Ingredients:

- 4 catfish fillets
- ¼ cup Louisiana Fish fry
- 1 tablespoon olive oil
- 1 tablespoon parsley, chopped
- 1 lemon, sliced
- Fresh herbs, to garnish

Directions:

1. Mix fish fry with olive oil, and parsley then liberally rub over the catfish.
2. Place two fillets in each of the crisper plate.
3. Return the crisper plates to the Ninja Foodi Dual Zone Air Fryer.
4. Choose the Air Fry mode for Zone 1 and set the temperature to 390 degrees F and the time to 17 minutes.
5. Select the "MATCH" button to copy the settings for Zone 2.
6. Initiate cooking by pressing the START/STOP button.
7. Garnish with lemon slices and herbs.
8. Serve warm.

Nutrition:

- (Per serving) Calories 275 | Fat 1.4g |Sodium 582mg | Carbs 31.5g | Fiber 1.1g | Sugar 0.1g | Protein 29.8g

Scallops

Servings: 4
Cooking Time: 5 Minutes

Ingredients:

- ½ cup Italian breadcrumbs
- ½ teaspoon garlic powder
- ¼ teaspoon salt
- ½ teaspoon black pepper
- 2 tablespoons butter, melted
- 1 pound sea scallops, rinsed and pat dry

Directions:

1. Combine the breadcrumbs, garlic powder, salt, and pepper in a small bowl. Pour the melted butter into another shallow bowl.
2. Dredge each scallop in the melted butter, then roll it in the breadcrumb mixture until well covered.
3. Place a crisper plate in each drawer. Put the scallops in a single layer in each drawer. Insert the drawers into the unit.
4. Select zone 1, then AIR FRY, then set the temperature to 360 degrees F/ 180 degrees C with a 5-minute timer. To match zone 2 settings to zone 1, choose MATCH. To begin, select START/STOP.
5. Press START/STOP to pause the unit when the timer reaches 3 minutes. Remove the drawers. Use tongs to carefully flip the scallops over. To resume cooking, re-insert the drawers into the unit and press START/STOP.
6. Remove the scallops from the drawers after the timer has finished.

Nutrition:

- (Per serving) Calories 81 | Fat 6g | Sodium 145mg | Carbs 3g | Fiber 4g | Sugar 1g | Protein 3g

Furikake Salmon

Servings: 4
Cooking Time: 10 Minutes

Ingredients:

- ½ cup mayonnaise
- 1 tablespoon shoyu

- 455gsalmon fillet
- Salt and black pepper to taste
- 2 tablespoons furikake

Directions:

1. Mix shoyu with mayonnaise in a small bowl.
2. Rub the salmon with black pepper and salt.
3. Place the salmon pieces in the air fryer baskets.
4. Top them with the mayo mixture.
5. Return the air fryer basket 1 to Zone 1, and basket 2 to Zone 2 of the Ninja Foodi 2-Basket Air Fryer.
6. Choose the "Air Fry" mode for Zone 1 at 400 degrees F and 10 minutes of cooking time.
7. Select the "MATCH COOK" option to copy the settings for Zone 2.
8. Initiate cooking by pressing the START/PAUSE BUTTON.
9. Serve warm.

Nutrition:

- (Per serving) Calories 297 | Fat 1g |Sodium 291mg | Carbs 35g | Fiber 1g | Sugar 9g | Protein 29g

Herb Tuna Patties

Servings: 10

Cooking Time: 12 Minutes

Ingredients:

- 2 eggs
- 425g can tuna, drained & diced
- ½ tsp garlic powder
- ½ small onion, minced
- 1 celery stalk, chopped
- 42g parmesan cheese, grated
- 50g breadcrumbs
- ½ tsp dried oregano
- ½ tsp dried basil
- ½ tsp dried thyme
- 15ml lemon juice
- 1 lemon zest
- Pepper
- Salt

Directions:

1. In a bowl, mix tuna with remaining ingredients until well combined.
2. Insert a crisper plate in the Ninja Foodi air fryer baskets.
3. Make patties from the tuna mixture and place them in both baskets.
4. Select zone 1, then select "bake" mode and set the temperature to 380 degrees F for 12 minutes. Press "match" to match zone 2 settings to zone 1. Press "start/stop" to begin. Turn halfway through.

Nutrition:

- (Per serving) Calories 86 | Fat 1.5g |Sodium 90mg | Carbs 4.5g | Fiber 0.4g | Sugar 0.6g | Protein 12.8g

Lemon Pepper Salmon With Asparagus
Servings:2
Cooking Time:18
Ingredients:

- 1 cup of green asparagus
- 2 tablespoons of butter
- 2 fillets of salmon, 8 ounces each
- Salt and black pepper, to taste
- 1 teaspoon of lemon juice
- ½ teaspoon of lemon zest
- oil spray, for greasing

Directions:

1. Rinse and trim the asparagus.
2. Rinse and pat dry the salmon fillets.
3. Take a bowl and mix lemon juice, lemon zest, salt, and black pepper.
4. Brush the fish fillet with the rub and place it in the zone 1 basket.
5. Place asparagus in zone 2 basket.
6. Spray the asparagus with oil spray.
7. Set zone 1 to AIRFRY mode for 18 minutes at 390 degrees F.
8. Set the zone 2 to 5 minutes at 390 degrees F, at air fry mode.
9. Hit the smart finish button to finish at the same time.
10. Once done, serve and enjoy.

Nutrition:

- (Per serving) Calories 482| Fat 28g| Sodium209 mg | Carbs 2.8g | Fiber1.5 g | Sugar1.4 g | Protein 56.3g

Honey Teriyaki Tilapia
Servings: 4
Cooking Time: 10 Minutes
Ingredients:

- 8 tablespoons low-sodium teriyaki sauce
- 3 tablespoons honey
- 2 garlic cloves, minced
- 2 tablespoons extra virgin olive oil
- 3 pieces tilapia (each cut into 2 pieces)

Directions:

1. Combine all the first 4 ingredients to make the marinade.
2. Pour the marinade over the tilapia and let it sit for 20 minutes.
3. Place a crisper plate in each drawer. Place the tilapia in the drawers. Insert the drawers into the unit.
4. Select zone 1, then AIR FRY, then set the temperature to 360 degrees F/ 180 degrees C with a 10-minute timer. To match zone 2 settings to zone 1, choose MATCH. To begin, select START/STOP.

5. Remove the tilapia from the drawers after the timer has finished.

Nutrition:

- (Per serving) Calories 350 | Fat 16.4g | Sodium 706mg | Carbs 19.3g | Fiber 0.1g | Sugar 19g | Protein 29.3g

Crusted Tilapia
Servings: 4
Cooking Time: 17 Minutes.
Ingredients:

- ¾ cup breadcrumbs
- 1 packet dry ranch-style dressing
- 2 ½ tablespoons vegetable oil
- 2 eggs beaten
- 4 tilapia fillets
- Herbs and chilies to garnish

Directions:

1. Thoroughly mix ranch dressing with panko in a bowl.
2. Whisk eggs in a shallow bowl.
3. Dip each fish fillet in the egg, then coat evenly with the panko mixture.
4. Set two coated fillets in each of the crisper plate.
5. Return the crisper plates to the Ninja Foodi Dual Zone Air Fryer.
6. Choose the Air Fry mode for Zone 1 and set the temperature to 390 degrees F and the time to 17 minutes.
7. Select the "MATCH" button to copy the settings for Zone 2.
8. Initiate cooking by pressing the START/STOP button.
9. Serve warm with herbs and chilies.

Nutrition:

- (Per serving) Calories 196 | Fat 7.1g |Sodium 492mg | Carbs 21.6g | Fiber 2.9g | Sugar 0.8g | Protein 13.4g

Pecan-crusted Catfish Nuggets With "fried" Okra
Servings:4
Cooking Time: 17 Minutes
Ingredients:

- FOR THE CATFISH NUGGETS
- 1 cup whole milk
- 1 pound fresh catfish nuggets (or cut-up fillets)
- 1 large egg
- 2 to 3 dashes Louisiana-style hot sauce (optional)
- ¼ cup finely chopped pecans
- ½ cup all-purpose flour
- Nonstick cooking spray
- Tartar sauce, for serving (optional)
- FOR THE OKRA

- ½ cup fine yellow cornmeal
- ¼ cup all-purpose flour
- ½ teaspoon garlic powder
- ½ teaspoon paprika
- 1 teaspoon kosher salt
- 1 large egg
- 8 ounces frozen cut okra, thawed
- Nonstick cooking spray

Directions:

1. To prep the catfish: Pour the milk into a large zip-top bag. Add the catfish and turn to coat. Set in the refrigerator to soak for at least 1 hour or up to overnight.
2. Remove the fish from the milk, shaking off any excess liquid.
3. In a shallow dish, whisk together the egg and hot sauce (if using). In a second shallow dish, combine the pecans and flour.
4. Dip each piece of fish into the egg mixture, then into the nut mixture to coat. Gently press the nut mixture to adhere to the fish. Spritz each nugget with cooking spray.
5. To prep the okra: Set up a breading station with two small shallow bowls. In the first bowl, stir together the cornmeal, flour, garlic powder, paprika, and salt. In the second bowl, whisk the egg.
6. Dip the okra first in the cornmeal mixture, then the egg, then back into the cornmeal. Spritz with cooking spray.
7. To cook the catfish and okra: Install a crisper plate in each of the two baskets. Place the fish in a single layer in the Zone 1 basket and insert the basket in the unit. Place the okra in the Zone 2 basket and insert the basket in the unit.
8. Select Zone 1, select AIR FRY, set the temperature to 390°F, and set the timer to 17 minutes.
9. Select Zone 2, select AIR FRY, set the temperature to 400°F, and set the timer to 12 minutes. Select SMART FINISH.
10. Press START/PAUSE to begin cooking.
11. When cooking is complete, the fish should be cooked through and the okra golden brown and crispy. Serve hot.

Nutrition:

- (Per serving) Calories: 414; Total fat: 24g; Saturated fat: 2.5g; Carbohydrates: 30g; Fiber: 3g; Protein: 23g; Sodium: 569mg

Keto Baked Salmon With Pesto

Servings:2

Cooking Time:18

Ingredients:

- 4 salmon fillets, 2 inches thick
- 2 ounces green pesto
- Salt and black pepper
- ½ tablespoon of canola oil, for greasing
- 1-1/2 cup mayonnaise
- 2 tablespoons Greek yogurt
- Salt and black pepper, to taste

Directions:

1. Rub the salmon with pesto, salt, oil, and black pepper.
2. In a small bowl, whisk together all the green sauce ingredients.

3. Divide the fish fillets between both the baskets.
4. Set zone 1 to air fry mode for 18 minutes at 390 degrees F.
5. Select MATCH button for Zone 2 basket.
6. Once the cooking is done, serve it with green sauce drizzle.
7. Enjoy.

Nutrition:

- (Per serving) Calories 1165 | Fat80.7 g| Sodium 1087 mg | Carbs 33.1g | Fiber 0.5g | Sugar11.5 g | Protein 80.6g

Sesame Honey Salmon

Servings: 4

Cooking Time: 10minutes

Ingredients:

- 4 salmon fillets
- 85g honey
- 15ml sesame oil
- 1 tbsp garlic, minced
- 2 tbsp soy sauce
- 1 tbsp sriracha
- Pepper
- Salt

Directions:

1. In a bowl, coat fish fillets with oil, garlic, honey, sriracha, soy sauce, pepper, and salt. Cover and place in refrigerator for 30 minutes.
2. Insert a crisper plate in the Ninja Foodi air fryer baskets.
3. Place the marinated fish fillets in both baskets.
4. Select zone 1, then select "air fry" mode and set the temperature to 375 degrees F for 10 minutes. Press "match" to match zone 2 settings to zone 1. Press "start/stop" to begin.

Nutrition:

- (Per serving) Calories 341 | Fat 14.4g |Sodium 596mg | Carbs 19.5g | Fiber 0.2g | Sugar 17.6g | Protein 35.2g

Honey Sriracha Mahi Mahi

Servings: 4

Cooking Time: 7 Minutes

Ingredients:

- 3 pounds mahi-mahi
- 6 tablespoons honey
- 4 tablespoons sriracha
- Salt, to taste
- Cooking spray

Directions:

1. In a small bowl, mix the sriracha sauce and honey. Mix well.
2. Season the fish with salt and pour the honey mixture over it. Let it sit at room temperature for 20 minutes.
3. Place a crisper plate in each drawer. Put the fish in a single layer in each. Insert the drawers into the unit.
4. Select zone 1, then AIR FRY, then set the temperature to 400 degrees F/ 200 degrees C with a 7-minute timer. To match zone 2 settings to zone 1, choose MATCH. To begin, select START/STOP.
5. Remove the fish from the drawers after the timer has finished.

Nutrition:

- (Per serving) Calories 581 | Fat 22g | Sodium 495mg | Carbs 26g | Fiber 4g | Sugar 26g | Protein 68g

Bang Bang Shrimp With Roasted Bok Choy

Servings:4

Cooking Time: 13 Minutes

Ingredients:

- FOR THE BANG BANG SHRIMP
- ½ cup all-purpose flour
- 2 large eggs
- 1 cup panko bread crumbs
- 1 pound peeled shrimp (tails removed), thawed if frozen
- Nonstick cooking spray
- ½ cup mayonnaise
- ¼ cup Thai sweet chili sauce
- ¼ teaspoon sriracha
- FOR THE BOK CHOY
- 1 tablespoon reduced-sodium soy sauce
- 1 teaspoon minced garlic
- 1 teaspoon sesame oil
- 1 teaspoon minced fresh ginger
- 1½ pounds baby bok choy, halved lengthwise
- 1 tablespoon toasted sesame seeds

Directions:

1. To prep the shrimp: Set up a breading station with three small shallow bowls. Place the flour in the first bowl. In the second bowl, whisk the eggs. Place the panko in the third bowl.
2. Bread the shrimp in this order: First, dip them into the flour, coating both sides. Then, dip into the beaten egg. Finally, coat them in the panko, gently pressing the bread crumbs to adhere to the shrimp. Spritz both sides of the shrimp with cooking spray.
3. To prep the bok choy: In a small bowl, whisk together the soy sauce, garlic, sesame oil, and ginger.
4. To cook the shrimp and bok choy: Install a crisper plate in the Zone 1 basket. Place the shrimp in the basket in a single layer and insert the basket in the unit. Place the boy choy cut-side up in the Zone 2 basket. Pour the sauce over the bok choy and insert the basket in the unit.
5. Select Zone 1, select AIR FRY, set the temperature to 390°F, and set the timer to 13 minutes.
6. Select Zone 2, select BAKE, set the temperature to 370°F, and set the timer to 8 minutes. Select SMART FINISH.
7. Press START/PAUSE to begin cooking.
8. When cooking is complete, the shrimp should be cooked through and golden brown and the bok choy soft and slightly caramelized.
9. In a large bowl, whisk together the mayonnaise, sweet chili sauce, and sriracha. Add the shrimp and toss to coat.

10. Sprinkle the bok choy with the sesame seeds and serve hot alongside the shrimp.

Nutrition:

- (Per serving) Calories: 534; Total fat: 33g; Saturated fat: 4g; Carbohydrates: 29g; Fiber: 3g; Protein: 31g; Sodium: 789mg

Scallops With Greens

Servings: 8

Cooking Time: 13 Minutes.

Ingredients:

- ¾ cup heavy whipping cream
- 1 tablespoon tomato paste
- 1 tablespoon chopped fresh basil
- 1 teaspoon garlic, minced
- ½ teaspoons salt
- ½ teaspoons pepper
- 12 ounces frozen spinach thawed
- 8 jumbo sea scallops
- Vegetable oil to spray

Directions:

1. Season the scallops with vegetable oil, salt, and pepper in a bowl
2. Mix cream with spinach, basil, garlic, salt, pepper, and tomato paste in a bowl.
3. Pour this mixture over the scallops and mix gently.
4. Divide the scallops in the Air Fryers Baskets without using the crisper plate.
5. Return the crisper plate to the Ninja Foodi Dual Zone Air Fryer.
6. Choose the Air Fry mode for Zone 1 and set the temperature to 390 degrees F and the time to 13 minutes.
7. Select the "MATCH" button to copy the settings for Zone 2.
8. Initiate cooking by pressing the START/STOP button.
9. Serve right away

Nutrition:

- (Per serving) Calories 266 | Fat 6.3g |Sodium 193mg | Carbs 39.1g | Fiber 7.2g | Sugar 5.2g | Protein 14.8g

Shrimp Skewers

Servings: 4

Cooking Time: 10minutes

Ingredients:

- 453g shrimp
- 15ml lemon juice
- 15ml olive oil
- 1 tbsp old bay seasoning
- 1 tsp garlic, minced

Directions:

1. Toss shrimp with old bay seasoning, garlic, lemon juice, and olive oil in a bowl.
2. Thread shrimp onto the soaked skewers.
3. Insert a crisper plate in the Ninja Foodi air fryer baskets.
4. Place the shrimp skewers in both baskets.
5. Select zone 1, then select "air fry" mode and set the temperature to 390 degrees F for 10 minutes. Press "match" to match zone 2 settings to zone 1. Press "start/stop" to begin.

Nutrition:

- (Per serving) Calories 167 | Fat 5.5g |Sodium 758mg | Carbs 2g | Fiber 0g | Sugar 0.1g | Protein 25.9g

Sweet & Spicy Fish Fillets

Servings: 4

Cooking Time: 8 Minutes

Ingredients:

- 4 salmon fillets
- 1 tsp smoked paprika
- 1 tsp chilli powder
- ½ tsp red pepper flakes, crushed
- ½ tsp garlic powder
- 85g honey
- Pepper
- Salt

Directions:

1. In a small bowl, mix honey, garlic powder, chilli powder, paprika, red pepper flakes, pepper, and salt.
2. Brush fish fillets with honey mixture.
3. Insert a crisper plate in the Ninja Foodi air fryer baskets.
4. Place fish fillets in both baskets.
5. Select zone 1, then select "air fry" mode and set the temperature to 390 degrees F for 8 minutes. Press "match" and then"start/stop" to begin.

Nutrition:

- (Per serving) Calories 305 | Fat 11.2g |Sodium 125mg | Carbs 18.4g | Fiber 0.6g | Sugar 17.5g | Protein 34.8g

Delicious Haddock

Servings: 4

Cooking Time: 10 Minutes

Ingredients:

- 1 egg
- 455g haddock fillets
- 1 tsp seafood seasoning
- 136g flour
- 15ml olive oil

- 119g breadcrumbs
- Pepper
- Salt

Directions:

1. In a shallow dish, whisk egg. Add flour to a plate.
2. In a separate shallow dish, mix breadcrumbs, pepper, seafood seasoning, and salt.
3. Brush fish fillets with oil.
4. Coat each fish fillet with flour, then dip in egg and finally coat with breadcrumbs.
5. Insert a crisper plate in the Ninja Foodi air fryer baskets.
6. Place coated fish fillets in both baskets.
7. Select zone 1, then select "air fry" mode and set the temperature to 360 degrees F for 10 minutes. Press "match" to match zone 2 settings to zone 1. Press "start/stop" to begin.

Nutrition:

- (Per serving) Calories 393 | Fat 7.4g |Sodium 351mg | Carbs 43.4g | Fiber 2.1g | Sugar 1.8g | Protein 35.7g

Flavorful Salmon With Green Beans

Servings: 4

Cooking Time: 10 Minutes

Ingredients:

- 4 ounces green beans
- 1 tablespoon canola oil
- 4 (6-ounce) salmon fillets
- 1⁄3 cup prepared sesame-ginger sauce
- Kosher salt, to taste
- Black pepper, to taste

Directions:

1. Toss the green beans with a teaspoon each of salt and pepper in a large bowl.
2. Place a crisper plate in each drawer. Place the green beans in the zone 1 drawer and insert it into the unit. Place the salmon into the zone 2 drawer and place it into the unit.
3. Select zone 1, then AIR FRY, and set the temperature to 390 degrees F/ 200 degrees C with a 10-minute timer.
4. Select zone 2, then AIR FRY, and set the temperature to 390 degrees F/ 200 degrees C with a 15-minute timer. Select SYNC. To begin cooking, press the START/STOP button.
5. Press START/STOP to pause the unit when the zone 2 timer reaches 9 minutes. Remove the salmon from the drawer and toss it in the sesame-ginger sauce. To resume cooking, replace the drawer in the device and press START/STOP.
6. When cooking is complete, serve the salmon and green beans immediately.

Nutrition:

- (Per serving) Calories 305 | Fat 16g | Sodium 535mg | Carbs 8.7g | Fiber 1g | Sugar 6.4g | Protein 34.9g

Roasted Salmon And Parmesan Asparagus
Servings: 4
Cooking Time: 27 Minutes
Ingredients:

- 2 tablespoons Montreal steak seasoning
- 3 tablespoons brown sugar
- 3 uncooked salmon fillets (6 ounces each)
- 2 tablespoons canola oil, divided
- 1-pound asparagus, ends trimmed
- Kosher salt, as desired
- Ground black pepper, as desired
- ¼ cup shredded parmesan cheese, divided

Directions:

1. Combine the steak spice and brown sugar in a small bowl.
2. Brush 1 tablespoon of oil over the salmon fillets, then thoroughly coat with the sugar mixture.
3. Toss the asparagus with the remaining 1 tablespoon of oil, salt, and pepper in a mixing bowl.
4. Place a crisper plate in both drawers. Put the fillets skin-side down in the zone 1 drawer, then place the drawer in the unit. Insert the zone 2 drawer into the device after placing the asparagus in it.
5. Select zone 1, then ROAST, then set the temperature to 390 degrees F/ 200 degrees C with a 17-minute timer. To match the zone 2 settings to zone 1, choose MATCH. To begin cooking, press the START/STOP button.
6. When the zone 2 timer reaches 7 minutes, press START/STOP. Remove the zone 2 drawer from the unit. Flip the asparagus with silicone-tipped tongs. Re-insert the drawer into the unit. Continue cooking by pressing START/STOP.
7. When the zone 2 timer has reached 14 minutes, press START/STOP. Remove the zone 2 drawer from the unit. Sprinkle half the parmesan cheese over the asparagus, and mix lightly. Re-insert the drawer into the unit. Continue cooking by pressing START/STOP.
8. Transfer the fillets and asparagus to a serving plate once they've finished cooking. Serve with the remaining parmesan cheese on top of the asparagus.

Nutrition:

- (Per serving) Calories 293 | Fat 15.8g | Sodium 203mg | Carbs 11.1g | Fiber 2.4g | Sugar 8.7g | Protein 29g

Desserts Recipes

Cinnamon Sugar Dessert Fries
Servings: 4
Cooking Time: 15 Minutes
Ingredients:

- 2 sweet potatoes
- 1 tablespoon butter, melted
- 1 teaspoon butter, melted
- 2 tablespoons sugar
- ½ teaspoon ground cinnamon

Directions:

1. Peel and cut the sweet potatoes into skinny fries.

2. Coat the fries with 1 tablespoon of butter.
3. Install a crisper plate into each drawer. Place half the sweet potatoes in the zone 1 drawer and half in zone 2's, then insert the drawers into the unit.
4. Select zone 1, select AIR FRY, set temperature to 390 degrees F/ 200 degrees C, and set time to 15 minutes. Select MATCH to match zone 2 settings to zone 1. Press the START/STOP button to begin cooking.
5. When the time reaches 11 minutes, press START/STOP to pause the unit. Remove the drawers and flip the fries. Re-insert the drawers into the unit and press START/STOP to resume cooking.
6. Meanwhile, mix the 1 teaspoon of butter, the sugar, and the cinnamon in a large bowl.
7. When the fries are done, add them to the bowl, and toss them to coat.
8. Serve and enjoy!

Nutrition:

- (Per serving) Calories 110 | Fat 4g | Sodium 51mg | Carbs 18g | Fiber 2g | Sugar 10g | Protein 1g

Mini Strawberry And Cream Pies

Servings:2

Cooking Time:10

Ingredients:

- 1 box Store-Bought Pie Dough, Trader Joe's
- 1 cup strawberries, cubed
- 3 tablespoons of cream, heavy
- 2 tablespoons of almonds
- 1 egg white, for brushing

Directions:

1. Take the store brought pie dough and flatten it on a surface.
2. Use a round cutter to cut it into 3-inch circles.
3. Brush the dough with egg white all around the parameters.
4. Now add almonds, strawberries, and cream in a very little amount in the center of the dough, and top it with another circular.
5. Press the edges with the fork to seal it.
6. Make a slit in the middle of the dough and divide it into the baskets.
7. Set zone 1 to AIR FRY mode 360 degrees for 10 minutes.
8. Select MATCH for zone 2 basket.
9. Once done, serve.

Nutrition:

- (Per serving) Calories 203| Fat12.7g| Sodium 193mg | Carbs20 g | Fiber 2.2g | Sugar 5.8g | Protein 3.7g

Bread Pudding

Servings: 4

Cooking Time: 15 Minutes

Ingredients:

- 2 cups bread cubes
- 1 egg

- ⅔ cup heavy cream
- ½ teaspoon vanilla extract
- ¼ cup sugar
- ¼ cup chocolate chips

Directions:

1. Grease two 4 inches baking dish with a cooking spray.
2. Divide the bread cubes in the baking dishes and sprinkle chocolate chips on top.
3. Beat egg with cream, sugar and vanilla in a bowl.
4. Divide this mixture in the baking dishes.
5. Place one pan in each air fryer basket.
6. Return the air fryer basket 1 to Zone 1, and basket 2 to Zone 2 of the Ninja Foodi 2-Basket Air Fryer.
7. Choose the "Air Fry" mode for Zone 1 at 350 degrees F and 15 minutes of cooking time.
8. Select the "MATCH COOK" option to copy the settings for Zone 2.
9. Initiate cooking by pressing the START/PAUSE BUTTON.
10. Allow the pudding to cool and serve.

Nutrition:

- (Per serving) Calories 149 | Fat 1.2g |Sodium 3mg | Carbs 37.6g | Fiber 5.8g | Sugar 29g | Protein 1.1g

Monkey Bread

Servings: 12

Cooking Time: 10 Minutes

Ingredients:

- Bread
- 12 Rhodes white dinner rolls
- ½ cup brown sugar
- 1 teaspoon cinnamon
- 4 tablespoons butter melted
- Glaze
- ½ cup powdered sugar
- 1-2 tablespoons milk
- ½ teaspoon vanilla

Directions:

1. Mix brown sugar, cinnamon and butter in a bowl.
2. Cut the dinner rolls in half and dip them in the sugar mixture.
3. Place these buns in a greased baking pan and pour the remaining butter on top.
4. Place the buns in the air fryer baskets.
5. Return the air fryer basket 1 to Zone 1, and basket 2 to Zone 2 of the Ninja Foodi 2-Basket Air Fryer.
6. Choose the "Air Fry" mode for Zone 1 at 350 degrees F and 10 minutes of cooking time.
7. Initiate cooking by pressing the START/PAUSE BUTTON.
8. Flip the rolls once cooked halfway through.
9. Meanwhile, mix milk, vanilla and sugar in a bowl.
10. Pour the glaze over the air fried rolls.
11. Serve.

Nutrition:

- (Per serving) Calories 192 | Fat 9.3g |Sodium 133mg | Carbs 27.1g | Fiber 1.4g | Sugar 19g | Protein 3.2g

Apple Nutmeg Flautas
Servings: 8
Cooking Time: 8 Minutes.
Ingredients:

- ¼ cup light brown sugar
- ⅛ cup all-purpose flour
- ¼ teaspoon ground cinnamon
- Nutmeg, to taste
- 4 apples, peeled, cored & sliced
- ½ lemon, juice, and zest
- 6 (10-inch) flour tortillas
- Vegetable oil
- Caramel sauce
- Cinnamon sugar

Directions:

1. Mix brown sugar with cinnamon, nutmeg, and flour in a large bowl.
2. Toss in apples in lemon juice. Mix well.
3. Place a tortilla at a time on a flat surface and add ½ cup of the apple mixture to the tortilla.
4. Roll the tortilla into a burrito and seal it tightly and hold it in place with a toothpick.
5. Repeat the same steps with the remaining tortillas and apple mixture.
6. Place two apple burritos in each of the crisper plate and spray them with cooking oil.
7. Return the crisper plates to the Ninja Foodi Dual Zone Air Fryer.
8. Choose the Air Fry mode for Zone 1 and set the temperature to 400 degrees F and the time to 8 minutes.
9. Select the "MATCH" button to copy the settings for Zone 2.
10. Initiate cooking by pressing the START/STOP button.
11. Flip the burritos once cooked halfway through, then resume cooking.
12. Garnish with caramel sauce and cinnamon sugar.
13. Enjoy!

Nutrition:

- (Per serving) Calories 157 | Fat 1.3g |Sodium 27mg | Carbs 1.3g | Fiber 1g | Sugar 2.2g | Protein 8.2g

Delicious Apple Fritters
Servings: 10
Cooking Time: 8 Minutes
Ingredients:

- 236g Bisquick
- 2 apples, peel & dice
- 158ml milk
- 30ml butter, melted
- 1 tsp cinnamon

- 24g sugar

Directions:

1. In a bowl, mix Bisquick, cinnamon, and sugar.
2. Add milk and mix until dough forms. Add apple and stir well.
3. Insert a crisper plate in Ninja Foodi air fryer baskets.
4. Make fritters from the mixture and place in both baskets. Brush fritters with melted butter.
5. Select zone 1 then select "air fry" mode and set the temperature to 360 degrees F for 10 minutes. Press "match" to match zone 2 settings to zone 1. Press "start/stop" to begin.

Nutrition:

- (Per serving) Calories 171 | Fat 6.7g |Sodium 352mg | Carbs 25.8g | Fiber 1.7g | Sugar 10.8g | Protein 2.7g

Dehydrated Peaches

Servings: 4

Cooking Time: 8 Hours

Ingredients:

- 300g canned peaches

Directions:

1. Insert a crisper plate in the Ninja Foodi air fryer baskets.
2. Place peaches in both baskets.
3. Select zone 1, then select "dehydrate" mode and set the temperature to 135 degrees F for 8 hours. Press "start/stop" to begin.

Nutrition:

- (Per serving) Calories 30 | Fat 0.2g |Sodium 0mg | Carbs 7g | Fiber 1.2g | Sugar 7g | Protein 0.7g

Air Fryer Sweet Twists

Servings:2

Cooking Time:9

Ingredients:

- 1 box store-bought puff pastry
- ½ teaspoon cinnamon
- ½ teaspoon sugar
- ½ teaspoon black sesame seeds
- Salt, pinch
- 2 tablespoons Parmesan cheese, freshly grated

Directions:

1. Place the dough on a work surface.
2. Take a small bowl and mix cheese, sugar, salt, sesame seeds, and cinnamon.
3. Press this mixture on both sides of the dough.

4. Now, cut the pastry into 1" x 3" strips.
5. Twist each of the strips 2 times and then lay it onto the flat.
6. Transfer to both the air fryer baskets.
7. Select zone 1 to air fry mode at 400 degrees F for 9-10 minutes.
8. Select the MATCH button for the zone 2 basket.
9. Once cooked, serve.

Nutrition:

- (Per serving) Calories 140| Fat9.4g| Sodium 142mg | Carbs 12.3g | Fiber0.8 g | Sugar 1.2g | Protein 2g

"air-fried" Oreos Apple Fries

Servings:4

Cooking Time: 10 Minutes

Ingredients:

- FOR THE "FRIED" OREOS
- 1 teaspoon vegetable oil
- 1 cup all-purpose flour
- 1 tablespoon granulated sugar
- 1 tablespoon baking powder
- ½ teaspoon baking soda
- ¼ teaspoon kosher salt
- 1 large egg
- ¼ cup unsweetened almond milk
- ½ teaspoon vanilla extract
- 8 Oreo cookies
- Nonstick cooking spray
- 1 tablespoon powdered sugar (optional)
- FOR THE APPLE FRIES
- 1 teaspoon vegetable oil
- 1 cup all-purpose flour
- 1 tablespoon granulated sugar
- 1 tablespoon baking powder
- ½ teaspoon baking soda
- ¼ teaspoon kosher salt
- 1 large egg
- ¼ cup unsweetened almond milk
- ½ teaspoon vanilla extract
- 2 Granny Smith apples
- 2 tablespoons cornstarch
- ½ teaspoon apple pie spice
- Nonstick cooking spray
- 1 tablespoon powdered sugar (optional)

Directions:

1. To prep the "fried" Oreos: Brush a crisper plate with the oil and install it in the Zone 1 basket.
2. In a large bowl, combine the flour, granulated sugar, baking powder, baking soda, and salt. Mix in the egg, almond milk, and vanilla to form a thick batter.

3. Using a fork or slotted spoon, dip each cookie into the batter, coating it fully. Let the excess batter drip off, then place the cookies in the prepared basket in a single layer. Spritz each with cooking spray.
4. To prep the apple fries: Brush a crisper plate with the oil and install it in the Zone 2 basket.
5. In a large bowl, combine the flour, granulated sugar, baking powder, baking soda, and salt. Mix in the egg, almond milk, and vanilla to form a thick batter.
6. Core the apples and cut them into ½-inch-thick French fry shapes. Dust lightly with the cornstarch and apple pie spice.
7. Using a fork or slotted spoon, dip each apple into the batter, coating it fully. Let the excess batter drip off, then place the apples in the prepared basket in a single layer. Spritz with cooking spray.
8. To cook the "fried" Oreos and apple fries: Insert both baskets in the unit.
9. Select Zone 1, select AIR FRY, set the temperature to 400°F, and set the timer to 8 minutes.
10. Select Zone 2, select AIR FRY, set the temperature to 400°F, and set the timer to 10 minutes. Select SMART FINISH.
11. Press START/PAUSE to begin cooking.
12. When cooking is complete, the batter will be golden brown and crisp. If desired, dust the cookies and apples with the powdered sugar before serving.

Nutrition:

- (Per serving) Calories: 464; Total fat: 21g; Saturated fat: 3.5g; Carbohydrates: 66g; Fiber: 2.5g; Protein: 7g; Sodium: 293mg

Cake In The Air Fryer

Servings:2

Cooking Time:30

Ingredients:

- 90 grams all-purpose flour
- Pinch of salt
- 1/2 teaspoon of baking powder
- ½ cup of tutti fruitti mix
- 2 eggs
- 1 teaspoon of vanilla extract
- 10 tablespoons of white sugar

Directions:

1. Take a bowl and add all-purpose flour, salt, and baking powder.
2. Stir it in a large bowl.
3. Whisk two eggs in a separate bowl and add vanilla extract, sugar and blend it with a hand beater.
4. Now combine wet ingredients with the dry ones.
5. Mix it well and pour it between two round pan that fits inside baskets.
6. Place the pans in both the baskets.
7. Now set the zone 1 basket to BAKE function at 310 for 30 minutes.
8. Select MATCH for zone two baskets.
9. Once it's done, serve and enjoy.

Nutrition:

- (Per serving) Calories 711| Fat4.8g| Sodium 143mg | Carbs 161g | Fiber 1.3g | Sugar 105g | Protein 10.2g

Mocha Pudding Cake Vanilla Pudding Cake
Servings:8
Cooking Time: 25 Minutes
Ingredients:

- FOR THE MOCHA PUDDING CAKE
- 1 cup all-purpose flour
- ⅔ cup granulated sugar
- 1 cup packed light brown sugar, divided
- 5 tablespoons unsweetened cocoa powder, divided
- 2 teaspoons baking powder
- ¼ teaspoon kosher salt
- ½ cup unsweetened almond milk
- 2 teaspoons vanilla extract
- 2 tablespoons vegetable oil
- 1 cup freshly brewed coffee
- FOR THE VANILLA PUDDING CAKE
- 1 cup all-purpose flour
- ⅔ cup granulated sugar, plus ½ cup
- 2 teaspoons baking powder
- ¼ teaspoon kosher salt
- ½ cup unsweetened almond milk
- 2½ teaspoons vanilla extract, divided
- 2 tablespoons vegetable oil
- ¾ cup hot water
- 2 teaspoons cornstarch

Directions:

1. To prep the mocha pudding cake: In a medium bowl, combine the flour, granulated sugar, ½ cup of brown sugar, 3 tablespoons of cocoa powder, the baking powder, and salt. Stir in the almond milk, vanilla, and oil to form a thick batter.
2. Spread the batter in the bottom of the Zone 1 basket. Sprinkle the remaining ½ cup brown sugar and 2 tablespoons of cocoa powder in an even layer over the batter. Gently pour the hot coffee over the batter (do not mix).
3. To prep the vanilla pudding cake: In a medium bowl, combine the flour, ⅔ cup of granulated sugar, the baking powder, and salt. Stir in the almond milk, 2 teaspoons of vanilla, and the oil to form a thick batter.
4. Spread the batter in the bottom of the Zone 2 basket.
5. In a small bowl, whisk together the hot water, cornstarch, and remaining ½ cup of sugar and ½ teaspoon of vanilla. Gently pour over the batter (do not mix).
6. To cook both pudding cakes: Insert both baskets in the unit.
7. Select Zone 1, select BAKE, set the temperature to 330°F, and set the timer to 25 minutes. Select MATCH COOK to match Zone 2 settings to Zone 1.
8. Press START/PAUSE to begin cooking.
9. When cooking is complete, the tops of the cakes should be dry and set.
10. Let the cakes rest for 10 minutes before serving. The pudding will thicken as it cools.

Nutrition:

- (Per serving) Calories: 531; Total fat: 8g; Saturated fat: 1g; Carbohydrates: 115g; Fiber: 3.5g; Protein: 5g; Sodium: 111mg

Grilled Peaches
Servings: 2
Cooking Time: 5 Minutes
Ingredients:

- 2 yellow peaches, peeled and cut into wedges
- ¼ cup graham cracker crumbs
- ¼ cup brown sugar
- ¼ cup butter diced into tiny cubes
- Whipped cream or ice cream

Directions:

1. Toss peaches with crumbs, brown sugar, and butter in a bowl.
2. Spread the peaches in one air fryer basket.
3. Return the air fryer basket to the Ninja Foodi 2 Baskets Air Fryer.
4. Choose the "Air Fry" mode for Zone 1 and set the temperature to 350 degrees F and 5 minutes of cooking time.
5. Initiate cooking by pressing the START/PAUSE BUTTON.
6. Serve the peaches with a scoop of ice cream.

Nutrition:

- (Per serving) Calories 327 | Fat 14.2g |Sodium 672mg | Carbs 47.2g | Fiber 1.7g | Sugar 24.8g | Protein 4.4g

Chocolate Cookies
Servings: 18
Cooking Time: 7 Minutes
Ingredients:

- 96g flour
- 57g butter, softened
- 15ml milk
- 7.5g cocoa powder
- 80g chocolate chips
- ½ tsp vanilla
- 35g sugar
- ¼ tsp baking soda
- Pinch of salt

Directions:

1. In a bowl, mix flour, cocoa powder, sugar, baking soda, vanilla, butter, milk, and salt until well combined.
2. Add chocolate chips and mix well.
3. Insert a crisper plate in Ninja Foodi air fryer baskets.
4. Make cookies from the mixture and place in both baskets.
5. Select zone 1 then select "air fry" mode and set the temperature to 360 degrees F for 7 minutes. Press "match" to match zone 2 settings to zone 1. Press "start/stop" to begin.

Nutrition:

- (Per serving) Calories 82 | Fat 4.1g |Sodium 47mg | Carbs 10.7g | Fiber 0.4g | Sugar 6.2g | Protein 1g

Apple Fritters

Servings: 14

Cooking Time: 10 Minutes

Ingredients:

- 2 large apples
- 2 cups all-purpose flour
- ½ cup granulated sugar
- 1 tablespoon baking powder
- 1 teaspoon salt
- 1 teaspoon ground cinnamon
- ½ teaspoon ground nutmeg
- ¼ teaspoon ground cloves
- ¾ cup apple cider or apple juice
- 2 eggs
- 3 tablespoons butter, melted
- 1 teaspoon vanilla extract
- For the apple cider glaze:
- 2 cups powdered sugar
- ¼ cup apple cider or apple juice
- ½ teaspoon ground cinnamon
- ¼ teaspoon ground nutmeg

Directions:

1. Peel and core the apples, then cut them into ¼-inch cubes. Spread the apple chunks out on a kitchen towel to absorb any excess moisture.
2. In a mixing bowl, combine the flour, sugar, baking powder, salt, and spices.
3. Add the apple chunks and combine well.
4. Whisk together the apple cider, eggs, melted butter, and vanilla in a small bowl.
5. Combine the wet and dry ingredients in a large mixing bowl.
6. Install a crisper plate in both drawers. Use an ice cream scoop to scoop 3 to 4 dollops of fritter dough into the zone 1 drawer and 3 to 4 dollops into the zone 2 drawer. Insert the drawers into the unit. You may need to cook in batches.
7. Select zone 1, select BAKE, set temperature to 390 degrees F/ 200 degrees C, and set time to 10 minutes. Select MATCH to match zone 2 settings to zone 1. Press the START/STOP button to begin cooking.
8. Meanwhile, make the glaze: Whisk the powdered sugar, apple cider, and spices together until smooth.
9. When the fritters are cooked, drizzle the glaze over them. Let sit for 10 minutes until the glaze sets.

Nutrition:

- (Per serving) Calories 221 | Fat 3g | Sodium 288mg | Carbs 46g | Fiber 2g | Sugar 29g | Protein 3g

Fried Dough With Roasted Strawberries

Servings:4

Cooking Time: 20 Minutes

Ingredients:

- FOR THE FRIED DOUGH
- 6 ounces refrigerated pizza dough, at room temperature
- 2 tablespoons all-purpose flour, for dusting
- 4 tablespoons vegetable oil
- 2 tablespoons powdered sugar
- FOR THE ROASTED STRAWBERRIES
- 2 cups frozen whole strawberries
- 2 tablespoons granulated sugar

Directions:

1. To prep the fried dough: Divide the dough into four equal portions.
2. Dust a clean work surface with the flour. Place one dough portion on the surface and use a rolling pin to roll to a ⅛-inch thickness. Rub both sides of the dough with 1 tablespoon of oil. Repeat with remaining dough portions and oil.
3. To prep the strawberries: Place the strawberries in the Zone 2 basket. Sprinkle the granulated sugar on top.
4. To cook the fried dough and strawberries: Install a crisper plate in the Zone 1 basket. Place 2 dough portions in the basket and insert the basket in the unit. Insert the Zone 2 basket in the unit.
5. Select Zone 1, select AIR FRY, set the temperature to 400°F, and set the timer to 18 minutes.
6. Select Zone 2, select ROAST, set the temperature to 330°F, and set the timer to 20 minutes. Select SMART FINISH.
7. Press START/PAUSE to begin cooking.
8. When both timers read 8 minutes, press START/PAUSE. Remove the Zone 1 basket and transfer the fried dough to a cutting board. Place the 2 remaining dough portions in the basket, then reinsert the basket. Remove the Zone 2 basket and stir the strawberries. Reinsert the basket and press START/PAUSE to resume cooking.
9. When cooking is complete, the dough should be cooked through and the strawberries soft and jammy.
10. Sprinkle the fried dough with powdered sugar. Gently mash the strawberries with a fork. Spoon the strawberries onto each fried dough portion and serve.

Nutrition:

- (Per serving) Calories: 304; Total fat: 15g; Saturated fat: 2.5g; Carbohydrates: 38g; Fiber: 0.5g; Protein: 3g; Sodium: 421mg

Pumpkin Muffins

Servings:4

Cooking Time:20

Ingredients:

- 1 and ½ cups of all-purpose flour
- ½ teaspoon baking soda
- ½ teaspoon of baking powder
- 1 and 1/4 teaspoons cinnamon, groaned
- 1/4 teaspoon ground nutmeg, grated
- 2 large eggs
- Salt, pinch
- 3/4 cup granulated sugar
- 1/2 cup dark brown sugar

- 1 and 1/2 cups of pumpkin puree
- 1/4 cup coconut milk

Directions:

1. Take 4 ramekins that are the size of a cup and layer them with muffin papers.
2. Crack an egg in a bowl and add brown sugar, baking soda, baking powder, cinnamon, nutmeg, and sugar.
3. Whisk it all very well with an electric hand beater.
4. Now, in a second bowl, mix the flour, and salt.
5. Now, mix the dry ingredients slowly with the wet ingredients.
6. Now, at the end fold in the pumpkin puree and milk, mix it well
7. Divide this batter into 4 ramekins.
8. Now, divide ramekins between both zones.
9. Set the time for zone 1 to 18 minutes at 360 degrees Fat AIRFRY mode.
10. Select the MATCH button for the zone 2 basket.
11. Check if not done, and let it AIR FRY for one more minute.
12. Once it is done, serve.

Nutrition:

- (Per serving) Calories 291| Fat6.4 g| Sodium 241mg | Carbs 57.1g | Fiber 4.4g | Sugar42 g | Protein 5.9g

Cinnamon-sugar "churros" With Caramel Sauce

Servings:4

Cooking Time: 10 Minutes

Ingredients:

- FOR THE "CHURROS"
- 1 sheet frozen puff pastry, thawed
- Butter-flavored cooking spray
- 1 tablespoon granulated sugar
- 1 teaspoon ground cinnamon
- FOR THE CARAMEL SAUCE
- ½ cup packed light brown sugar
- 2 tablespoons unsalted butter, cut into small pieces
- ¼ cup heavy (whipping) cream
- 2 teaspoons vanilla extract
- ⅛ teaspoon kosher salt

Directions:

1. To prep the "churros": Cut the puff pastry crosswise into 4 rectangles. Fold each piece in half lengthwise to make a long thin "churro."
2. To prep the caramel sauce: Measure the brown sugar, butter, cream, and vanilla into an ovenproof ramekin or bowl (no need to stir).
3. To cook the "churros" and caramel sauce: Install a crisper plate in the Zone 1 basket. Place the "churros" in the basket and insert the basket in the unit. Place the ramekin in the Zone 2 basket and insert the basket in the unit.
4. Select Zone 1, select AIR FRY, set the temperature to 330°F, and set the timer to 10 minutes.
5. Select Zone 2, select BAKE, set the temperature to 350°F, and set the timer to 10 minutes. Select SMART FINISH.
6. Press START/PAUSE to begin cooking.

7. When the Zone 2 timer reads 5 minutes, press START/PAUSE. Remove the basket and stir the caramel. Reinsert the basket and press START/PAUSE to resume cooking.
8. When cooking is complete, the "churros" will be golden brown and cooked through and the caramel sauce smooth.
9. Spritz each "churro" with cooking spray and sprinkle generously with the granulated sugar and cinnamon.
10. Stir the salt into the caramel sauce. Let cool for 5 to 10 minutes before serving. Note that the caramel will thicken as it cools.

Nutrition:

- (Per serving) Calories: 460; Total fat: 26g; Saturated fat: 14g; Carbohydrates: 60g; Fiber: 1.5g; Protein: 5g; Sodium: 254mg

Moist Chocolate Espresso Muffins
Servings: 8
Cooking Time: 18 Minutes
Ingredients:

- 1 egg
- 177ml milk
- ½ tsp baking soda
- ½ tsp espresso powder
- ½ tsp baking powder
- 50g cocoa powder
- 78ml vegetable oil
- 1 tsp apple cider vinegar
- 1 tsp vanilla
- 150g brown sugar
- 150g all-purpose flour
- ½ tsp salt

Directions:

1. In a bowl, whisk egg, vinegar, oil, brown sugar, vanilla, and milk.
2. Add flour, cocoa powder, baking soda, baking powder, espresso powder, and salt and stir until well combined.
3. Pour batter into the silicone muffin moulds.
4. Insert a crisper plate in Ninja Foodi air fryer baskets.
5. Place muffin moulds in both baskets.
6. Select zone 1 then select "bake" mode and set the temperature to 320 degrees F for 18 minutes. Press match cook to match zone 2 settings to zone 1. Press "start/stop" to begin.

Nutrition:

- (Per serving) Calories 222 | Fat 11g |Sodium 251mg | Carbs 29.6g | Fiber 2g | Sugar 14.5g | Protein 4g

Lemon Sugar Cookie Bars Monster Sugar Cookie Bars
Servings:12
Cooking Time: 18 Minutes
Ingredients:

- FOR THE LEMON COOKIE BARS
- Grated zest and juice of 1 lemon
- ½ cup granulated sugar
- 4 tablespoons (½ stick) unsalted butter, at room temperature
- 1 large egg yolk
- 1 teaspoon vanilla extract
- ⅛ teaspoon baking powder
- ½ cup plus 2 tablespoons all-purpose flour
- FOR THE MONSTER COOKIE BARS
- ½ cup granulated sugar
- 4 tablespoons (½ stick) unsalted butter, at room temperature
- 1 large egg yolk
- 1 teaspoon vanilla extract
- ⅛ teaspoon baking powder
- ½ cup plus 2 tablespoons all-purpose flour
- ¼ cup rolled oats
- ¼ cup M&M's
- ¼ cup peanut butter chips

Directions:

1. To prep the lemon cookie bars: In a large bowl, rub together the lemon zest and sugar. Add the butter and use a hand mixer to beat until light and fluffy.
2. Beat in the egg yolk, vanilla, and lemon juice. Mix in the baking powder and flour.
3. To prep the monster cookie bars: In a large bowl, with a hand mixer, beat the sugar and butter until light and fluffy.
4. Beat in the egg yolk and vanilla. Mix in the baking powder and flour. Stir in the oats, M&M's, and peanut butter chips.
5. To cook the cookie bars: Line both baskets with aluminum foil. Press the lemon cookie dough into the Zone 1 basket and insert the basket in the unit. Press the monster cookie dough into the Zone 2 basket and insert the basket in the unit.
6. Select Zone 1, select BAKE, set the temperature to 330°F, and set the timer to 18 minutes. Press MATCH COOK to match Zone 2 settings to Zone 1.
7. Press START/PAUSE to begin cooking.
8. When cooking is complete, the cookies should be set in the middle and have begun to pull away from the sides of the basket.
9. Let the cookies cool completely, about 1 hour. Cut each basket into 6 bars for a total of 12 bars.

Nutrition:

- (Per serving) Calories: 191; Total fat: 8.5g; Saturated fat: 5g; Carbohydrates: 27g; Fiber: 0.5g; Protein: 2g; Sodium: 3mg

Biscuit Doughnuts
Servings: 8
Cooking Time: 15 Minutes.
Ingredients:

- ½ cup white sugar
- 1 teaspoon cinnamon
- ½ cup powdered sugar

- 1 can pre-made biscuit dough
- Coconut oil
- Melted butter to brush biscuits

Directions:

1. Place all the biscuits on a cutting board and cut holes in the center of each biscuit using a cookie cutter.
2. Grease the crisper plate with coconut oil.
3. Place the biscuits in the two crisper plates while keeping them 1 inch apart.
4. Return the crisper plates to the Ninja Foodi Dual Zone Air Fryer.
5. Choose the Air Fry mode for Zone 1 and set the temperature to 375 degrees F and the time to 15 minutes.
6. Select the "MATCH" button to copy the settings for Zone 2.
7. Initiate cooking by pressing the START/STOP button.
8. Brush all the donuts with melted butter and sprinkle cinnamon and sugar on top.
9. Air fry these donuts for one minute more.
10. Enjoy!

Nutrition:

- (Per serving) Calories 192 | Fat 9.3g |Sodium 133mg | Carbs 27.1g | Fiber 1.4g | Sugar 19g | Protein 3.2g

Blueberry Pie Egg Rolls

Servings: 12

Cooking Time: 5 Minutes

Ingredients:

- 12 egg roll wrappers
- 2 cups of blueberries
- 1 tablespoon of cornstarch
- ½ cup of agave nectar
- 1 teaspoon of lemon zest
- 2 tablespoons of water
- 1 tablespoon of lemon juice
- Olive oil or butter flavored cooking spray
- Confectioner's sugar for dusting

Directions:

1. Mix blueberries with cornstarch, lemon zest, agave and water in a saucepan.
2. Cook this mixture for 5 minutes on a simmer.
3. Allow the mixture to cool.
4. Spread the roll wrappers and divide the filling at the center of the wrappers.
5. Fold the two edges and roll each wrapper.
6. Wet and seal the wrappers then place them in the air fryer basket 1.
7. Spray these rolls with cooking spray.
8. Return the air fryer basket 1 to Zone 1 of the Ninja Foodi 2-Basket Air Fryer.
9. Choose the "Air Fry" mode for Zone 1 at 350 degrees F and 5 minutes of cooking time.
10. Initiate cooking by pressing the START/PAUSE BUTTON.
11. Dust the rolls with confectioner' sugar.
12. Serve.

Nutrition:

- (Per serving) Calories 258 | Fat 12.4g |Sodium 79mg | Carbs 34.3g | Fiber 1g | Sugar 17g | Protein 3.2g

S'mores Dip With Cinnamon-sugar Tortillas

Servings:4

Cooking Time: 5 Minutes

Ingredients:

- FOR THE S'MORES DIP
- ½ cup chocolate-hazelnut spread
- ¼ cup milk chocolate or white chocolate chips
- ¼ cup graham cracker crumbs
- ½ cup mini marshmallows
- FOR THE CINNAMON-SUGAR TORTILLAS
- 4 (6-inch) flour tortillas
- Butter-flavored cooking spray
- 1 teaspoon granulated sugar
- ½ teaspoon ground cinnamon
- ¼ teaspoon ground cardamom (optional)

Directions:

1. To prep the s'mores dip: Spread the chocolate- hazelnut spread in the bottom of a shallow ovenproof ramekin or dish.
2. Scatter the chocolate chips and graham cracker crumbs over the top. Arrange the marshmallows in a single layer on top of the crumbs.
3. To prep the tortillas: Spray both sides of each tortilla with cooking spray. Cut each tortilla into 8 wedges and sprinkle both sides evenly with sugar, cinnamon, and cardamom (if using).
4. To cook the dip and tortillas: Install a crisper plate in each of the two baskets. Place the ramekin in the Zone 1 basket and insert the basket in the unit. Place the tortillas in the Zone 2 basket and insert the basket in the unit.
5. Select Zone 1, select BAKE, set the temperature to 330°F, and set the timer to 5 minutes.
6. Select Zone 2, select AIR FRY, set the temperature to 375°F, and set the timer to 5 minutes. Select SMART FINISH.
7. Press START/PAUSE to begin cooking.
8. When the Zone 2 timer reads 3 minutes, press START/PAUSE. Remove the basket and shake it to redistribute the chips. Reinsert the basket and press START/PAUSE to resume cooking.
9. When cooking is complete, the dip will be bubbling and golden brown and the chips crispy.
10. If desired, toast the marshmallows more: Select Zone 1, select AIR BROIL, set the temperature to 450°F, and set the timer to 1 minute. Cook until the marshmallows are deep golden brown.
11. Let the dip cool for 2 to 3 minutes. Serve with the cinnamon-sugar tortilla chips.

Nutrition:

- (Per serving) Calories: 404; Total fat: 18g; Saturated fat: 7g; Carbohydrates: 54g; Fiber: 2.5g; Protein: 6g; Sodium: 346mg

Chocolate Chip Cake

Servings:4

Cooking Time:15

Ingredients:

- Salt, pinch
- 2 eggs, whisked
- ½ cup brown sugar
- ½ cup butter, melted
- 10 tablespoons of almond milk
- ¼ teaspoon of vanilla extract
- ½ teaspoon of baking powder
- 1 cup all-purpose flour
- 1 cup of chocolate chips
- ½ cup of cocoa powder

Directions:

1. Take 2 round baking pan that fits inside the baskets of the air fryer.
2. layer it with baking paper, cut it to the size of a baking pan.
3. In a bowl, whisk the egg, brown sugar, butter, almond milk, and vanilla extract.
4. Whisk it all very well with an electric hand beater.
5. In a second bowl, mix the flour, cocoa powder, baking powder, and salt.
6. Now, mix the dry ingredients slowly with the wet ingredients.
7. Now, at the end fold in the chocolate chips.
8. Incorporate all the ingredients well.
9. Divide this batter into the round baking pan.
10. Set the time for zone 1 to 16 minutes at 350 degrees F at AIR FRY mode.
11. Select the MATCH button for the zone 2 baskets.
12. Check if not done, and let it AIR FRY for one more minute.
13. Once it is done, serve.

Nutrition:

- (Per serving) Calories 736| Fat45.5g| Sodium 356mg | Carbs 78.2g | Fiber 6.1g | Sugar 32.7g | Protein11.5 g

Walnut Baklava Bites Pistachio Baklava Bites

Servings:12

Cooking Time: 10 Minutes

Ingredients:

- FOR THE WALNUT BAKLAVA BITES
- ¼ cup finely chopped walnuts
- 2 teaspoons cold unsalted butter, grated
- 2 teaspoons granulated sugar
- ½ teaspoon ground cinnamon
- 6 frozen phyllo shells (from a 1.9-ounce package), thawed
- FOR THE PISTACHIO BAKLAVA BITES
- ¼ cup finely chopped pistachios
- 2 teaspoons very cold unsalted butter, grated
- 2 teaspoons granulated sugar
- ¼ teaspoon ground cardamom (optional)
- 6 frozen phyllo shells (from a 1.9-ounce package), thawed
- FOR THE HONEY SYRUP

- ¼ cup hot water
- ¼ cup honey
- 2 teaspoons fresh lemon juice

Directions:

1. To prep the walnut baklava bites: In a small bowl, combine the walnuts, butter, sugar, and cinnamon. Spoon the filling into the phyllo shells.
2. To prep the pistachio baklava bites: In a small bowl, combine the pistachios, butter, sugar, and cardamom (if using). Spoon the filling into the phyllo shells.
3. To cook the baklava bites: Install a crisper plate in each of the two baskets. Place the walnut baklava bites in the Zone 1 basket and insert the basket in the unit. Place the pistachio baklava bites in the Zone 2 basket and insert the basket in the unit.
4. Select Zone 1, select BAKE, set the temperature to 330°F, and set the timer to 10 minutes. Press MATCH COOK to match Zone 2 settings to Zone 1.
5. Press START/PAUSE to begin cooking.
6. When cooking is complete, the shells will be golden brown and crisp.
7. To make the honey syrup: In a small bowl, whisk together the hot water, honey, and lemon juice. Dividing evenly, pour the syrup over the baklava bites (you may hear a crackling sound).
8. Let cool completely before serving, about 1 hour.

Nutrition:

- (Per serving) Calories: 262; Total fat: 16g; Saturated fat: 3g; Carbohydrates: 29g; Fiber: 1g; Protein: 2g; Sodium: 39mg

Pumpkin Hand Pies Blueberry Hand Pies

Servings:4
Cooking Time: 15 Minutes

Ingredients:

- FOR THE PUMPKIN HAND PIES
- ½ cup pumpkin pie filling (from a 15-ounce can)
- ⅓ cup half-and-half
- 1 large egg
- ½ refrigerated pie crust (from a 14.1-ounce package)
- 1 large egg yolk
- 1 tablespoon whole milk
- FOR THE BLUEBERRY HAND PIES
- ¼ cup blueberries
- 2 tablespoons granulated sugar
- 1 tablespoon grated lemon zest (optional)
- ¼ teaspoon cornstarch
- 1 teaspoon fresh lemon juice
- ⅛ teaspoon kosher salt
- ½ refrigerated pie crust (from a 14.1-ounce package)
- 1 large egg yolk
- 1 tablespoon whole milk
- ½ teaspoon turbinado sugar

Directions:

1. To prep the pumpkin hand pies: In a small bowl, mix the pumpkin pie filling, half-and-half, and whole egg until well combined and smooth.
2. Cut the dough in half to form two wedges. Divide the pumpkin pie filling between the wedges. Fold the crust over to completely encase the filling. Using a fork, crimp the edges, forming a tight seal.
3. In a small bowl, whisk together the egg yolk and milk. Brush over the pastry. Carefully cut two small vents in the top of each pie.
4. To prep the blueberry hand pies: In a small bowl, combine the blueberries, granulated sugar, lemon zest (if using), cornstarch, lemon juice, and salt.
5. Cut the dough in half to form two wedges. Divide the blueberry filling between the wedges. Fold the crust over to completely encase the filling. Using a fork, crimp the edges, forming a tight seal.
6. In a small bowl, whisk together the egg yolk and milk. Brush over the pastry. Sprinkle with the turbinado sugar. Carefully cut two small vents in the top of each pie.
7. To cook the hand pies: Install a crisper plate in each of the two baskets. Place the pumpkin hand pies in the Zone 1 basket and insert the basket in the unit. Place the blueberry hand pies in the Zone 2 basket and insert the basket in the unit.
8. Select Zone 1, select AIR FRY, set the temperature to 350°F, and set the timer to 15 minutes. Select MATCH COOK to match Zone 2 settings to Zone 1.
9. Press START/PAUSE to begin cooking.
10. When cooking is complete, the pie crust should be crisp and golden brown and the filling bubbling.
11. Let the hand pies cool for at least 30 minutes before serving.

Nutrition:

- (Per serving) Calories: 588; Total fat: 33g; Saturated fat: 14g; Carbohydrates: 68g; Fiber: 0.5g; Protein: 10g; Sodium: 583mg

Apple Crisp

Servings: 8
Cooking Time: 14 Minutes.

Ingredients:

- 3 cups apples, chopped
- 1 tablespoon pure maple syrup
- 2 teaspoons lemon juice
- 3 tablespoons all-purpose flour
- ⅓ cup quick oats
- ¼ cup brown sugar
- 2 tablespoons light butter, melted
- ½ teaspoon cinnamon

Directions:

1. Toss the chopped apples with 1 tablespoon of all-purpose flour, cinnamon, maple syrup, and lemon juice in a suitable bowl.
2. Divide the apples in the two air fryer baskets with their crisper plates.
3. Whisk oats, brown sugar, and remaining all-purpose flour in a small bowl.
4. Stir in melted butter, then divide this mixture over the apples.
5. Return the crisper plate to the Ninja Foodi Dual Zone Air Fryer.
6. Select the Bake mode for Zone 1 and set the temperature to 375 degrees F and the time to 14 minutes.
7. Select the "MATCH" button to copy the settings for Zone 2.

8. Initiate cooking by pressing the START/STOP button.
9. Enjoy fresh.

Nutrition:

- (Per serving) Calories 258 | Fat 12.4g |Sodium 79mg | Carbs 34.3g | Fiber 1g | Sugar 17g | Protein 3.2g

Chocó Lava Cake

Servings: 4

Cooking Time: 10 Minutes

Ingredients:

- 3 eggs
- 3 egg yolks
- 70g dark chocolate, chopped
- 168g cups powdered sugar
- 96g all-purpose flour
- 1 tsp vanilla
- 113g butter
- ½ tsp salt

Directions:

1. Add chocolate and butter to a bowl and microwave for 30 seconds. Remove from oven and stir until smooth.
2. Add eggs, egg yolks, sugar, flour, vanilla, and salt into the melted chocolate and stir until well combined.
3. Pour batter into the four greased ramekins.
4. Insert a crisper plate in Ninja Foodi air fryer baskets.
5. Place ramekins in both baskets.
6. Select zone 1 then select "air fry" mode and set the temperature to 390 degrees F for 10 minutes. Press "match" to match zone 2 settings to zone 1. Press "start/stop" to begin.

Nutrition:

- (Per serving) Calories 687 | Fat 37.3g |Sodium 527mg | Carbs 78.3g | Fiber 1.5g | Sugar 57.4g | Protein 10.7g

Churros

Servings: 8

Cooking Time: 10 Minutes

Ingredients:

- 1 cup water
- 1⁄3 cup unsalted butter, cut into cubes
- 2 tablespoons granulated sugar
- ¼ teaspoon salt
- 1 cup all-purpose flour
- 2 large eggs
- 1 teaspoon vanilla extract
- Cooking oil spray
- For the cinnamon-sugar coating:

- ½ cup granulated sugar
- ¾ teaspoon ground cinnamon

Directions:

1. Add the water, butter, sugar, and salt to a medium pot. Bring to a boil over medium-high heat.
2. Reduce the heat to medium-low and stir in the flour. Cook, stirring constantly with a rubber spatula until the dough is smooth and comes together.
3. Remove the dough from the heat and place it in a mixing bowl. Allow 4 minutes for cooling.
4. In a mixing bowl, beat the eggs and vanilla extract with an electric hand mixer or stand mixer until the dough comes together. The finished product will resemble gluey mashed potatoes. Press the lumps together into a ball with your hands, then transfer to a large piping bag with a large star-shaped tip. Pipe out the churros.
5. Install a crisper plate in both drawers. Place half the churros in the zone 1 drawer and half in zone 2's, then insert the drawers into the unit.
6. Select zone 1, select AIR FRY, set temperature to 390 degrees F/ 200 degrees C, and set time to 12 minutes. Select MATCH to match zone 2 settings to zone 1. Press the START/STOP button to begin cooking.
7. In a shallow bowl, combine the granulated sugar and cinnamon.
8. Immediately transfer the baked churros to the bowl with the sugar mixture and toss to coat.

Nutrition:

- (Per serving) Calories 204 | Fat 9g | Sodium 91mg | Carbs 27g | Fiber 0.3g | Sugar 15g | Protein 3g

Honey Lime Pineapple

Servings: 4

Cooking Time: 10 Minutes

Ingredients:

- 562g pineapple chunks
- 55g brown sugar
- 30ml lime juice
- 63g honey

Directions:

1. In a bowl, mix pineapple, honey, lime juice, and brown sugar. Cover and place in refrigerator for 1 hour.
2. Insert a crisper plate in Ninja Foodi air fryer baskets.
3. Remove pineapple chunks from the marinade and place in both baskets.
4. Select zone 1 then select "air fry" mode and set the temperature to 390 degrees F for 10 minutes. Press "match" to match zone 2 settings to zone 1. Press "start/stop" to begin. Stir halfway through.

Nutrition:

- (Per serving) Calories 153 | Fat 0.2g |Sodium 5mg | Carbs 40.5g | Fiber 2g | Sugar 35.7g | Protein 0.8g

Fried Oreos

Servings: 8

Cooking Time: 8 Minutes

Ingredients:

- 1 can Pillsbury Crescent Dough (or equivalent)
- 8 Oreo cookies
- 1–2 tablespoons powdered sugar

Directions:

1. Open the crescent dough up and cut it into the right-size pieces to completely wrap each cookie.
2. Wrap each Oreo in dough. Make sure that there are no air bubbles and that the cookies are completely covered.
3. Install a crisper plate in both drawers. Place half the Oreo cookies in the zone 1 drawer and half in zone 2's. Sprinkle the tops with the powdered sugar, then insert the drawers into the unit.
4. Select zone 1, select AIR FRY, set temperature to 390 degrees F/ 200 degrees C, and set time to 8 minutes. Select MATCH to match zone 2 settings to zone 1. Press the START/STOP button to begin cooking.
5. Serve warm and enjoy!

Nutrition:

- (Per serving) Calories 338 | Fat 21.2g | Sodium 1503mg | Carbs 5.1g | Fiber 0.3g | Sugar 4.6g | Protein 29.3g

Baked Apples
Servings: 4
Cooking Time: 15 Minutes
Ingredients:

- 4 apples
- 6 teaspoons raisins
- 2 teaspoons chopped walnuts
- 2 teaspoons honey
- ½ teaspoon cinnamon

Directions:

1. Chop off the head of the apples and scoop out the flesh from the center.
2. Stuff the apples with raisins, walnuts, honey and cinnamon.
3. Place these apples in the air fryer basket 1.
4. Return the air fryer basket 1 to Zone 1 of the Ninja Foodi 2-Basket Air Fryer.
5. Choose the "Air Fry" mode for Zone 1 and set the temperature to 350 degrees F and 15 minutes of cooking time.
6. Initiate cooking by pressing the START/PAUSE BUTTON.
7. Serve.

Nutrition:

- (Per serving) Calories 175 | Fat 13.1g |Sodium 154mg | Carbs 14g | Fiber 0.8g | Sugar 8.9g | Protein 0.7g

Cinnamon Bread Twists
Servings: 4
Cooking Time: 15 Minutes
Ingredients:

- Bread Twists Dough
- 120g all-purpose flour

- 1 teaspoon baking powder
- ¼ teaspoon salt
- 150g fat free Greek yogurt
- Brushing
- 2 tablespoons light butter
- 2 tablespoons granulated sugar
- 1-2 teaspoons ground cinnamon, to taste

Directions:

1. Mix flour, salt and baking powder in a bowl.
2. Stir in yogurt and the rest of the dough ingredients in a bowl.
3. Mix well and make 8 inches long strips out of this dough.
4. Twist the strips and place them in the air fryer baskets.
5. Return the air fryer basket 1 to Zone 1, and basket 2 to Zone 2 of the Ninja Foodi 2-Basket Air Fryer.
6. Choose the "Air Fry" mode for Zone 1 at 375 degrees F and 15 minutes of cooking time.
7. Select the "MATCH COOK" option to copy the settings for Zone 2.
8. Initiate cooking by pressing the START/PAUSE BUTTON.
9. Flip the twists once cooked halfway through.
10. Mix butter with cinnamon and sugar in a bowl.
11. Brush this mixture over the twists.
12. Serve.

Nutrition:

- (Per serving) Calories 391 | Fat 24g |Sodium 142mg | Carbs 38.5g | Fiber 3.5g | Sugar 21g | Protein 6.6g

Strawberry Nutella Hand Pies

Servings: 8

Cooking Time: 10 Minutes

Ingredients:

- 1 tube pie crust dough
- 3–4 strawberries, finely chopped
- Nutella
- Sugar
- Coconut oil cooking spray

Directions:

1. Roll out the pie dough and place it on a baking sheet. Cut out hearts using a 3-inch heart-shaped cookie cutter as precisely as possible.
2. Gather the leftover dough into a ball and roll it out thinly to make a few more heart shapes. For 8 hand pies, I was able to get 16 hearts from one tube of pie crust.
3. Set aside a baking tray lined with parchment paper.
4. Spread a dollop of Nutella (approximately 1 teaspoon) on one of the hearts. Add a few strawberry pieces to the mix. Add a pinch of sugar to the top.
5. Place another heart on top and use a fork to tightly crimp the edges. Gently poke holes in the top of the pie with a fork. Place on a baking sheet. Repeat for all the pies.
6. All of the pies on the tray should be sprayed with coconut oil.

7. Install a crisper plate in both drawers. Place half the pies in the zone 1 drawer and half in zone 2's, then insert the drawers into the unit.
8. Select zone 1, select BAKE, set temperature to 390 degrees F/ 200 degrees C, and set time to 10 minutes. Select MATCH to match zone 2 settings to zone 1. Press the START/STOP button to begin cooking.

Nutrition:

- (Per serving) Calories 41 | Fat 2.1g | Sodium 18mg | Carbs 5.5g | Fiber 0.4g | Sugar 4.1g | Protein 0.4g

Zesty Cranberry Scones
Servings: 8
Cooking Time: 16 Minutes.
Ingredients:

- 4 cups of flour
- ½ cup brown sugar
- 2 tablespoons baking powder
- ½ teaspoon ground nutmeg
- ½ teaspoon salt
- ½ cup butter, chilled and diced
- 2 cups fresh cranberry
- ⅔ cup sugar
- 2 tablespoons orange zest
- 1 ¼ cups half and half cream
- 2 eggs

Directions:

1. Whisk flour with baking powder, salt, nutmeg, and both the sugars in a bowl.
2. Stir in egg and cream, mix well to form a smooth dough.
3. Fold in cranberries along with the orange zest.
4. Knead this dough well on a work surface.
5. Cut 3-inch circles out of the dough.
6. Divide the scones in the crisper plates and spray them with cooking oil.
7. Return the crisper plates to the Ninja Foodi Dual Zone Air Fryer.
8. Choose the Air Fry mode for Zone 1 and set the temperature to 375 degrees F and the time to 16 minutes.
9. Select the "MATCH" button to copy the settings for Zone 2.
10. Initiate cooking by pressing the START/STOP button.
11. Flip the scones once cooked halfway and resume cooking.
12. Enjoy!

Nutrition:

- (Per serving) Calories 204 | Fat 9g |Sodium 91mg | Carbs 27g | Fiber 2.4g | Sugar 15g | Protein 1.3g

Lemony Sweet Twists
Servings:2
Cooking Time:9

Ingredients:

- 1 box store-bought puff pastry
- ½ teaspoon lemon zest
- 1 tablespoon of lemon juice
- 2 teaspoons brown sugar
- Salt, pinch
- 2 tablespoons Parmesan cheese, freshly grated

Directions:

1. Put the puff pastry dough on a clean work area.
2. In a bowl, combine Parmesan cheese, brown sugar, salt, lemon zest, and lemon juice.
3. Press this mixture on both sides of the dough.
4. Now, cut the pastry into 1" x 4" strips.
5. Twist each of the strips.
6. Transfer to both the air fryer baskets.
7. Select zone 1 to air fry mode at 400 degrees F for 9-10 minutes.
8. Select match for zone 2 basket.
9. Once cooked, serve and enjoy.

Nutrition:

- (Per serving) Calories 156| Fat10g| Sodium 215mg | Carbs 14g | Fiber 0.4g | Sugar3.3 g | Protein 2.8g

Oreo Rolls

Servings: 9

Cooking Time: 8 Minutes.

Ingredients:

- 1 crescent sheet roll
- 9 Oreo cookies
- Cinnamon powder, to serve
- Powdered sugar, to serve

Directions:

1. Spread the crescent sheet roll and cut it into 9 equal squares.
2. Place one cookie at the center of each square.
3. Wrap each square around the cookies and press the ends to seal.
4. Place half of the wrapped cookies in each crisper plate.
5. Return the crisper plates to the Ninja Foodi Dual Zone Air Fryer.
6. Select the Bake mode for Zone 1 and set the temperature to 360 degrees F and the time to 4-6 minutes.
7. Select the "MATCH" button to copy the settings for Zone 2.
8. Initiate cooking by pressing the START/STOP button.
9. Check for the doneness of the cookie rolls if they are golden brown, else cook 1-2 minutes more.
10. Garnish the rolls with sugar and cinnamon.
11. Serve.

Nutrition:

- (Per serving) Calories 175 | Fat 13.1g |Sodium 154mg | Carbs 14g | Fiber 0.8g | Sugar 8.9g | Protein 0.7g

Printed in Great Britain
by Amazon

39955069R00104